COOKING WITH
Mushrooms

A Culinary Guide to Chef Pisto's Favorite Fungi

BY JOHN PISTO

Introduction by: David Arora

Photography by: Cheryl Pisto

Cover photo by: Taylor F. Lockwood

Illustrations by: Susannah Kelly

Design by: Riddell & Riddell
172 16th St., Pacific Grove, CA 93950

Published by:
Pisto's Kitchen
P.O. Box 51201, Pacific Grove, CA 93950
(800) 45-PISTO

COOKING WITH

Mushrooms

*A Culinary Guide to
Chef Pisto's Favorite Fungi*

Other Pisto's Kitchen Books In Print
Monterey's Cookin' Pisto Style
"from Sicily to Monterey" 1994

ISBN 0-9640828-1-0

*Dedicated to the thousands of responsible mushroom collectors who
harvest only what they use and to the innovators in mushroom farming
who are even now discovering the cultivation secrets of fungi.*

MY FRIEND DAVID ARORA (MR MUSHROOM) A bright and knowledgeable mycologist, David has shared his enthusiasm with me on mushroom adventures from California to Mongolia.

The experience of hunting, cooking, and eating mushrooms has become a hobby that I enjoy as much as the search for and collection of fine wines and good cigars. However, it is the sharing of these passions with others that truly enriches my life.

I have met some of my favorite people on mushroom forays. One of them, California's own mushroom guru, David Arora, is responsible for much of the newly found interest in mushrooms here in the States. David shares his overwhelming enthusiasm and expertise with any and all interested. His two mushroom identification books are considered bibles in the field. David is also largely responsible for my growing dedication to the hobby, and I greatly appreciate the time we have spent together.

A CUPBOARD Stocked with all the essentials, including fresh and dried mushrooms

TABLE OF CONTENTS

JOHN PISTO Holding a plug of domestically grown oyster mushrooms.

Americans are finally becoming educated to what the rest of the world has known for centuries—mushrooms are delicious! Because of the ever-growing culinary interest, mushrooms are now being cultivated throughout the United States.

An unique and at times unpredictable process, mushroom cultivation is still considered experimental. Yet, growers are determined to learn the secrets of the fungi's finnicky growing cycle. Some varieties have already yielded success, including shiitake, champignon, portabello, and oyster mushrooms.

MUSHROOMS REDISCOVERED

By David Arora

North Americans are finally beginning to discover what Europeans, Asians, and Africans have known for centuries—that there are dozens of delicious mushrooms in our forests and fields (and increasingly, in our delicatessens and supermarkets), and dozens of ways to prepare and enjoy them. This book should boost this discovery process, introducing a few of John Pisto's favorite mushrooms and mushroom recipes to the reader with passion and authority.

When I see a restaurant menu that features "mushroom soup" or "sautéed mushrooms" I am immediately turned off in the same way someone would be discouraged by "roasted meat" or "green plant soup." It is much too generic a label, connoting ignorance or indifference rather than familiarity and respect. Mushrooms after all are not one vegetable, but many, each with its own individual flavor, fragrance, texture, appearance, and sound (yes, *sound*; if you've ever thunked a solid king bolete then you know what I mean). To identify different kinds of mushrooms with individual names should be done, not as a matter of culinary ethics or pretense, but for the same practical reason that we distinguish broccoli from eggplant and caviar from calamari—because they are *different*.

DAVID ARORA Mr. Mushroom, author of *Mushrooms Demystified & All That the Rain Promises and More*

I was delighted, then, when I first visited (John Pisto's) Whaling Station (restaurant) in Monterey, to find a tantalizing array of mushroom entrees with nary a mention of the word *mushroom*; instead, there was truffle chicken, filet mignon in porcini sauce, porter house steak with sautéed shiitakes, grilled portabello over polenta, candy cap mushroom pasta, and grilled bleeding agaricus. I chose the latter, one of my favorites but not served by any other restaurants that I know of, plus the candy caps over pasta. Both were delicious, and my delight doubled when I discovered that John Pisto, the man behind these revelations, was as passionate about the *search* for mushrooms as he was about their ultimate fate in the kitchen. One mushroom hunt in particular stands out.

I came to Monterey one day with three young visitors from Singapore. They were in low spirits—homesick, perhaps—and I wasn't sure what to do with them. John kindly offered to drive us around town. Naturally I expected him to show us Pebble Beach, Lover's Point, Fisherman's Wharf, and maybe some restaurants or real estate. Instead he gave us something much more memorable and personal—a frenzied whirlwind tour of all the significant cypress trees in Monterey (and by significant I mean all those known to produce delicious and elusive giant cypress agaricus underneath them).

"This is *my* tree!," John would shout, screeching to a halt and jumping to snare three giant, rock hard mushrooms visible only as hairline cracks in the hard-packed earth beneath a giant old cypress. Never mind that the tree was on public property— a historical monument—it was *his* tree because he found it. *He* was the one that knew about the giant cypress agaricus that grew there, and *he* alone appreciated the tree as a provider of delectable fungal fruit.

My friends from Singapore had never picked wild mushrooms before. The notion of picking *anything* to eat that wasn't off a shelf was alien to them, And getting out to do it in the middle of traffic, with everybody *watching*—forget it! They were taken aback, even horrified. But John's passion for the hunt is infectious, to say the least. Here were beautiful, delectable, *free* mushrooms growing right in the middle of town, overlooked by thousands of people—tourists and residents alike! It was so improbable and fantastic that within half an hour the three staid Singaporeans (one of whom was a flight attendant) had shed their timidity *and* their troubles and were beating us to the mushrooms—leaping out of the car in the middle of traffic to snag giant cypress agarics from culverts, parking medians, and people's yards before John and I could see them! They were so completely captivated by the experience and by John's cooking afterward, that they began laying plans for similar forays in the parks and streets of Singapore.

This cookbook by John Pisto should be equally inspiring, for it is infused with the same spirit that so impressed the Singaporeans, passion and knowledge and flair that have made John's restaurants and television show so popular and have made me come back to Monterey again and again, for more. Welcome to John Pisto's kitchen, and welcome to the wonderful world of mushrooms!

David Arora

JOHN PISTO On the set of "Monterey's Cookin'"

COOKING WITH MUSHROOMS

COOKING WITH JOHN PISTO

Most professional chefs, myself included, do not cook from recipes. I'm not saying that I don't look at recipes. In fact, I have hundreds of cookbooks at home. Chefs are always on the lookout for new ideas, but you will never find me in the kitchen with a cookbook open, doling out ingredients with a menagerie of measuring cups and teaspoons. I cook by taste, by memory, by touch, and, most often, by inspiration.

I've done my best to translate my pinches, dashes, and handfuls into teaspoons, tablespoons, and cups, but if you're not completely satisfied with the flavor, for heaven's sake, experiment. Above all, taste it . . . taste it as you're cooking it . . . and taste it after you're finished with it. Learning how to identify what you taste is what makes a good cook.

People are always asking me what the secret is to my cooking. I believe the key to fine cooking is to never cook because you have to. You should cook only when there is joy in your heart and you want to share that joy with those at the table.

If its been a long day and your heart is not in it, I recommend you order pizza, heavy on the mushrooms!

Cooking with mushrooms has brought new levels of enjoyment to my cooking. The variety of colors, textures, and flavors they offer will, I'm sure, give me many more years of experimentation. Yet, sharing my passion with others is what makes me happiest of all.

I hope you enjoy this humble book and that it encourages you to experiment with and experience the lighter, warmer, funnier side of cooking with mushrooms.

Lastly, many of the enclosed recipes use spices of my own making. We, of course, make these available to you, via mail order, in the back of the book (pg. 109); you may also find them at your local grocer. In any case, I also offer simple suggestions for substitutes that can be found on page 126.

Good Cookin'
John Pisto

GOURMET PRODUCTS From Pisto's Kitchen
(see page 109 for more information)

KING BOLETE One of Chef Pisto's favorite mushrooms

MUSHROOMS

Chef Pisto's Favorite Fungi

In Search of Mushrooms • Collecting Fungi • Tools of the Trade • Mushroom Diagram • Oyster Mushroom • Shiitake Mushroom • Morel • Black Elfin Saddle • Lobster Mushroom • Hawk Wing • Hedgehog • King Bolete (Porcini) • Champignon (Portabella) • Prince • Giant Cypress Agaricus • White Matsutake • Wood Ear • Oregon White Truffle • Chanterelle • Candy Cap • An Appetite for Mushrooms • Introducing Mushrooms into Your Diet

IN SEARCH OF MUSHROOMS

By John Pisto

I become excited right after the first rains, thinking of the treasures beginning to blossom beneath the earth. After five to seven days of good moisture, mushrooms can be found almost every-where—sprouting up overnight in many cases.

Everyone in our house looks forward to the hunt. It's an event. We pack up the car with all our hunting and picnic supplies and make an adventure of it.

Sometimes I use mushrooms as an excuse to call an old buddy I haven't seen in a while for a day of foraging and catching up. We don't always find mush-rooms, but we do find ourselves enjoying the camaraderie, the outdoors, and the spirit of the hunt.

Sometimes I go alone to what I pretend are my secret hunting grounds, in remote locations a few hours from home. For me it's like hunting for treasure without a map, armed with clues about habitat and distinguishable features.

I have found the excitement of uncovering a massive shrump (a bevy of mushrooms) under an old oak tree to be exhilarating.

I've had the amazing experience of run-ning across a meadow covered in giant Elfin Saddles.

Mushrooms have added a new dimen-sion to my life. It's an unusual hobby, yet I am not alone. All sorts of people are passionate about mushrooms, and you can find these people almost everywhere. I've seen them high in the Sierra, clutching David Arora's *Mushrooms Demystified* brimming with yellow Post-It notes and alongside busy freeways, on their hands and knees retriev-ing lucky finds. They are restaurant owners, photographers, dentists, and hairdressers—folks from every walk of life—all waiting for the next rain.

COLLECTING FUNGI

Every region's mushroom season is different. In California you can generally find a large variety of mushrooms from October through March. Of course, this depends entirely on the weather—no rain means, for the most part. no mushrooms.

Most often mushroom hunts begin at dawn, during or just after a period of heavy rain. Overcast or foggy days offer the greatest promise.

Continued from previous page

Beginners should consider joining their local mycologist club or finding a local person who is knowledgeable in the field to act as guide.

When mushrooms are spotted, the mycologist should identify the mushrooms before harvesting them. Where and how the mushroom grows are important identification clues.

There are some 40,000 known mushrooms. I hunt for about six to eight specific varieties and have become adept at identifying my favorites.

When hunting mushrooms we harvest only the best specimens, leaving small or imperfect shrooms for reproduction. To harvest ground mushrooms, clear away leaves and other natural matter and, with a knife, cut at the base of the stalk.

Examine for bugs or worms. Brush away dirt and place mushrooms in bags. If you collect specimens for later identification, remember that mushrooms can look quite different just hours later. No mushroom should be consumed unless you are *absolutely certain* about its identity.

TOOLS OF THE TRADE

The basic tools for this hobby are well within everyone's budget. To carry the mushrooms, you will need a loose weave basket, a collapsible wire basket, or any lightweight container. I always keep a collapsible basket under the seat of my truck for treasures I spot from the road.

Bring along wax paper and/or wax or paper bags to keep mushrooms separated by type and to protect them during your hunt. Never store mushrooms in plastic.

TOOLS OF THE TRADE
Your basic mushroom-hunting tools

A walking stick or preferably a mushroom stick with a forked end is used for investigating suspicious looking mounds or bumps (called *shrumps*).

Also carry a pocket knife and a small painter's brush to harvest and clean the mushrooms.

Finally, everyone in our group always carrys a coach's whistle for attracting attention when he or she finds mushrooms. Whistles are also helpful for locating lost members of the party who have wandered off.

MUSHROOM DIAGRAM
A GUIDE TO DISTINGUISHING CHARACTERISTICS

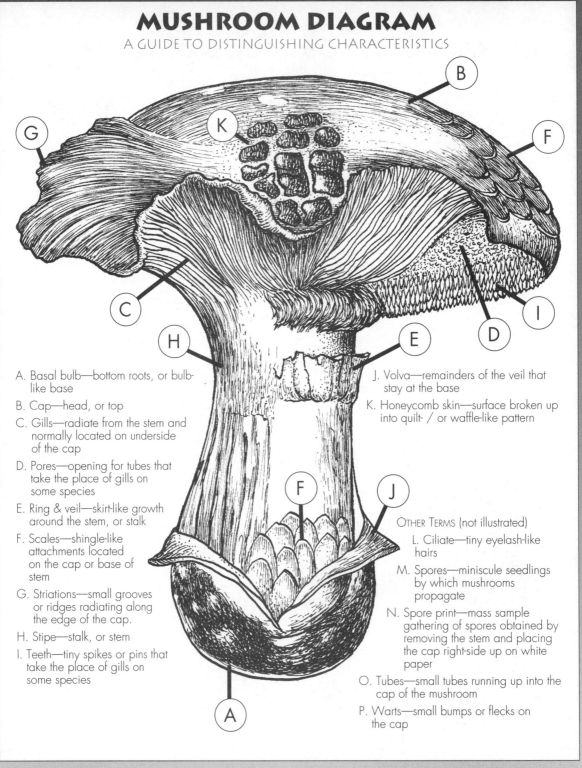

A. Basal bulb—bottom roots, or bulb-like base

B. Cap—head, or top

C. Gills—radiate from the stem and normally located on underside of the cap

D. Pores—opening for tubes that take the place of gills on some species

E. Ring & veil—skirt-like growth around the stem, or stalk

F. Scales—shingle-like attachments located on the cap or base of stem

G. Striations—small grooves or ridges radiating along the edge of the cap.

H. Stipe—stalk, or stem

I. Teeth—tiny spikes or pins that take the place of gills on some species

J. Volva—remainders of the veil that stay at the base

K. Honeycomb skin—surface broken up into quilt- / or waffle-like pattern

OTHER TERMS (not illustrated)

L. Ciliate—tiny eyelash-like hairs

M. Spores—miniscule seedlings by which mushrooms propagate

N. Spore print—mass sample gathering of spores obtained by removing the stem and placing the cap right-side up on white paper

O. Tubes—small tubes running up into the cap of the mushroom

P. Warts—small bumps or flecks on the cap

OYSTER MUSHROOM
(PLEUROTUS OSTREATUS)

This interesting mushroom is plentiful throughout California and other coastal areas. A mild, yet distinctly flavorful mushroom, the oyster is versatile in the kitchen.

NOTABLE CHARACTERISTICS:
Oysters can be found in clusters on dead trees—in particular, oak, willow, and beech trees or other hardwoods. When clustered on a tree limb these mushrooms have the appearance of flat, oval shells, with color of caps ranging from light blue-grey when young to creamy pale brown when mature. Gills are pale, sometimes white. Stalk is not always present or often very short. The flesh is tender when young, toughening as the mushroom matures. Look for small, young mushrooms for best flavor.

FUNGI FACTS
There are almost 40,000 known mushrooms, some of which are poisonous, such as the *Amanita phalloides,* or death cap, of which a single mushroom can prove fatal.

SHIITAKE MUSHROOM
(LENTINUS EDODES)

Not native to North America, shiitake mushrooms (also called black mushrooms) originally came from Japan. Now cultivated widely throughout the world, including North America, it's only a matter of time before we find them in our forests—perhaps on oak trees or other hardwoods.

NOTABLE CHARACTERISTICS:
Cap color is brown to dark brown, often with serrated or jagged gills. Veil remnants are often present. These mushrooms have a meaty, earthy taste and are often used in asian cuisine. Price for domestically cultivated Shiitakes has become more affordable because of the proliferation of growers. Today they represent a culinary bargain.

MOREL

(MORCHELLA ESCULENTA)

The morel is one of the most sought after of all mushrooms. In France, it is said ardent lovers of this mushroom, which is known to grow in the wake of forest fires, actually set fire to woodland areas and then harvest morels the following season.

Morels offer a rich, earthy flavor for entrees. They are wonderful both fresh and reconstituted. (Always cook this mushroom before eating it.)

NOTABLE CHARACTERISTICS:
The head, or cap, of a morel tends to be round or slightly conical. The cap comprises cup-like pits, appearing almost sponge-like. Color is ocher-brown to yellow-brown. The cap is hollow and exudes a distinct fragrance.

Morels are found in sandy soil in woodlands, pastures, and orchards.

BLACK ELFIN SADDLE

(HELVELLA LACUNOSA)

Its Latin translation "with holes" evidently refers to the elfin's stalk, which appears to have tree-ring-like holes. Despite this mushroom's appearance, it has a delicious apricot flavor when cooked.

NOTABLE CHARACTERISTICS:
Elfin caps are normally tri-lobed, with a smooth finish and heavy, sharpei-dog wrinkles. Color ranges from dark gray to black. The stem is white to dark gray, even black, with grooves forming deep pockets and holes.

Black elfin saddles are prevalent along the California coast. They prefer sandy soil.

FUNGI FACTS

Mushrooms don't reproduce with seeds; instead they release spores. Spores are often so tiny that they are visible to the naked eye only in large quantities.

Often mushrooms can release as many as 25 million or more spores in a single hour.

Experienced mushroom collectors often leave several mushrooms in a given area to resow the mushrooms and thus continue the growing cycle.

LOBSTER MUSHROOM
(HYPOMYCES LACTIFLUORUM)

This unusual mushroom is an excellent ingredient in seafood dishes. I sometimes combine this mushroom with its namesake for a visually interesting and incredibly tasty meal. The mature mushroom is crisp when fresh and gets softer as it ages.

NOTABLE CHARACTERISTICS:
This mushroom's cap and stem color ranges from bright orange or red to deep violet-red.

Looking a bit like an intense chanterelle mushroom, the lobster mushroom is sometimes confused with its lighter-skinned cousin.

The lobster's cap is medium size and sometimes lighter or yellower than the reverse side.

FUNGI FACTS

Several mushrooms glow in the dark, including the *Omphalotus olearius* and the *Omphalotus olivascens*, or jack o'lantern, both of which have phosphorescent gills.

Both are poisonous. Occasionally these mushrooms are mistaken for chanterelles despite the fact that they are normally found growing on trees.

HAWK WING
(SARCODON IMBRICATUM)

Hawk wing mushrooms are excellent when sautéed thoroughly. They can be dried and/or reduced to powder and used as a fantastic food flavoring.

NOTABLE CHARACTERISTICS:
This mushroom derives its Latin name from the expression "covered with tiles." Its stunning appearance resembles a beautiful "hawk wing" or a tiled roof.

The cap is convex and medium to large-size, with scales that are often raised or peeled back, looking much like a feathered wing. Colors vary from brown to dark brown, even black. Hawk wing stems are short, thick, and smooth, most often the color of the cap.

Hawk wings are often found growing in groups under broad-leaf conifers.

HEDGEHOG

(HYDNUM REPANDUM)

This mushroom's common name relates to
the tiny spines found under its cap.
Hedgehog mushrooms should always be
cooked. The delicate flavor is similar to
the chanterelle. They can be stewed,
fried, sautéed, or baked.

NOTABLE CHARACTERISTICS:
The hedgehog is identifiable by the small,
brittle spines, or teeth, that grow along
the underside of the cap. Spines can easily be removed, which should be done
with older mushrooms. Cap color is pale
yellow to tan. Cap is irregular, convex to
flat. The stalk tends to be a lighter color
than cap, smooth and relatively thick.

Hedgehogs are often found in groups,
strings, or rings growing at the edge of
forests, especially near conifers.

KING BOLETE

(BOLETUS EDULIS)

Often referred to as porcini or cep, the
Boletus edulis gets its name from the Latin
word "edible." An Italian favorite, this
mushroom is now popular in America.
The bolete's sweet taste is reminiscent of
hazelnut and is intensified by drying. This
is one of the main ingredients in traditional Italian risotto.

NOTABLE CHARACTERISTICS:
The king bolete is a fairly large, meaty
mushroom, with a medium to large convex cap. The stem is thick—usually
greater than 1 inch and always lighter
than the cap (white or light tan).

Cap colors range from medium tan to
chestnut or deep red-brown. Underside
of cap is soft and spongy when young
and normally the same color as the stem.

This mushroom is often found
in California's wood-
ed areas. Hunt at
the woods' edge,
beneath conifers
and broad-leaf trees
such as oak and
pine.

CHAMPIGNON
(AGARICUS CAMPESTRIS)

Champignon mushrooms (meadow mushrooms) are related to the *Agaricus bisporus* (button mushroom) and the popular portabella. All are commonly found in local markets. Most people, when they speak of mushrooms, have champignons in mind.

Champignons are delicious raw and are often found sliced in salads or spaghetti.

NOTABLE CHARACTERISTICS:
The cap of the champignon is white, often with a smattering of brown specks and fibers. It is round to convex and securely fastened to the stem. Stem is thick (often 1/2 inch or thicker), and similar to the cap in color. When sliced, meat is white, and gills are tan to dark brown. Their cousins, *Agaricus bisporus,* have been cultivated at least since the 1800s and are one of the most common mushrooms available.

Champignons are primarily found in grasses or pastures, often growing in rings or groups.

FUNGI FACTS

Mushrooms were one of the first plants used to make dyes and are still in use in many countries for dyeing wool, hair, and other materials.

Among those sought after by dyers include the northern & western red-dye, jack o'lantern, and hawk wing, to name a few.

PRINCE
(AGARICUS AUGUSTUS)

This mushroom derives its name from the Latin *augustus* or "majestic." Prince mushrooms offer a beautiful fragrance and a wonderful taste. When the stem is cut or bruised, its fragrance is often associated with almonds. Taste is sweet and quite delicious.

NOTABLE CHARACTERISTICS:
Cap is convex with a flat spot on top and is covered with golden-brown scales cascading downward. Mushroom is notable for its marshmallow-shaped cap when young. Stem is white, about 1/2 inch thick, and normally has a skirt-like veil.

The prince can usually be found in grassy or wooded areas. It is common on the West Coast and is particularly prevalent in fog belts.

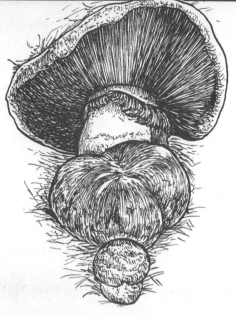

GIANT CYPRESS AGARICUS

(AGARICUS LILACEPS)

This delicious fungus gets its name from its favorite habitat at the base of cypress trees. Still unappreciated in America, the cypress is a culinary treat.

NOTABLE CHARACTERISTICS:
The cypress cap is domed and normally dark tan to brown in color. Occasionally habitat conditions can cause the cap to vary to shades of yellow, orange, lilac, or even pink.

The meat of this mushroom is firm and will stain red when roughly cut. The stem, or stalk, is 1 inch thick or more in a mature specimen. A veil is often present, covering gills until the mushroom is fully mature.

WHITE MATSUTAKE

(TRICHOLOMA MAGNIVELARE)

The matsutake is wonderfully complex and especially favored by the Japanese. They are excellent sautéed, fried, or grilled and make a hearty soup.

NOTABLE CHARACTERISTICS:
The cap is white to yellow-ocher in color, often with dark spots or stains. The stem is thick, and a veil is present, forming a prominent ring around the stem. Gills are white and do not run down the stem.

The matsutake can also be distinguished by its spicy, cinnamon-like aroma. This smell is easily detected and memorable.

This mushroom prefers sandy soil, often under pines.

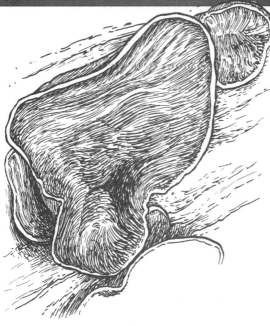

WOOD EAR
(AURICULARIA AURICULA)

This mushroom is delicious in soups and sauces. Like the shiitake, it has long been a staple in Chinese restaurants. I find the taste similar to pork.

In China, the wood ear is also valued for its medicinal properties, including for reducing bad cholesterol levels.

NOTABLE CHARACTERISTICS:
The cap is usually a rich brown color and is shaped much like an inverted cup or ear. No stem or stalk is present. Wood ear meat is described as jelly-like.

You may find several ear-like lobes growing on logs, dead branches, or the stumps of hardwoods.

OREGON WHITE TRUFFLE
(TUBER GIBBOSUM)

Truffles are difficult to locate and identify; however, they are one of the most sought-after fungi. Prized for their rich and complex taste, some truffles can bring as much as $350.00 an ounce.

Although not quite as rich, Oregon white truffles are considered by some chefs to be as good as Europe's famous Black Forest truffles.

NOTABLE CHARACTERISTICS:
Oregon white truffles often resemble small, rather deformed potatoes. Cut open, their meat is firm and marbled with veins.

Outside color is tan to brown and becomes darker with maturity. Inside color is lighter.

Truffles grow underground; thus they are difficult to find. In Europe people use special truffle-hunting pigs to "smell out" the truffle's location, usually under Douglas firs.

CHANTERELLE
(CANTHARELLUS CIBARIUS)

Sought after by chefs around the world, the chanterelle is one of my favorite mushrooms. In fact, its Latin name is a derivative of the phrase "good to eat." Its sweet flavor and fragrance are often compared to those of an apricot.

NOTABLE CHARACTERISTICS:
Chanterelle cap and stem color ranges from bright orange to yolk-yellow, or to yellow-orange, as in the popular variety illustrated above.

The cap of a mature chanterelle is often shaped like an abstract vase or trumpet with striations and forked gills. The stalk, or stem, is fibrous and will not break clean.

Chanterelles are generally found beneath coniferous and broad-leaf trees through-out North America.

CANDY CAP
(LACTARIUS FRAGILIS)

This mushroom is a sleeper. I've found it to be the most exciting mushroom on the market today. This mushroom's rich maple flavor and aroma are intensified by drying and then reconstituting.

An exciting ingredient for desserts, pasta, and sauces, just a handful of candy caps will send the sweet smell of maple syrup throughout the house.

NOTABLE CHARACTERISTICS:
The cap of this mushroom ranges from golden honey brown to reddish-brown or orange-brown. Cap texture is matte or dull, never shiny. A mature cap is often flat to slightly concave.

Candy cap stalks are usually much paler than cap color. The stalk is slender and will snap clean.

This mushroom is often found under pine and oak trees throughout the Pacific Northwest.

CLEANING MUSHROOMS John carefully cleaning a day's pick of king boletes

One of the joys of mushroom collecting is bringing home your find, spreading out some newspaper, pouring yourself a glass of wine, and cleaning your trophies. Leisurely inspecting, brushing, and cutting, occasionally bringing the mushroom to your nose to inhale the fresh, clean smell of the forest—the essence of nature.

One of the reasons mushrooms are a popular ingredient in today's cooking is that they absorb butter, garlic, and liquids quickly. For this reason, avoid soaking fresh mushrooms in water.

Mushrooms should be cleaned dry. Using a firm brush, lightly clean off any visible dirt or sand. Some mushrooms may benefit from being wiped clean with a soft rag or having the first layer of skin peeled off. As a last resort for cleaning gritty mushrooms, quickly rinse under water and pat dry. Once clean, mushrooms should be carefully inspected for bugs and worm holes. Cut suspected mushrooms in half and cut away any infected portions. A mushroom need not be discarded because of a worm hole or two.

AN APPETITE FOR MUSHROOMS

By John Pisto

With this cookbook, I strive to inspire you to learn more about mushrooms, their unique characteristics, and their natural habitats. After browsing through these pages filled with stories of my mushroom adventures you may even be encouraged to partake in the hunt. It's a rewarding experience that my family and I look forward to each winter. One thing is certain: you will no longer think of mushrooms as those white buttons in the spaghetti sauce.

It has been more than two decades since I first whet my appetite for wild mushrooms. Since that time, mushrooms have added their subtle flavors and beautiful aromas to many of my recipes both at home and in my restaurants.

The incredible variety of mushrooms available in the markets today offer endless possibilities for unique pasta dishes, entrees, soups, and sauces.

You are sure to be impressed with the mushroom's unique and distinctive culinary attributes.

Mushrooms also supply important vitamins and nutrients while livening up a quick pasta dish. They can add flavor, color,

CHEF JOHN PISTO With a find from the forest

texture, and the element of surprise to almost any meal.

I remember the first time I smelled the sweet maple fragrance of the candy cap (maple cap) mushroom. The strong and defining aroma reminded me of awakening to the beckon of a pancake breakfast with homemade maple syrup. I couldn't wait to experiment with this unusual fungus.

Those new to the tremendous variety of wild mushrooms should take note of the following page's words of caution.

INTRODUCING MUSHROOMS INTO YOUR DIET

As with any new ingredient you add to your family's meals, I recommend you introduce mushrooms into the diet slowly. This allows time to determine if your family members are allergic to any kind of mushroom. I recommend serving only those wild mushrooms that have been purchased from a reputable grocer. Very few mushrooms are deadly, yet identification is critical. The purpose of the descriptions in this book is to inform you, generally, of the varieties of mushrooms available and their culinary uses. THIS IS NOT A PICKER'S GUIDE. Please do not even consider using this information to identify wild mushrooms. Collecting mushrooms with the scant information contained in this cookbook would be foolhardy at best and potentially fatal at worst.

For those interested in hunting mushrooms, I recommend David Arora's detailed field guides.

David's fungi afficionado bible, *Mushrooms Demystified,* and the handy pocket guide, *All That The Rain Promises and More,* both feature full-color photographs, identification charts, habitat information, harvest time information, and information about edibility. Even with Arora's books in hand you should harvest mushrooms for consumption only if you have your finds inspected by a local mycologist. Mushrooms can fool you during their many stages of growth; some of the most deadly can be mistaken for the most delicious. I also recommend taking part in the many mushroom festivals and organized hunts springing up across the country. Spend a couple of years in the field before you serve your finds to the family. All my recipes can be prepared with mushrooms available at your local supermarket or gourmet store.

CANDY CAP MUSHROOM
For description & known habitat see page 12

MUSHROOM GREEN SALAD Recipe on page 33

STARTERS

Julia's Mushrooms • Wild Mushrooms with Onions • Sautéed Wild Mushrooms • Sautéed King Boletes • Marinated Champignons • Deep-Fried Mushrooms • Chanterelle Mushroom Antipasti • Mushroom Green Salad • Grilled Portabella over Polenta • BBQ Wild Mushrooms

JULIA'S MUSHROOMS
A TASTY APPETIZER FOR 2

½ lb   king bolete mushroom caps, ¼" slices; stems chopped
3 Tbs   parsley, Italian flat-leaf (leaves only), chopped
3 cups   olive oil, extra virgin   salt & pepper to taste

Heat a large skillet filled with 2¾ cups of olive oil until simmering. Add mushrooms to skillet and fry over medium heat for 10–12 minutes, turning occasionally. Mushrooms should be crisp on the outside and soft on the inside. Season lightly with salt & pepper. Remove mushrooms and place on paper towels to drain, then set aside.

Place stems in a second skillet. Add remaining olive oil and sauté stems over medium heat. Stems are done when they are lightly brown. Place on paper towels to absorb oil. Lightly season with salt & pepper, and sprinkle with chopped parsley.

Place sautéed caps on serving platter; sprinkle stems over caps, and serve.

WILD MUSHROOMS WITH ONIONS
SERVES 3-4 AS AN APPETIZER

½ lb each   shiitake, hedgehog, champignon (or other mushrooms), ¼" slices
6 Tbs   olive oil, extra virgin   1   shallot, chopped
6 Tbs   butter, unsalted   1 cup   Madeira or dry sherry
1 large   onion, chopped   1 loaf   French bread, sliced
6 cloves   garlic, chopped   salt & pepper to taste

In a preheated (medium heat), medium-size skillet coated with olive oil and butter, add mushrooms. Add onion, garlic, and shallot and fry for 2–3 minutes. Carefully add wine and sauté for 5 more minutes. Remove from skillet. Season lightly with salt and pepper,

Serve mushroom sauce from skillet in a small bowl with toasted French bread surrounding dish. To eat, dip french bread into sauce, add mushrooms to bread, and enjoy!

Serve with a nice light red wine.

FRIENDS SAL BALESTERI, JULIA CHILD, LINDA BALESTERI, & JOHN PISTO
(L to rt) On the set of "Monterey's Cookin' Pisto Style" television show

Friends and fungi go together well. I am pictured here with a few people who have played important roles in my life. Sal, who was instrumental in the success of my television show, and his lovely wife, Linda, have been my close friends for many years. I was introduced to Julia Child and her late husband Paul back in the early '70s. Since that time we have shared a number of culinary adventures.

Soon after my television show, "Monterey's Cookin' Pisto Style," went national, Julia happened to be in California and offered to make an appearance. We spent the day experimenting with each other's mushroom recipes. I sent her home with a bag of dried candy caps. She called a few days later. Her voice expressed surprise and excitement as she told me of her experience: "These fabulous little mushrooms have flavored my entire house with the aroma of maple syrup!"

Julia shares my love for fresh, bold flavors and isn't afraid to experiment. More than that, to me she epitomizes the culinary spirit . . . there is nothing more enjoyable than the combination of good food, wine, and friends.

SAUTÉED WILD MUSHROOMS
SERVES 4-6 AS AN APPETIZER

2 each	portabello, hedgehog, wood ear (or your favorite assorted wild mushrooms), sliced into large bite-size pieces
¼ cup	olive oil, extra virgin (more if required)
3 cloves	garlic, 2 chopped coarsely / 1 whole
1	shallot, chopped coarsely
½ bunch	savory, chopped coarsely
½ bunch	parsley, Italian flat-leaf, chopped coarsely
1 tsp	Pisto's Pepper & Garlic Blend
1 cup	white wine, dry
1 tsp	balsamic vinegar
½ loaf	French bread, sliced
2 Tbs	Pisto's Sensational Seasoning

salt to taste

Coat bottom of a medium-size skillet with olive oil, and heat over medium heat. Add mushrooms to skillet and sauté for 4–6 minutes, stirring frequently. Add chopped garlic, shallot, savory, parsley, and Pisto's Pepper & Garlic Blend (see spice substitutes page 126). When ingredients begin to soften, stir in wine and balsamic vinegar, and increase heat to high. Cook for 1½ to 2 minutes. Drain excess liquid. Season lightly with salt then put aside.

Coat bread slices with a bit of olive oil, sprinkle with Sensational Seasoning, and grill on cast iron grill or in broiler. Lightly toast, then remove slices and rub a raw garlic clove over toasted side. Add mushrooms and a bit of the sautéed ingredients to top of each slice.

Arrange finished slices on a serving platter. Place remainder of sautéed mushrooms around bread decoratively and serve.

SAUTÉED KING BOLETES
SIMPLE & QUICK, SERVES 3–4 AS AN APPETIZER

3–4 lg	king bolete mushrooms, vertically sliced 1/4" thick		
1 Tbs	butter, unsalted	2 Tbs	balsamic vinegar
4 Tbs	olive oil, extra virgin	3 Tbs	thyme, fresh chopped
2 Tbs	garlic, chopped	salt & pepper to taste	

In a preheated (medium heat), medium-size skillet add butter and 1 tablespoon olive oil. Add mushrooms, seasoned lightly with salt and pepper. Sauté on each side about 5 to 6 minutes, or until slightly browned. Remove from skillet and allow to cool. Arrange mushrooms on serving platter.

In same skillet carefully add remaining olive oil, garlic, vinegar, and thyme. Sauté ingredients about 3 minutes at medium heat. Pour over mushrooms and enjoy!

MARINATED CHAMPIGNONS
SERVES 4–6 AS AN APPETIZER

1 lb	champignon mushrooms	1 Tbs	thyme, fresh chopped
½ cup	lemon juice	1 tsp	Pisto's Old California Spice
1 cup	olive oil, extra virgin	1 tsp	salt
2 Tbs	parsley, flat-leaf, chopped	1 head	romaine lettuce
¼ tsp	celery seed, whole	6 sprigs	parsley, Italian flat-leaf
1	bay leaf	1	lemon, quartered
1 tsp	basil, fresh chopped		

In a large bowl add mushrooms, lemon juice, olive oil, chopped parsley, celery seed, bay leaf, basil, thyme, Pisto's Old California Spice (see spice substitutes page 126), and salt. With a zester add several shavings of lemon rind and mix together well. Cover with plastic wrap and allow to marinate in refrigerator at least 2 hours or overnight. Occasionally stir mushrooms, allowing liquid to cover mushrooms.

To serve prepare a platter with a bed of romaine lettuce; place mushrooms on platter and garnish with parsley sprigs and lemon quarters. Remix remaining liquid well and drizzle over mushrooms. Mushrooms can be served as part of an antipasti plate or by themselves.

DEEP-FRIED MUSHROOMS

A TASTY APPETIZER THAT SERVES 6

4 each	portabello, hawk wing, and giant cypress mushrooms or other large mushrooms, sliced vertically
1 cup	flour
1 cup	cracker meal
2	eggs, scrambled well, with 1 tsp. water
3 Tbs	Pisto's Sensational Seasoning
½ bunch	parsley, Italian flat-leaf, chopped (save a few of sprigs for garnish)
4 cups	olive oil, extra virgin
1	lemon, quartered
1 loaf	French bread, sliced

salt & pepper to taste

Prepare bread first by painting each slice with olive oil and sprinkling it with Sensational Seasoning (see spice substitutes page 126). Toast bread lightly on cast iron stovetop grill or in broiler.

Place three pie pans on table top. Place flour in first pan, cracker meal in second pan, and add well-whisked eggs to third pan. Divide Pisto's Sensational Seasoning between pans containing flour and cracker meal. Add parsley to pan with cracker meal, and mix contents of all pans well.

Pour olive oil into a large saucepan and heat over medium-high heat until simmering. Coat mushrooms lightly with flour, then egg, and, finally, with cracker meal.

Carefully place coated mushrooms into oil and fry until golden. When mushrooms are done, remove from hot oil and place on paper towels to drain.

Once excess oil is drained, arrange mushrooms on a serving platter. Garnish with quartered lemon and parsley. Serve with toasted French bread.

GIA PISTO Holding one of her many mushroom finds

Gia Pisto, my youngest daughter, is an avid mushroom hunter. She accompanied me on her first hunt at age 5 and has been tagging along ever since. Now, as with all mushroom afficionados, she doesn't wait for a weekend trek—she is always on the hunt.

One day Gia was on her way to a doctor's appointment with her sister Kim. There in the landscaped gardens of the complex she spotted a cluster of valuable morel mushrooms just alongside the path.

"I saw the mushrooms and first thought they might be elfin saddle," said Gia, "but I plucked one up and realized that they were morels. . . In no time at all, I had two pounds picked and wrapped up in my sweatshirt."

Finding mushrooms in Monterey County is common; however, finding morel mushrooms is another matter indeed. They are rarely found in coastal areas, much less in downtown Monterey. Morels (*Morchella esculenta*) are usually found in colder climates and at much higher altitudes. Gia's discovery made the front page of the local daily newspaper. I was especially proud.

CHANTERELLE MUSHROOM ANTIPASTI

SERVES 8 AS AN APPETIZER

1¼ cups	chanterelles, sliced vertically; small mushrooms can be left whole		
2 each	green, red, yellow bell peppers		
¾ cup	olive oil, extra virgin	3 Tbs	Reggiano parmesan cheese, grated
4 cloves	garlic, chopped	¼ cup	Pisto's Gourmet Vinegar
3 Tbs	Pisto's Sensational Seasoning	2	shallots, chopped
1 head	romaine lettuce	1 med	red onion, chopped
4 baby	artichokes, steamed & quartered	1 tsp	basil, fresh chopped
3	tomatoes, sliced	1 loaf	French bread, sliced
½ cup	calamata olives		salt & pepper to taste
½ tin	anchovy fillets		

Roast bell peppers over open flame or in broiler until all sides are blackened. Place bell peppers in paper bag to cool for 15 minutes. Remove bell peppers and peel off bitter skin using a flat knife to scrape blackened skin off. Remove seeds and cut bell peppers into ½-inch strips.

Prepare dressing: In a medium-size bowl add ¼ cup of olive oil, vinegar, garlic, shallots, red onion, basil, 1 teaspoon Sensational Seasoning (see spice substitutes page 126), salt, and pepper. Mix ingredients well.

Then prepare bread: Paint each slice with olive oil and sprinkle with remaining Sensational Seasoning. Toast bread lightly on cast iron stovetop grill or in broiler.

In a medium skillet over medium heat, sauté chanterelle mushrooms for 2 to 3 minutes in ¼ cup olive oil with 2 cloves of garlic. Season lightly with salt & pepper and 1 teaspoon of Sensational Seasoning.

On a large platter covered with romaine lettuce leaves, decoratively place baby artichokes in center with alternating strips of bell peppers. Place sliced tomatoes, chanterelles, olives, and anchovy fillets to platter. Drizzle dressing over top. Season with fresh ground pepper, and sprinkle cheese over mushrooms. Serve with toasted French bread.

MUSHROOM GREEN SALAD

A WONDERFUL GREEN SALAD WITH VINAIGRETTE DRESSING

1½ cups	champignon and portabello (or sautéd chanterelles) mushrooms, sliced
6 Tbs	olive oil, extra virgin
2 Tbs	Pisto's Gourmet Herb-Infused Red Wine Vinegar
1	lemon, juiced
2 cloves	garlic
2	roma tomatoes, quartered and seeded
½ lb	lettuce leaves, cooled in refrigerator
1 Tbs	Reggiano parmesan cheese, grated

fresh ground black pepper to taste

In a large bowl add mushrooms, olive oil, red wine vinegar, lemon juice, and garlic. Whisk together well; then let stand for 2–3 hours. Remove garlic cloves, add tomatoes and lettuce; toss well.

Place portions on salad plates. Add a dash of fresh black pepper and grated cheese and serve immediately.

Chanterelle Mushroom Antipasti, opposite page

GRILLED PORTABELLO OVER POLENTA

A WONDERFUL APPETIZER FOR 6 PERSONS

½ lb	portabella mushrooms, chopped fine
½ cup	butter, unsalted
1 Tbs	olive oil, extra virgin
2 cloves	garlic, chopped
2 cups	polenta (cornmeal)
6 cups	beef stock
1 cup	gorgonzola cheese, grated
½ cup	Reggiano parmesan cheese, grated
1 cup	heavy cream

salt & fresh ground black pepper to taste

In a medium-size skillet add 1 tablespoon butter, olive oil, chopped garlic, and mushrooms and sauté over medium heat for 4 to 6 minutes, or until done. Season lightly with salt and pepper.

Preheat oven to 350°.

Put cornmeal in a large pot, and slowly whisk in beef stock. Add salt and bring cornmeal to a boil. Lower heat to a simmer, and cook cornmeal for approximately 25 minutes, stirring often until mixture thickens. Slowly add 3 tablespoons butter, ⅔ cup gorgonzola, and Reggiano parmesan to polenta, stirring briskly to melt and combine ingredients. Add cream and stir briskly with a wooden spoon. Continue cooking for another 10 minutes or so until cornmeal has thickened. Stir in a couple of tablespoons of water if mixture becomes difficult to stir.

Pour cooked polenta into a well-buttered baking dish, spreading polenta with a plastic spatula to form a layer of uniform thickness. Place polenta in fridge for 20 to 30 minutes, until cooled. Using a cookie cutter or sturdy glass, cut firm polenta into 3- to 4-inch circles.

Place polenta circles on greased baking dish. Place some sautéed mushrooms on each circle and add a bit of grated gorgonzola cheese. Place baking dish in preheated oven and bake for 15 minutes. Remove from oven and allow to cool for several minutes before serving.

BBQ WILD MUSHROOMS
SERVES 4–6 PERSONS AS AN APPETIZER

1 lb	wild mushrooms, (hawk wing, giant cypress or other large mushrooms), sliced vertically ¼" thick
¼ cup	olive oil, extra virgin
2 Tbs	Pisto's Sensational Seasoning
1 loaf	French bread, sliced
2 Tbs	butter, unsalted melted
6 sprigs	parsley, Italian flat-leaf

salt & pepper to taste

Lightly brush bread slices with olive oil and melted butter. Lightly season with Sensational Seasoning (see spice substitutes page 126), and toast in broiler or on a cast iron, stovetop grill.

Lightly brush mushrooms with olive oil and season with Sensational Seasoning.

Preheat cast iron, stovetop grill to medium-high heat. Place mushrooms on grill and cook for 2–3 minutes; then flip over and grill on other side for 2–3 minutes. A barbecue or broiler can also be used.

Place mushrooms on a large platter covered with a bed of shredded lettuce. Garnish with sprigs of parsley. Season lightly with salt and pepper, and serve with toasted French bread.

LOBSTER, LOBSTER SOUP Recipe on page 47

COOKING WITH MUSHROOMS

SOUPS & SAUCES

Mushroom Beef Stock • Mushroom Chicken Stock • Wild Mushroom Stock • Cream of Candy Cap Soup • Wild Mushroom Potato Soup • Cream of Porcini Mushroom Soup • Wild Mushroom Egg Drop Soup • Lobster, Lobster Soup • Pisto's Mushroom Steak Sauce • Matsutake Sauce with Tomatoes • Candy Cap Wine Sauce

MUSHROOM BEEF STOCK

A TRADITIONAL SOUP STOCK WITH A TWIST

3 lbs	meaty beef bones, sawed into pieces	4 qts	water
1	carrot, peeled & sliced	1 Tbs	Pisto's Sensational Seasoning
1 med	white onion, quartered	1 tsp	Pisto's Pepper & Garlic Blend
2 stalks	celery, chopped	1 tsp	salt
½ cup	assorted dried mushrooms		

Preheat oven to 450°.

In a roasting dish add beef bones and brown bones in oven for 35 to 45 minutes. (Bones can be had at any butcher shop and can be stored in your freezer until needed.) Add carrot, onion, celery. after 15 minutes.

In a 6-quart saucepan add roasted ingredients, mushrooms, and 4 quarts of water. Bring water to a boil, and skim off foam. Add Pisto's Sensational Seasoning, Pisto's Pepper & Garlic Blend (see spice substitutes page 126), and salt. Reduce heat to low, cover, and allow broth to simmer for at least 4 hours, skimming off foam occasionally. Add more water if needed.

When done, strain liquid through a colander or sieve and discard all but liquid. Broth may be covered and refrigerated for a day or two or frozen for later use.

A SHRUMP UNCOVERED A king bolete (porcini) carefully uncovered before harvesting

A shrump is a mound of leaves or needles hiding a mushroom from view. Mushroom hunters (called *shroomers*) become quite adept at locating mushrooms by canvassing the forest or hillside looking for shrumps. When a suspicious looking mound presents itself, the shroomer carefully investigates it with a trusty, forked walking stick.

MUSHROOM CHICKEN STOCK
A DELICIOUS ADDITION TO MANY SOUPS & SAUCES

4 lbs	chicken parts/bones, chopped	6 oz	porcini, oyster, champignon
3 stalks	celery, chopped coarsely		mushrooms, dried
1 lg	white onion, quartered	2	bay leaves
1 lg	yellow onion, quartered	1 bunch	parsley, Italian flat-leaf
3	carrots, chopped coarsely	2 sprigs	thyme, fresh
3–4	shallots, chopped coarsely		salt & pepper to taste
4 qts	water		

In a large skillet brown chicken parts and bones for 15 minutes or so. Add celery, onions, carrots, and shallots about half way through. After chicken is well browned, leave fat in skillet and place rest of ingredients in a 6-quart pot.

Add water, mushrooms, bay leaves, parsley, and thyme to pot. Bring water to a boil, and skim off foam. Reduce heat to low, and allow to simmer for at least 2 hours, skimming off foam occasionally. Add water if necessary to keep ingredients covered.

When done, strain liquid through a colander or sieve, discarding all but liquid. Degrease liquid by chilling it in refrigerator, allowing fat to congeal on top for easy removal by skimming or lifting off. Broth can be covered and refrigerated or frozen for later use.

WILD MUSHROOM STOCK
MY FAVORITE FUNGI SOUP STOCK

1 oz each	porcini, champignon, oyster (or other favorite mushrooms), dried		
½ cup	sherry, dry	¼ cup	green onions, chopped
2 qts	water	1 stalk	celery, chopped
1	white onion, chopped		salt & pepper to taste

Reconstitute mushrooms in a bowl filled with sherry; soak for 30 minutes. Set aside sherry.

In a medium saucepan add mushrooms, sherry, 2 quarts of water, onions, celery, pepper, and salt. Allow ingredients to simmer for at least 1 hour; then strain mushrooms (discard) and use liquid as a stock.

CREAM OF CANDY CAP SOUP

SERVES 4

1 oz	candy cap mushrooms, dried
3 cups	heavy cream
3 Tbs	Plugrá, European-style sweet butter
2 med	shallots, sliced
½ bunch	parsley, Italian flat-leaf, chopped; save several sprigs for garnish
3 cups	mushroom chicken stock (page40)
½ tsp	white pepper
salt & pepper to taste	

Reconstitute mushrooms in ½ cup cream for 20 minutes. When reconstituted, remove mushrooms, set aside cream, and chop mushrooms finely.

In a medium saucepan, add butter and melt at low heat. Add chopped mushrooms, shallots, and parsley. Sauté for 10 minutes, stirring frequently. Cover saucepan during last 3 minutes or so. When done, shallots will be translucent. Drain excess butter.

Whisk in 3 cups (hot) chicken mushroom stock. Then stir in remaining cream and cream that mushrooms were reconstituted in. Bring mixture to a gentle simmer, and allow to reduce for 20 to 25 minutes. Stir contents frequently. During last few minutes, add white pepper and adjust seasoning.

Serve in small bowls garnished with parsley sprigs.

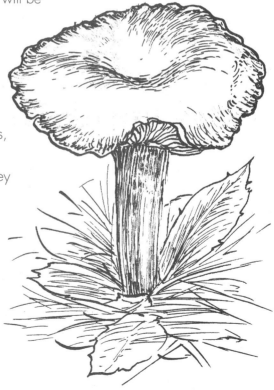

WILD MUSHROOM POTATO SOUP

A DELICIOUS AND FILLING MAIN DISH—SERVES 4

2 cups	chanterelle, oyster, morel, champignon, prince or other assorted mushrooms, dried
2 lbs	baking potatoes, peeled & quartered
2	carrots, peeled & sectioned
2 stalks	celery, chopped
1 lg	onion, diced
6 cloves	garlic, chopped
1	shallot, diced
1 Tbs	Pisto's Pepper & Garlic Blend
4 cups	wild mushroom stock (page 40)
3 Tbs	green onions, chopped

Reconstitute mushrooms in water for 20 minutes. When reconstituted, remove mushrooms, set aside water, and chop mushrooms finely.

Boil potatoes for 25 to 30 minutes, adding carrots during last 15 minutes. Drain and allow to cool. Dice potatoes and place in a large, well-oiled saucepan. Add mushrooms, carrots, celery, onion, garlic, shallot, and Pisto's Pepper & Garlic Blend (see spice substitutes page 126). Sauté at low heat for 6 to 8 minutes.

Add wild mushroom stock and water from reconstituted mushrooms. Simmer for 20 minutes.

Serve in small bowls with fresh, chopped green onions sprinkled on top.

JOHN PISTO HOLDS A PRINCE MUSHROOM Found by his wife Cheryl.

Novice hunters are often surprised at how large certain species of mushrooms are. I've seen mushrooms that were the size of a large dog . . . well, maybe a small dog anyway.

This particular find was shared with friends and took three days of meals to eat—not before everyone had his or her opportunity to pose with it, of course.

CREAM OF PORCINI MUSHROOM SOUP

SERVES 4

1 lb	porcini mushrooms, fresh (or substitute ⅓ lb dried), chopped
3 Tbs	Plugrá, European-style sweet butter
1 med	white onion, diced
½ bunch	parsley, Italian flat-leaf, chopped; save several sprigs for garnish
½ bunch	thyme, fresh chopped
2 stalks	celery, chopped
3 cups	mushroom chicken stock, hot (page 40)
3 cups	heavy cream
1 Tbs	cornstarch (optional)
2 Tbs	water (optional)
1 tsp	white pepper

salt to taste

In a medium saucepan, add butter and melt at medium-low heat. Add mushrooms, onion, parsley, and thyme, and sauté for 10 minutes, stirring frequently. Cover saucepan during last 3 minutes; onions should be translucent.

Stir in celery, hot chicken mushroom stock, and cream. Bring mixture to a gentle simmer, and allow to reduce for 20 to 25 minutes.

For a thicker soup, stir together a tablespoon of cornstarch and two tablespoons of water, and add to soup 10 minutes before soup is done.

During last couple of minutes, add white pepper, and season to taste.

Serve in small bowls garnished with parsley sprigs.

MY GOOD FRIEND TONY RICCIARDI Probably California's best-dressed mushroom hunter

The Ricciardi Hunting Ensemble: Color-coordinated (preferable earth tones) water-resistant, elastic-waist pants (keeps the ticks out) and jacket with strategically placed pockets for easy access to matches, protein bars, aspirin, and assorted pocket knives; complementary two-tone duck bill rubber boots and hunting hat; his trusty, hand-carved mushroom stick, used for unearthing shrumps and warding off mountain lions; wool scarf (on sale at Eddie Bauer); matching brown backpack filled with insect repellent, bandaids, poison oak medication, toilet paper, and who knows what else, with Tony.

WILD MUSHROOM EGG DROP SOUP

SERVES 4

½ lb	assorted wild mushrooms, sliced vertically ¼" thick
2 Tbs	olive oil, extra virgin
8 cups	mushroom chicken stock, (pg. 40)
3	eggs
¼ cup	cream
3 Tbs	parsley, Italian flat-leaf, chopped; reserve several sprigs for garnish
3 Tbs	Reggiano parmesan cheese, grated

salt & pepper to taste

Bring chicken mushroom soup stock to a simmer in a large saucepan.

Sauté mushrooms in a nonstick skillet lightly coated with olive oil for 4 to 5 minutes at medium-high heat. Remove from heat, and place mushrooms on paper towels to drain.

In a bowl, whisk together 3 whole eggs and ¼ cup of cream. Add chopped parsley, Reggiano parmesan, and lightly season with salt and pepper. Slowly add this to simmering soup stock. Add mushrooms, reduce heat to a gentle simmer, and cook for 5 minutes.

Serve in bowls garnished with parsley sprigs.

LOBSTER, LOBSTER SOUP

SERVES 4-6

1 or 2	lobsters, fresh cooked	6 cloves	garlic, chopped
¼ cup	olive oil, extra virgin	4 Tbs	dry sherry
1	leek, chopped	¼ bunch	basil, fresh chopped
2	celery stalks, chopped	½	tomato, chopped
½ lg	yellow onion, chopped	¼ cup	brandy
2	carrots, chopped	2 qts.	water
2 tsp	tarragon, fresh chopped	2 Tbs	tomato paste
2 tsp	thyme, fresh chopped	pinch	saffron
1 cup	lobster mushrooms, sliced		

Remove all white meat from lobsters and set aside. Reserve any lobster juice. Discard egg sack and lungs. Use a mallet to break up head, legs, and remaining shell.

Place a medium, well-oiled skillet over medium-high heat. When skillet is hot add lobster meat, leek, and one-half of celery, onions, and carrots to skillet. Sauté until carrots begin to soften. Stir in 1 teaspoon each of tarragon and thyme. Set aside in bowl. Using same skillet, add more olive oil, and heat over medium heat. Add lobster mushrooms and one-half of garlic, stirring well. Carefully add 2 tablespoons sherry, and flambé ingredients. Add fresh basil, and set ingredients aside.

Cover the bottom of a large stock pot with 3 tablespoons olive oil, and heat to medium. Add lobster shells and juice to pot. Add remaining carrots, onion, celery, and garlic. Add tomato, remaining thyme, and tarragon. Sauté for 15 minutes. Add brandy, remaining dry sherry, and stir. Let reduce (1 to 2 minutes). Add 2 quarts water, tomato paste, and a pinch of saffron. Bring to a boil. Reduce heat to medium-low, and simmer for 45 minutes to an hour, stirring occasionally.

Strain ingredients retaining the liquid. Add sautéed lobster meat, and mushroom mixture and continue cooking for another 15 minutes.

Pour soup into large bowl, and add some lobster meat and mushrooms to each dish.

PISTO'S MUSHROOM STEAK SAUCE
GREAT ON STEAK, VENISON, BUFFALO, & GAME

1 cup	bolete, oyster, morel, or other favorite mushrooms, cleaned & sliced		
2	shallots, chopped	1 Tbs	Pisto's Old California Spice
3 cloves	garlic, chopped	1 Tbs	Pisto's Sensational Seasoning
¼ cup	butter, unsalted	½ cup	cream
2 oz	brandy (optional)	1 tsp	tabasco sauce
1 cup	mushroom beef stock (page 38)	1 Tbs	Worcestershire sauce
1 tsp	sugar		salt & fresh ground black pepper
1 Tbs	Pisto's Pepper & Garlic Blend		

In a large skillet, (at medium heat) sauté mushrooms, shallots, garlic, and butter for 8 to 10 minutes. Add brandy, and flambé ingredients for a more robust taste (optional).

Add mushroom beef stock, and season with sugar, Pisto's Pepper and Garlic Blend, Old California Seasoning, and Sensational Seasoning (see spice substitutes page 126). Add cream, and bring to a fast simmer, allowing mixture to reduce by half (Take care to stir mixture and not allow sauce to scorch).

Add tabasco and Worcestershire sauce. Season lightly with salt, and continue cooking for additional 6–8 minutes. When done, sauce should coat the back of a wooden spoon.

OYSTER MUSHROOMS IN A TREE Along the roadside in Carmel Valley

During mushroom season, my wife and I look for every opportunity to jump in the truck and go exploring. Even if it's just for a couple of hours, early in the morning. One such morning, we spotted a group of oyster mushrooms from the road. They were growing on large sycamore trees—about 25 feet above our heads. As true fungi fanatics, we went back to investigate. After much consideration, I rigged a series of fallen branches together and asked my wife (who weighs much less than I) to climb this makeshift ladder. Cheryl did just that and used her mushroom stick to dislodge the mushrooms from the tree, aiming for my strategically placed box below. One bunch was so large that, when it fell and hit me in the chest, it literally knocked me to the ground. We collected almost 50 pounds of oysters that day!

MATSUTAKE SAUCE WITH TOMATOES
A GREAT SAUCE FOR SEAFOOD & POULTRY

½ lb	matsutake mushrooms, sliced
3 Tbs	butter, unsalted
2 Tbs	olive oil, extra virgin
1 med	onion, chopped finely
1 Tbs	basil, fresh chopped
2 med	roma tomatoes, chopped & mashed
1 tsp	lemon zest
1½ Tbs	flour
2 cups	mushroom beef stock (page 38)
⅛ cup	tomato puree
1	bay leaf, dried
4–6	calamata olives, pitted & chopped
½ Tbs	capers
1 sprig	parsley, Italian flat-leaf, chopped
1 pinch	cayenne pepper
1 cup	red wine, cabernet, merlot, etc.

salt & pepper to taste

In a medium-size skillet, melt 3 tablespoons butter over medium heat. Add a tablespoon of olive oil. Add onion, basil, tomatoes, and lemon zest, and simmer for 2 minutes. Lightly season with salt and pepper. Stir in flour; then add mushroom beef stock, stirring frequently. Add tomato puree, bay leaf, and simmer for 10 to 15 minutes over medium heat. Strain contents of skillet through a colander into a medium-size bowl. Then pour sauce back into skillet and discard other ingredients.

Add to skillet mushrooms, olives, capers, parsley, cayenne pepper, and simmer for an additional 10 minutes. Stir in wine during last few minutes of cooking.

CANDY CAP WINE SAUCE

DELICIOUS SAUCE FOR VEAL OR PORK

⅔ cup	candy cap mushrooms, sliced (or 1½ oz dried mushrooms reconstituted in cream for 20 minutes)
2 Tbs	olive oil, extra virgin
¼ cup	white onion, chopped
¼ cup	shallots, chopped
1 Tbs	lemon juice
½ tsp	Pisto's Moroccan Seasoning
¾ cup	white wine
6 Tbs	butter, unsalted
4 cups	wild mushroom stock (pg. 40)
1 cup	heavy cream

salt & pepper to taste

In a medium skillet coated with olive oil, add onion, shallots, mushrooms, lemon juice, Moroccan Seasoning (see page 126 for spice substitutes), and 4 tablespoons of butter, and sauté ingredients for 8 to 10 minutes. Deglaze pan with wine, and set ingredients aside.

In a medium saucepan, add 3 cups wild mushroom stock, and heat to medium-high. Bring to a fast boil, then reduce to a simmer and cook for 10 minutes, or until liquid has been reduced by two-thirds. Add cream.

Add ingredients from skillet, and whisk in last cup of wild mushroom stock. Continue to simmer for 15 minutes. Season to taste with salt and pepper.

CANDY CAP MUSHROOM PASTA Recipe on page 56

MUSHROOMS WITH
PASTA

Sautéed Mushrooms Rigatoni • Candy Cap Mushroom Pasta • Mushroom Veggie Lasagna • Marinara Sauce • Salmon & Morel Pasta • White Matsutake Pasta • Fresh Herb Pasta • Pisto's Mushroom Pesto • Shiitake Alfredo Fettuccine

SAUTÉED MUSHROOMS RIGATONI

SERVES 2-4 PERSONS

2 ea	king bolete, portabella, hedgehog (or your favorite mushrooms), sliced into ¼" thick pieces			
1 lb	rigatoni pasta	1 tsp	savory, fresh chopped
¼ cup	olive oil, extra virgin	1 tsp	crushed red pepper
3 cloves	garlic, chopped	2 Tbs	basil, fresh chopped
2	shallots, chopped coarsely	1 Tbs	butter, unsalted
2	lemons	¼ bunch	parsley, Italian flat-leaf
¼ cup	white wine, dry	½ cup	cream
2 Tbs	Reggiano parmesan cheese, grated	¾ cup	mushroom chicken stock (pg. 40)

salt & pepper to taste

Prepare pasta according to package instructions (use salted water). Reserve a bit of pasta water.

In a large skillet coated with olive oil, add chopped mushrooms, garlic, shallots, and juice of one lemon. Season lightly with salt and pepper. Sauté for 6 to 8 minutes at medium heat.

Whisk in wine, cream, chicken stock, savory, crushed red pepper, basil, and butter to mushroom sauce. Simmer gently for 5 to 6 minutes.

Add pasta to mushroom sauce with a bit of pasta water and toss well. Serve topped with Reggiano parmesan cheese on a large platter. Garnish with sprigs of parsley and quartered lemon.

REFRIGERATION IS NOT The best alternative for long-term storage of mushrooms.

When fresh, mushrooms should be treated as a delicate vegetable. Their shelf life is fairly short, so I always consider my options immediately upon grasping my prize. *Shall I refrigerate it until dinner tomorrow?* When refrigerating mushrooms, place them in a brown paper bag, and they will last approximately 2 to 3 days. *Or dinner next week?* Some mushrooms (thick, meaty varieties like the bolete) freeze with fair results. *Or save them for appetizers at my next cigar dinner?* Pickled mushrooms can last several weeks, but they can also spoil if you don't know what you are doing. *No, I think I will savor this find for many months to come!* The best way to savor the flavor of mushrooms for months on end is to dry them. In fact, drying actually enhances the flavor of some mushrooms, such as the candy cap and the king bolete. Not all mushrooms fare well with this process—some, like chanterelles, are too fibrous.

CANDY CAP MUSHROOM PASTA
PERHAPS MY FAVORITE PASTA MUSHROOM RECIPE—SERVES 4

1½ oz	candy cap mushrooms, dried
2 cups	heavy cream
1 lb	penne pasta
2 Tbs	olive oil, extra virgin
½	onion, chopped
½ lb	bacon, chopped
3 Tbs	Plugrá, European-style sweet butter
2 cloves	garlic, chopped
1 cup	mushroom chicken stock (pg. 40)
1 Tbs	black pepper, fresh ground
¼ cup	Reggiano parmesan cheese, grated

Reconstitute mushrooms in heavy cream for approximately 30 minutes. Once reconstituted, remove mushrooms and chop finely. Hold cream for later use.

In a well-oiled, medium skillet preheated over medium heat, add onion and bacon; stir well. Sauté ingredients for 5 to 6 minutes. Add butter, garlic, and candy cap mushrooms. Sauté for 6 to 8 minutes more. Add chicken mushroom stock and fresh ground black pepper to taste. Allow mixture to reduce by about a third (approximately 8 to 10 minutes); then whisk in cream. Lower heat to a gentle simmer, and cook for approximately 10 to 15 minutes, stirring continuously. When sauce is ready, it should coat back of wooden spoon.

Prepare pasta using package instructions. Drain pasta, reserving a bit of the pasta water to mix with sauce. Spoon sauce over pasta, and toss well. Serve with grated Reggiano parmesan cheese and fresh ground black pepper.

MUSHROOM VEGGIE LASAGNA
DELICIOUS AND HEALTHY, TOO!—SERVES 6

½ lb	lasagna pasta	2 Tbs	olive oil, extra virgin
½ cup	king bolete mushrooms, chopped	1	eggplant, sliced thinly
1 lg	zucchini, green, sliced thinly	1 bunch	Swiss chard, parboiled
1 lg	yellow squash, sliced thinly	2 cups	mozzarella cheese
¼ cup	Asiago cheese, grated	¼ cup	riccota cheese
1 qt	marinara sauce (see below)	salt & pepper to taste	

Prepare marinara sauce (see below). Preheat oven to 350°.

Prepare pasta al dente, according to package instructions. When done, rinse in cool water, strain in colander, and set aside.

Coat a large glass baking dish with olive oil. Brush vegetables with olive oil, and lightly season with salt and pepper. Spread vegetables and mushrooms in baking dish, then place baking dish in preheated oven for 15 minutes, turning vegetables once to lightly brown.

Remove vegetables, and add 2 cups marinara sauce to baking dish. In layers, add pasta, then vegetables, then mozzarella cheese, coating each layer with ricotta and Asiago cheeses mixed with the remaining marinara sauce. Continue layering sauce, mozzarella, pasta, and vegetables until baking dish is almost full. Sprinkle top of dish with mozzarella cheese, and bake in preheated oven for approximately 45 minutes.

MARINARA SAUCE
GENERAL-PURPOSE GARLIC MARINARA SAUCE (APPROXIMATELY 1 QUART)

2 Tbs	olive oil, extra virgin	1½ qts	tomatoes, chopped
8 cloves	garlic, chopped	1 tsp	crushed red pepper
1 cup	onion, chopped	1 Tbs	sugar
1 bunch	parsley, Italian flat-leaf chopped	salt & pepper to taste	
½ bunch	basil, fresh chopped		

Coat a large skillet with olive oil, and place on medium heat. Add garlic, onion, parsley, and basil. Sauté ingredients until onion is soft. Add tomatoes, crushed red pepper, sugar, salt & pepper, and simmer for 15–20 minutes. Add a bit of water if sauce is too thick; stir frequently.

SALMON & MOREL PASTA

SERVES 2-4

½ lb	penne pasta
4 Tbs	olive oil, extra virgin
½ cup	morel mushrooms, sliced in half
2	salmon fillets, cleaned & boned
2 Tbs	capers
⅓ cup	calamata olives, pitted & sliced
2 cups	marinara sauce (page 57)
1 Tbs	Pisto's Pepper & Garlic Blend
1 Tbs	Pisto's Sensational Seasoning

salt & pepper to taste

Prepare marinara sauce.

Prepare pasta al dente, according to package instructions. When done, drain, add 2 tablespoons of olive oil, and toss well.

In a large skillet coated with olive oil, add morels and sauté over medium-high heat for 5–8 minutes, turning frequently. Make certain morels are well cooked.

Cut salmon fillets into 1-inch cubes and place in skillet. Add capers, olives, marinara sauce, Pisto's Pepper & Garlic Blend, and Sensational Seasoning to skillet (see spice substitutes page 126). Reduce heat to medium-low after 3–5 minutes. Cook sauce for another 25 minutes, or until salmon is done, stirring frequently as necessary to prevent scorching. Adjust seasoning.

Place pasta in large serving bowl, pour two-thirds of sauce over pasta, and toss well. Add last of sauce to top of pasta and serve.

DRIED MUSHROOMS

Dried mushrooms, when stored properly, can remain flavorful for more than a year, and drying fresh mushrooms is easier than you may think. Begin with fresh, clean mushrooms. Small mushrooms can be dried whole; large mushrooms should first be sliced vertically. When drying them, let the air circulate around the mushrooms. I recommend drying them on a framed screen or piece of cheesecloth. Also, gourmet specialty stores and asian markets often carry drying trays. Place the mushrooms in full sun for 8–16 hours, depending on the size and variety of mushroom. If weather isn't cooperative, mushrooms can be dried indoors in a well-ventilated room in about 4 to 7 days. Food dehydraters can simplify the procedure greatly, although you may lose a bit of the mushrooms' flavor. Thoroughly dehydrate mushrooms, or mold will occur.

Once mushrooms are completely free of moisture they can be stored in tightly covered jars (no refrigeration is necessary). Mushrooms can also be kept frozen in plastic bags, if desired.

WHITE MATSUTAKE PASTA
SERVES 4

½ lb	white matsutake mushrooms (or your favorite mushroom), chopped		
1 lb	penne pasta	½ Tbs	Pisto's Pepper & Garlic Blend
¼ cup	olive oil, extra virgin	1 Tbs	Pisto's Sensational Seasoning
6 cloves	garlic, chopped	1 Tbs	basil, fresh chopped
4 Tbs	butter, unsalted	4 Tbs	Reggiano parmesan cheese, grated

Prepare pasta al dente, according to package instructions, When done, drain, add 2 teaspoon olive oil, and toss well. Reserve ½ cup of pasta water.

In a large, nonstick saucepan coated with olive oil, add garlic, butter, mushrooms, Pisto's Pepper and Garlic Blend, and Sensational Seasoning (see spice substitutes page 126). Sauté over medium heat, stirring frequently, for 5 to 6 minutes.

Add pasta and pasta water to the saucepan and toss well. To serve, place pasta on a large serving platter, sprinkle with basil and cheese. Season lightly with Pisto's Pepper & Garlic Blend.

FRESH HERB PASTA
LIGHT & REFRESHING—SERVES 4 AS A SIDE DISH

½ lb	penne pasta	1 Tbs	sage, fresh chopped
¼ cup	butter, unsalted	1 Tbs	capers, chopped
1 cup	assorted mushrooms, sliced	1 cup	tomatoes, chopped
1 cup	spinach, chopped	3 Tbs	olive oil, extra virgin
3 cloves	garlic, chopped	3 Tbs	Reggiano parmesan cheese, grated
½	onion, chopped	salt & pepper to taste	
2 Tbs ea.	basil & thyme, fresh chopped		

Prepare pasta al dente, according to package instructions. Drain, rinse, and set aside.

In a medium saucepan, melt butter. Add mushrooms, spinach, garlic, and onion. Sauté several minutes at medium heat, turning frequently. Add basil, thyme, sage, capers, and tomatoes. Sauté over low heat for 3 to 4 more minutes.

Combine pasta, sautéed ingredients, and olive oil. Toss ingredients well. Adjust seasoning, and serve with a bit of cheese sprinkled on top.

PISTO'S MUSHROOM PESTO

SERVES 4 ITALIANS

1 lb	fettuccine pasta
½ lb	portabella, champignon, shiitake (or your favorite mushrooms), chopped into bite-sized pieces
6	baby artichokes
2 Tbs	butter, unsalted
½ cup	olive oil, extra virgin
½ cup	pine nuts
2	lemons, 1 quartered & 1 juiced
1 tsp	black pepper, fresh ground
2 cloves	garlic, crushed
1 bunch	basil leaves, fresh chopped
½ cup	Reggiano parmesan cheese, grated
½ cup	Asiago cheese, grated
½ loaf	French bread, sliced & toasted lightly

salt and pepper to taste

Prepare artichokes: Remove outer leaves of artichoke until only soft yellow leaves remain. Cut off top 15% of artichoke tip with a sturdy knife. Stalk of artichoke may be removed, or, alternatively, bitter outer skin can be peeled off and discarded. Quarter artichokes and place them in a bowl with the juice of one lemon and mix well (to prevent them from turning brown). Dry artichokes before sautéing.

Prepare pasta in salted boiling water according to package instructions. Drain, rinse, and set aside.

In a medium skillet, add butter, 2 tablespoon olive oil, mushrooms, pine nuts, artichokes, a bit of salt & pepper, and sauté over medium heat for 5 to 6 minutes. Remove from heat and set aside.

In a blender, add remaining olive oil, garlic, basil, and cheeses, blend well. Add to cooled skillet, and stir well with a wooden spoon.

Add sauce to pasta and toss well. Serve pasta hot with toasted french bread. Garnish with lemon wedges.

SHIITAKE ALFREDO FETTUCCINE
ROBUST AND TASTY—SERVES 6

1 lb	fettuccine pasta
½ cup	shiitake or morel mushrooms, sliced
2 Tbs	olive oil, extra virgin
⅓ cup	Plugrá, European-style sweet butter
3 oz	dry sherry or brandy
½ cup	Reggiano parmesan cheese, grated
½ cup	whipping cream
2	eggs
3 Tbs	parsley, Italian flat-leaf, chopped fine

Prepare pasta al dente according to package directions. Rinse, drain, and set aside. Reserve a bit of the pasta water.

In a large, nonstick saucepan, sauté mushrooms in 2 tablespoons each of olive oil and butter over medium heat for 5 to 6 minutes. Add sherry or brandy, and flambé for a moment to add a robust flavor. Remove mushrooms and set aside.

Add remaining butter, and blend in cheese, allowing it to melt. Stir in cream and blend well, allowing ingredients to reach a gentle simmer.

In a small bowl, scramble eggs well. Add 3 teaspoons of the simmering sauce to eggs; then transfer bowl's ingredients to saucepan. Reduce heat to low, and cook for 3 to 4 minutes, stirring frequently. Be careful not to over-cook sauce. Whisk in chopped parsley and mush-rooms, and remove from heat.

Add alfredo sauce to pasta, and toss well. Serve immediately, pasta should be served hot.

POWDERED MUSHROOMS Before food processors, powdered mushrooms were made with a mortar and pestle.

Mushroom powder is fast becoming a common flavoring additive. It can be a powerful ingredient, used like curry or cinnamon to add distinctive flavor. Just a dash of it in soups, pasta, and meat sauces will subtly enhance the dish. Try incorporating it into your bread dough or in your olive oil dip.

Mushroom powder can be made by grinding dried mushrooms in a food processor or a small coffee grinder. The powder is then stored in air-tight jars like any other seasoning.

PORTERHOUSE STEAK WITH SAUTÉED SHIITAKES Recipe on page 70

MEAT & POULTRY

Beef Tenderloin & Mushroom Sauce • Veal Marsala • Mushroom Marsala Sauce • Veal Stanton • Porterhouse Steak with Sautéed Shiitakes • Filet Mignon in Porcini Sauce • Truffle Chicken • Pheasant & Quail Stew • Breaded Rabbit • Fall Quail with Orange Glaze • Grilled Quail & Polenta • Stuffed Quail Vintner Style • Candy Cap Pork Chops

BEEF TENDERLOIN & MUSHROOM SAUCE

SERVES 4—JUICY AND DELICIOUS

1 lb	beef tenderloin, sliced
1 cup	assorted wild mushrooms, sliced
⅓ cup	Plugrá, European-style sweet butter
3 Tbs	shallots, chopped
2 Tbs	red onion, chopped
2 Tbs	flour
1 cup	wild mushroom stock (page 40)
2 Tbs	brandy
½ cup	port
1 Tbs	black peppercorns
1 Tbs	Pisto's Sensational Seasoning
½ cup	heavy cream
salt & pepper to taste	

In a large skillet over medium heat, melt 3 tablespoons butter, and sauté tenderloin lightly for approximately 1 minute on each side. Set aside and cover with foil. In same skillet add mushrooms, shallots, and onion. Cook for 2 to 3 minutes over medium-heat. Remove from heat and set aside.

Melt 3 tablespoons butter in a small saucepan and slowly whisk in flour, mixing well. Add mushroom stock, and continue to stir frequently over medium-low heat for 3 or 4 minutes.

Add contents of saucepan to skillet. Heat skillet over medium heat, and add brandy, port, black peppercorns, Sensational Seasoning, and cream (see spice substitutes page 126). Season lightly with salt and pepper. Mix all ingredients well; then add beef slices to skillet, spooning sauce over them. Bring contents to a quick boil, and remove from heat.

Place equal portions of tenderloin slices on four plates; smother with sauce and mushrooms.

FOR THE LOVE OF MUSHROOMS Barbara & Paige Ricciardi would climb the highest mountain.

North American mushroom hunters tend to be a secretive bunch. The reason for secrecy is simple. Mushrooms are produced by spores. Therefore, wherever you find a good crop of chanterelles or morels, the chances are good you will find them there again next season, or even the following week, after the next good rain.

There are some who covet their treasure maps so closely, they've developed secret location codes and recorded them in their field guides. I've seen hysteria on the face of an individual who misplaced her trusty, dusty old field guide. Many, shroomers take their hobby seriously.

VEAL MARSALA
SERVES 6

6	veal cutlets, medium-thick slices of range-fed veal
2 Tbs	olive oil, extra virgin
2 Tbs	butter, unsalted
2 cups	seasoned breadcrumbs
4 sprigs	parsley, Italian flat-leaf
1	lemon, cut in wedges

salt & pepper to taste

Prepare veal by sprinkling with water. Then cover each cutlet with plastic wrap and pound lightly. Unwrap and rub each cutlet with a drop or two of olive oil. Dredge cutlets in breadcrumbs, pressing hard so they adhere to the meat.

Heat a skillet, and add olive oil, butter, salt, and pepper. Place coated veal chops three at a time in skillet. Cook veal chops for 4–6 minutes on each side over medium-high heat. Clean skillet after each batch to avoid charred bread crumbs.

Serve veal chops on plate with marsala sauce (see below) drizzled over top and along sides. Garnish with lemon and sprigs of flat-leaf parsley or fresh basil.

MUSHROOM MARSALA SAUCE
SAUCE FOR VEAL MARSALA

1 cup	wild mushrooms (2 or 3 varieties if possible), sliced
¼ cup	water
3 cloves	garlic, chopped
6	green onions, sliced (white part only)
2 Tbs	olive oil, extra virgin
2 Tbs	parsley, Italian flat-leaf, chopped
½ cup	Marsala wine

In a large skillet, heat water, mushrooms, garlic, and onions over low heat and sauté a few minutes. Add olive oil and stir. Add parsley and wine; then stir until slightly reduced (approximately 4 to 5 minutes).

VEAL STANTON

SERVES 4

1 lb	veal, sliced ½" thick		½ cup	tomatoes, chopped
¼ cup	flour		½ tsp	sage, dried
3–4	white matsutake mushrooms (or your favorite mushrooms), sliced			
2 Tbs	olive oil, extra virgin		¼ cup	white wine, dry
1 Tbs	Plugrá, European-style sweet butter		½ cup	chicken mushroom stock
1 Tbs	garlic, chopped		4 sprigs	parsley, Italian flat-leaf
2 Tbs.	green onion, chopped		salt & fresh ground pepper to taste	

Salt and pepper veal slices lightly, then dredge in flour.

In a medium saucepan, add a tablespoon each of olive oil and butter. Heat saucepan to medium and carefully add veal. Sauté for 3 to 4 minutes on each side until lightly browned; remove from saucepan and keep warm.

In the same pan, add garlic, green onion, tomato, sage, salt, pepper, and mushrooms. Saute 3–4 minutes over medium heat. Increase heat to high and add remaining olive oil, wine, and chicken mushroom stock. Sauté 4 to 5 minutes, until slightly reduced.

Arrange veal on warm serving platter, and pour sauce over it. Garnish with parsley.

PORTERHOUSE STEAK WITH SAUTÉED SHIITAKES.

SIMPLY DELICIOUS—SERVES 2

24 oz	porterhouse steak
2 cups	shiitake mushrooms, sliced
4 Tbs	olive oil, extra virgin
3 tsp	Pisto's Sensational Seasoning
4 cloves	garlic, chopped
½ cup	red wine
¼ lb	spinach, fresh

salt & pepper to taste

Coat steak with olive oil, then sprinkle with a generous amount of Sensational Seasoning (see spice substitutes page 126), salt, and pepper. Pat or work spices into meat to lock in juices.

Preheat cast iron, stovetop grill or skillet over medium-high heat, and grill steak according to your preference.

Preheat a medium, well-oiled skillet over medium-high heat. Add mushrooms and 2 cloves of garlic. Sauté for 4–5 minutes, turning occasionally. Reduce heat to medium-low, then carefully add wine to skillet, and let reduce for 5 minutes or so.

Preheat a medium, well-oiled, skillet over medium-low heat. Add remaining garlic, and sauté until golden. Add spinach, and drizzle a bit of olive oil over spinach. Season with salt and pepper. Turn spinach continuously until slightly wilted. Prepare shortly before serving.

Cut steak into two portions and place on serving plates. Steaks can be sliced at an angle into strips if desired. Smother steaks with mushroom sauce, and place spinach on side of plate.

ALL THAT THE RAIN PROMISES AND MORE & MUSHROOMS DEMYSTIFIED Books by David Aura

Bird watchers and flower lovers look to the Audubon Society's field guides for on-the-spot identification and information. Mushroom afficionados live by David Arora's *Mushrooms Demystified* and carry the field companion *All That the Rain Promises and More* in their hip pockets. I've seen these books in the hands of people all over the world—their pages so worn from use they are held in place with tape and rubber bands, holding the bulge of scratch notes within.

Mushrooms Demystified offers over 2000 detailed descriptions and photographs of North American fungi.

All That the Rain Promises and More is a comprehensive, pocket-size field guide to approximately 200 wild mushrooms found in Western North America—all the way from the Rocky Mountains and the Pacific Coast to Mexico and Alaska. It, too, is filled with up-close and personal photos of each mushroom and all the necessary identification information.

FILET MIGNON IN PORCINI SAUCE

THE PERFECT COMBINATION OF MEAT & MUSHROOMS—SERVES 2

2 (12 oz)	filet mignon
2 cups	porcini (or your other favorite assorted mushrooms), thinly sliced

¼ cup	olive oil, extra virgin	2 Tbs	brandy
1 Tbs	shallot, chopped	¼ cup	heavy cream
4 cloves	garlic, chopped	2 Tbs	dijon mustard
4 Tbs	balsamic vinegar	salt & pepper to taste	

In a large preheated (medium heat) saucepan, add olive oil and sliced mushrooms; sauté for 5 to 6 minutes. About half way through add shallot and garlic to saucepan, stirring well. Add 2 tablespoons balsamic vinegar, lightly season with salt and black pepper, then simmer ingredients for 1 to 2 minutes and set aside.

Preheat a cast iron stovetop grill or skillet well coated with olive oil to medium-high heat. Lightly season filet with salt and pepper, then place on grill. Grill steaks according to your preference, approximately 2–3 minutes on each side for rare to medium-rare meat. When steaks are done, remove and set aside.

Deglaze grill or skillet with 2 tablespoons balsamic vinegar and brandy; and add ingredients to standing saucepan. Bring saucepan to a gentle simmer. Stir in cream and dijon mustard, and stir slowly with a wooden spoon until mixture thickens.

Place filets on plates, and smother steaks with shallots and mushrooms. Pour sauce over mushrooms and serve.

TRUFFLE CHICKEN

SERVES 4

4	chicken breast, boneless halves	¼ cup	pine nuts
2 Tbs	Pisto's Sensational Seasoning	2 Tbs	parsley, Italian flat-leaf chopped)
1 Tbs	lemon juice	2 slices	bacon, fried & crumbled
1½ cups	breadcrumbs	½ cup	flour
½ cup	olive oil, extra virgin	3	eggs
4 Tbs	Plugrá, European-style sweet butter	6	Oregon white truffles, thinly sliced*
¾ cup	Madeira wine	salt & fresh ground black pepper	
2 Tbs	Reggiano parmesan cheese, grated		

Preheat oven to 400º.

Place chicken breasts on cutting board and pound lightly. Season chicken with 1 teaspoon Pisto's Sensational Seasoning (see spice substitutes page 126), lemon juice, salt, and pepper, then set aside.

In a bowl add breadcrumbs, ¼ cup of olive oil, and 1 tablespoon of Sensational Seasoning; toss well. In a medium-size skillet, add 2 tablespoons butter, breadcrumbs, ¼ cup Madeira wine, cheese, and pine nuts. Sauté over medium-low heat for 5–6 minutes. Stir in chopped parsley and mix well.

On cutting board, lightly oil flattened chicken breasts. Place an equal amount of breadcrumb mixture (use about ½ of mixture) and a bit of bacon on each breast. Roll chicken breasts into tubes with stuffing inside. Use toothpicks to hold tubes together.

Add ½ cup of flour to remaining breadcrumb mixture. Season lightly with salt and pepper, and mix together well. In a separate bowl, whisk eggs, salt and black pepper to form a batter. Dip chicken tubes into batter, and then roll in breadcrumb mixture, coating chicken well. Grease baking dish lightly. Place chicken breasts in dish, and put a small piece of butter on each. Bake for 30–35 minutes. Check thickest part of chicken for doneness.

Remove chicken from baking dish, and deglaze pan with ½ cup of madeira wine. Add truffles.

Place chicken on plates, and add a bit of sauce and truffles to top of each serving. Note: If truffles are unavailable, substitute sautéed shiitake or white matsutake mushrooms.

*Truffles should be sliced very thin; if possible, use a French mandolin.

PHEASANT & QUAIL STEW

SERVES 6–8

1 med	pheasant, sectioned
6	quail, semi-boned
2 cups	white wine, dry
3 sprigs	rosemary
½ cup	king bolete mushrooms, dried
3 Tbs	olive oil, extra virgin
6 cloves	garlic, chopped coarsely
1 med	yellow onion, chopped coarsely
2 lg	leeks, sliced
2	carrots, peeled & sectioned
2 cups	roma tomatoes, chopped
¼ bunch	parsley, Italian flat-leaf, chopped coarsely
1 cup	chicken mushroom stock (recipe page 40)
¼ tsp.	crushed red pepper

salt & pepper to taste

Marinate pheasant and quail in white wine, rosemary, salt, and pepper for 1 hour. Reserve the wine marinade. Soak mushrooms in ½ cup water for 20 minutes to reconstitute.

Cover bottom of a large cast iron skillet with olive oil. Preheat skillet for 5–8 minutes over medium heat. When the skillet is hot, add pheasant and quail; brown all sides well.

Remove birds from skillet, and in their place add garlic, onion, leeks, carrots, and drained mushrooms. Sauté over medium heat until onions and garlic soften. Pour in wine marinade and stir. Add tomatoes, parsley, salt, chicken mushroom stock, crushed red pepper, and black pepper; and mix well.

Return birds to skillet, with the larger pieces on the bottom, and bring ingredients to a boil. Reduce heat to medium, and simmer for approximately 30 minutes, or until done.

Serve with traditional polenta, soft or grilled (page 34).

CHEF PISTO GRILLING Mushrooms and sausages, a perfect combination after a day of mushroom hunting.

Part of what makes the experience of hunting for mushrooms so enjoyable is the comradery with friends, old and new. We often bring a grill and necessary supplies to prepare a gourmet lunch or early supper on location. I prefer Italian sausage or quail. Yet, a simple picnic basket filled with crusty Italian bread, salami, cheese, and a good bottle of wine will do. It's a relaxing addition to an invigorating day.

BREADED RABBIT

SERVES 4

1 whole	rabbit, cut in pieces
½ cup	oyster, prince, giant cypress (or your favorite mushrooms), dried
1 cup	water
2 cups	flour
4 tsp	Pisto's Sensational Seasoning
4 Tbs	olive oil, extra virgin
3 Tbs	butter, unsalted
2 cloves	garlic, chopped coarsely
1½ cups	celery, chopped
1½ cups	carrots, diced
1½ cups	onions, chopped
½ cup	calamata olives, pitted
½ cup	white wine, dry
1 pinch	saffron

salt & pepper to taste

Soak mushrooms in water for 20 to 30 minutes to reconstitute. Reserve water. Squeeze excess water from mushrooms, and chop coarsely.

Mix flour, Sensational Seasoning (see spice substitutes page 126), salt, and pepper in a pie pan. Coat rabbit with flour mixture.

Cover the bottom of a cast iron skillet with butter and olive oil. Place skillet over high heat. When skillet is hot, add rabbit. When rabbit begins to brown, reduce heat and cook for approximately 20 minutes, turning the rabbit on all sides to brown.

Remove rabbit from pan, and set aside. In its place, add the garlic, celery, carrots, onions, and chopped mushrooms, stir well. Add olives, white wine, saffron, salt, and pepper. (You may add a bit of the water from the mushrooms for flavor, but don't use the residue that has accumulated on the bottom.)

Simmer for 5 minutes, stirring occasionally. Return rabbit to the pan, cover, and cook over medium heat for about 30 minutes, or until done.

Serve rabbit with vegetables on the side.

FALL QUAIL WITH ORANGE GLAZE

SERVES 4

8	quail, semi-boned	1¾ cup	white wine, dry
½ cup	champignon, king bolete mushrooms (or your favorite mushrooms), dried		
8 cloves	garlic	½ cup	raisins
1 cup	cream	½ lb	ground pork
½	asian pear, peeled & chopped	¼ cup	Pisto's Sensational Seasoning
½ cup	breadcrumbs, seasoned	1	egg
¼ bunch	parsley, Italian flat-leaf, chopped	3 Tbs	olive oil, extra virgin
½ cup	orange glaze (recipe below)		

Preheat oven to 400°. Prepare glaze (recipe below), and set aside

Marinate quail in 1 cup white wine and 4 cloves of crushed garlic for 45 minutes.

Soak raisins in ½ cup white wine for 20 minutes, or until plump.

Reconstitute dried mushrooms in 1 cup of cream for 20 to 30 minutes. Squeeze out cream, and chop mushrooms coarsely. .

Brown ground pork and remaining garlic (chopped) in well-oiled frying pan for 8 to 10 minutes. Add asian pear, raisins, and mushrooms. When pork is fully cooked, add remaining white wine, and deglaze pan. Transfer ingredients into a medium-size mixing bowl. Add 2 tablespoons of Sensational Seasoning (see spice substitutes page 126), fold in breadcrumbs, add egg and parsley, and mix to the consistency of meat loaf.

Stuff each marinated quail with 3 tablespoons of stuffing. In a large baking dish, prop quail breast up with legs crossed over cavity. Do not crowd dish. Paint quail with olive oil, and sprinkle a bit of Sensational Seasoning over birds.

Bake quail for approximately 15 minutes. Remove from oven, and paint with orange glaze. Return to oven and cook for an additional 5 minutes, or until done. Glaze quail again, and serve with remaining orange glaze on the side.

ORANGE GLAZE

3 cloves	garlic, minced	½ cup	orange juice
2 Tbs	onions, chopped	¼ cup	Grand Marnier liqueur
1 Tbs	butter, unsalted		

In a small frying pan, sauté garlic and onion in butter. Add orange juice and Grand Marnier, and reduce. Simmer until sauce has thickened.

GRILLED QUAIL & POLENTA

SERVES 2-3

4–6	quail, cleaned	1 cup	white wine, dry
4 cloves	garlic, crushed	1 Tbs	balsamic vinegar
2 Tbs	thyme, chopped	1 pkg	polenta, instant
2 Tbs	butter, unsalted	¼ cup	Asiago cheese, grated
2 Tbs	olive oil, extra virgin	salt & pepper to taste	

In a bowl, add wine, garlic, balsamic vinegar, thyme, salt, and pepper. Mix ingredients well. Add quail to bowl, and marinate for 2 hours or more.

Prepare polenta according to package instructions. When polenta thickens, just before serving, add butter and cheese. Mix well, and remove from heat. Cover polenta to keep warm until ready to serve.

Prepare mushroom sauce (see below).

Preheat well-oiled, cast iron stovetop grill or skillet to medium. Add quail, and grill for 2–3 minutes or more on each side, until done. Baste with marinade while grilling.

Place a bed of polenta down the center of a large platter, and spoon mushroom ragout sauce around the sides. Place quail on top of polenta, add a bit more sauce to top of quail, and serve.

RAGOUT (MUSHROOM SAUCE)

2 cups	portabella, oyster, shiitake (or your favorite mushrooms), stems removed & caps sliced		
2 Tbs	olive oil, extra virgin	3 Tbs	butter, unsalted
3 cloves	garlic, chopped	3	shallots, chopped
1 cup	chicken mushroom stock (page 40)		

In a nonstick skillet over medium heat, add olive oil, butter, mushrooms, garlic, and shallots. Sauté for 3 to 4 minutes. Reduce to low and add chicken stock. Simmer for 15 to 20 minutes.

A GOOD DAY'S WORK King boletes dominate the find of the day.

I often compare the adventure and rewards of mushroom hunting with panning for gold or a child's easter egg hunt. The thrill of the hunt and the excitement of the find are exhilarating.

When people hunt in groups, the hunt often becomes a contest, with the the biggest, most perfect mushroom taking honors that evening at dinner.

STUFFED QUAIL VINTNER STYLE

SERVES 6

12	quail, semi-boned	3 Tbs	olive oil, extra virgin
3 Tbs	white wine, dry	¼ cup	butter, unsalted

Preheat oven to 400°.

Prepare stuffing (see recipe opposite page).

Prepare vintner sauce (see below).

Stuff each quail with a tablespoon or two of stuffing. Preheat a well-oiled, cast iron stovetop grill or skillet over medium-high heat. Add quail and brown for 2 minutes or so on each side. Remove from heat. Dot quail with butter, splash with wine, and place in well-oiled baking dish, breast up with legs crossed over cavity. Bake about 15 minutes.

Prepare spinach (see recipe page 70).

Place a bed of spinach on a large serving platter, and place quail on top of spinach. Spoon vintner sauce over quail.

VINTNER SAUCE
WONDERFUL WITH QUAIL

¼ cup	candy cap mushrooms, chopped		
½ cup	butter, unsalted	2 Tbs	thyme, fresh chopped
2 cloves	garlic, chopped	2 Tbs	shallots, chopped
¼ cup	white wine, dry	¼ cup	red wine
1 cup ea	red & green seedless grapes, halved		
2 Tbs	parsley, Italian flat-leaf, chopped		

Melt ¼ cup butter in a saucepan. Add mushrooms, thyme, garlic, and shallots. Sauté over medium-low heat for 5 to 6 minutes. Add wine, grapes, salt, and pepper. Continue to sauté for 3–4 minutes. Add ¼ cup butter and parsley, and heat until butter is melted.

STUFFING

FOR USE WITH STUFFED QUAIL VINTNER STYLE

2 cups	champignon, king bolete, (or your favorite mushrooms), chopped fine*

3 Tbs	olive oil, extra virgin	2 cloves	garlic, chopped
2 Tbs	shallots, fresh chopped	½ cup	parsley, Italian flat-leaf, chopped
2 oz	white wine, dry	½ cup	milk
5 slices	soft white bread, cut into small cubes, crusts on		
1 Tbs ea	oregano, thyme, rosemary, lavender, fresh chopped		
2	eggs, scrambled	½ cup	Reggiano parmesan cheese, grated

salt & pepper to taste

Preheat a well-oiled skillet over medium–high heat. Add mushrooms, garlic, shallots, parsley, and white wine. Sauté over medium-high heat for approximately 8–10 minutes, stirring frequently.

Add milk, bread, oregano, thyme, rosemary, lavender, eggs, and cheese. Sauté over medium-high heat for about 10 minutes, stirring frequently. Remove from heat and place ingredients in bowl. Drain excess liquid, and allow to cool. Mix ingredients together well and use as stuffing for quail.

* If using dried mushrooms, reconstitute before using.

CANDY CAP PORK CHOPS
A HEARTY MEAL FOR 4

¼ lb	candy cap mushrooms (or your favorite mushrooms), dried		
4	pork chops, double loin rib	1 tsp	Pisto's Sensational Seasoning
½ cup	cream	½ tsp	basil, fresh chopped
¼ cup	Plugrá, European-style sweet butter	½ cups	sherry, dry
1 stalk	celery, chopped	3 Tbs	Dijon mustard
2 Tbs	shallots, chopped	1 bunch	mint leaves
1½ cups	bread cubes		salt & pepper to taste
2 Tbs	parsley, Italian flat-leaf chopped		

Reconstitute candy cap mushrooms for 20 minutes in cream. Gently squeeze excess cream from mushrooms, and chop coarsely.

Preheat a well-oiled skillet over medium–low heat. Add one half of butter, chopped celery, and shallots; sauté for 6 to 8 minutes. Add bread cubes, and cook gently until bread is golden brown, then remove skillet from heat. Add parsley, salt, Sensational Seasoning (see spice substitutes page 126), basil, and ¼ cup dry sherry. Mix ingredients well.

Create a pocket in each pork chop by cutting along one side. Tightly fill pocket with stuffing, and remove any remaining stuffing from skillet. In same skillet, add rest of butter and stuffed pork chops, and heat to medium. Brown pork chops on all sides. Reduce heat to a simmer, cover skillet, and cook pork chops for 20 minutes, turning them occasionally.

Add mushrooms and mustard to skillet. Continue to simmer for another 20 minutes, or until done, stirring occasionally. Remove pork chops and deglaze skillet with remaining sherry. Place pork chops on plate, and cover pork chops with mushrooms and sauce. Garnish with mint leaves.

Serve with garlic mashed potatoes and a bit of apple sauce.

CODY Our ever-faithful dog Cody and the bronze Pichon award

Everyone in our house loves mushrooms, even our dog, Cody. We used to take him on the hunts. Unfortunately, while we were collecting mushrooms, he was collecting ticks. Now, his mushroom hunting is restricted to our morning walks through the back streets of Monterey and an occasional dinner party.

Mushrooms are always a big hit at at our dinner parties. At one memorable dinner party Cody stole the show. I had prepared a dinner of roasted stuffed pork chops, grilled greens, and, as a special treat, potato gateau with Oregon white truffles.

The dinner was nearly complete when I slipped out of the kitchen to join our guests. Among them was the charming Comtesse de Lalande of the famed French Pichon Longueville vineyards. When I returned, Cody was just finishing off the potato gateau— truffles and all. The Comtesse seemed amused and quite taken with Cody, who spent the rest of the evening by her side. Before retiring she graciously presented us with a beautiful Pichon bronze hospitality medallion. Although I prize it in memory of her spirit, the medallion really belongs to Cody.

ALASKAN SALMON WITH MORELS Recipe on page 92

SEAFOOD

Salmon Cakes • Baked Rock Fish with Chanterelles • Baked Sole in Parchment • Fried Whole Trout with Shiitakes • Alaskan Salmon with Morels • Broiled Swordfish with Mushrooms • Monk Fish with Lobster Mushrooms

SALMON CAKES

A GREAT LUNCH OR BRUNCH TREAT—SERVES 6

1½ lb	salmon fillets, skin removed	3 Tbs	olive oil, extra virgin
1 cup	mushrooms, chopped fine	4 slices	bread, crusts removed
¼ cup	cream	4 Tbs	butter, unsalted
2	shallots, chopped fine	1 Tbs	mustard, dry
4 Tbs	parsley, Italian flat-leaf, chopped	1 Tbs	Pisto's Pepper & Garlic Blend
¼ cup	flour	2	eggs
1 cup	cracker meal	1 Tbs	Pisto's Sensational Seasoning
1 cup	tarter sauce	2	lemons, quartered

salt & pepper to taste

Paint both sides of salmon fillets with a bit of olive oil, and place them on a preheated cast iron stovetop grill or skillet, over medium-high heat. Grill on each side for 3 to 4 minutes. Remove from grill and place in a large bowl to cool.

In a separate bowl, place bread in cream, and allow to soak for 5 minutes. Remove bread and gently squeeze out majority of cream.

Sauté shallots, over medium-low heat in 1 tablespoon of butter for 5 minutes, or until soft and translucent.

When salmon is cool, flake salmon by hand into small pieces. Add chopped mushrooms, bread, dry mustard, parsley, and Pisto's Pepper & Garlic Blend (see spice substitutes page 126), and mash together well. Form 6 patties.

Place three pie pans on counter top. Fill one pan with flour. Fill second pan with well beaten eggs. Fill third pan with cracker meal seasoned with Sensational Seasoning, salt, and pepper.

Coat patties with flour, then eggs, then cracker meal. Grill patties on cast iron stovetop grill or in broiler for 2 to 3 minutes on each side. Put ½ teaspoon of butter on top of each patty after you flip it to cook the other side.

Garnish with quartered lemons, and serve with tarter sauce.

UNVEILING A SMALL CAULIFLOWER MUSHROOM Barbara Ricciardi kneels under a pine tree.

Cauliflower mushrooms are usually found under pine trees and grow very large (a single specimen can weigh up to 50 pounds). They resemble a yellow-white sponge or sea coral. Cauliflower mushrooms are edible when cooked, yet can be difficult to clean. Their delicious aroma and chewy texture compliment soups and casseroles.

BAKED ROCK FISH WITH CHANTERELLES

PREPARED IN PARCHMENT PAPER—SERVES 2

2 lg	rock fish fillets
3	chanterelles, sliced
½ cup	olive oil, extra virgin
2 Tbs	Pisto's Sensational Seasoning
1	yellow zucchini, sliced
1	green zucchini, sliced
2	roma tomatoes, chopped & seeded
6–8	snow pea pods
4 cloves	garlic, chopped
¼ bunch	basil, fresh chopped
2 tsp	butter, unsalted
3 oz	white wine, dry
2 sheets	parchment (24" x 24")
1	lemon, sliced

salt & pepper to taste

Preheat oven to 350°. Paint parchment paper thoroughly with olive oil on both sides. Place first sheet on large baking sheet.

Paint first fillet with olive oil on both sides. Sprinkle with Sensational Seasoning (see spice substitutes page 126). Place a portion of zucchini, tomatoes, peas, garlic, and basil in the center of the parchment and season with salt and pepper. Place fish on vegetables and mushrooms on top of fillet. Place a portion of lemon slices on fillet. Add some butter and wine. Fold parchment over, covering fish, and twist parchment ends and tops closed. Repeat process for second fillet. Place parchment packets side by side on large baking sheet. Bake fish in parchment for 20 to 30 minutes. Serve fish inside parchment. (Use kitchen scissors to cut open the top.)

NOTE: Cooking parchment paper should be available from your butcher or culinary specialty store. If unavailable, use clean, heavy duty, plain brown bags sliced open.

BAKED SOLE IN PARCHMENT

SERVES 6

6 lg	fillets of sole, cleaned & rinsed
½ lb	matsutake or shiitake mushrooms (or your favorite wild mushrooms), sliced
3	lemons, juiced
4 Tbs	butter, unsalted
2 cloves	garlic, chopped
3 Tbs	sherry, dry
4 Tbs	tarragon, fresh chopped
4 Tbs	basil, fresh chopped
4	roma tomatoes, chopped & seeded
1 Tbs	chives, fresh chopped
3 sheets	parchment (24" x24")
1	lemon, quartered
6 sprigs	parsley, Italian flat-leaf

salt & pepper to taste

Preheat oven to 350⁰.

In bowl, add fillets, mushrooms, lemon juice, salt, and pepper. Toss ingredients well to coat fillets and mushrooms. Set aside and allow to marinate for 10 minutes.

In a nonstick skillet, sauté mushrooms in 2 tablespoons butter for 5 to 6 minutes. Remove mushrooms and set aside. In same skillet, add remaining butter, garlic, sherry, tarragon, and basil, and sauté for 5 to 6 minutes.

Paint parchment paper thoroughly with olive oil on both sides. Paint fillets with olive oil. Place one piece of parchment on the baking sheet. Then place two fillets in its center. Put one-third of the chopped tomatoes, chives, mushrooms, and sautéed herbs on the fillets. Season lightly with salt and pepper. Fold over parchment and twist ends to secure each package. Repeat process for rest of fillets.

Place packages side by side on a large baking sheet. Bake fish in parchment for 25 to 30 minutes, or until done. To serve, open parchment with kitchen scissors and garnish with lemon wedges and sprigs of parsley.

NOTE: Cooking parchment paper should be available from your butcher or culinary specialty store. If unavailable, use clean, heavy duty, plain brown bags sliced open.

FRIED WHOLE TROUT WITH SHIITAKES

SERVES 4

4 small	trout, whole, cleaned	3 cups	shiitake, sliced very thinly
3 strips	bacon	½ cup	butter, unsalted
2 Tbs	olive oil, extra virgin	1 cup	flour
2	eggs	2 cups	cracker meal
1 Tbs	Pisto's Sensational Seasoning	1 bunch	watercress
3	lemons, quartered	salt & pepper to taste	

In a large skillet grill bacon well, then drain bacon and set aside bacon grease.

Wipe skillet with paper towel. Add olive oil, 3 tablespoons of butter, and sauté mushrooms for 3 or 4 minutes. Season lightly with salt and pepper. Remove mushrooms and set aside.

Place three pie pans on counter top. Fill one pan with flour. Fill second pan with well-beaten eggs. Fill third pan with cracker meal seasoned with Sensational Seasoning (see spice substitutes page 126), salt, and pepper.

Coat trout with flour, then eggs, then cracker meal. Add bacon grease and remaining butter to large skillet. Fry trout for 6 to 8 minutes on each side, or until done. To see if done, check thickest part of fish just behind gills. Fish is done when meat is solid white and still has a bit of spring to it. Remove trout and place each trout on an individual serving plate.

Place a portion of sautéed mushrooms around trout and sprinkle with bacon bits. Garnish with watercress and lemon wedges.

DADDY'S GIRL Gia shares a weekend adventure with pop hunting for mushrooms in the woods.

Although I highly recommend bringing the kids on mushroom hunts, it is important to remember that the hunts generally take place in the wild; therefore, children must be carefully supervised. I arm my myself and my daughter with whistles, just in case she wanders out of sight. My friend David Arora also gave me an interesting tip: A large umbrella, which can be used to unearth shrooms, is a good defense against large animals. The trick is to quickly open the umbrella on seeing an approaching animal, immediately frightening it away. He said he learned this trick while trekking through India, where they use this technique to ward off Bengal tigers. I haven't had an opportunity to see if it really works.

ALASKAN SALMON WITH MORELS

FROM THE GREAT STATE OF ALASKA COMES THIS DELICIOUS RECIPE—SERVES 3–4

1 lb	salmon fillet, boned & skin removed
3 oz	morels, dried
6	baby artichokes, cleaned and quartered
4	cedar blocks, ¼-inch thick
½ cup	soy sauce
3 Tbs	brown sugar
1 Tbs	sherry, dry
2 Tbs	Pisto's Sensational Seasoning
1 Tbs	butter, unsalted
1 clove	garlic, chopped
2 Tbs	shallots, chopped
3	roma tomatoes, chopped
2 Tbs	olive oil, extra virgin

salt & pepper to taste

Preheat oven to 300°.

In a bowl add soy sauce, brown sugar, sherry, Pisto's Sensational Seasoning (see spice substitutes page 126), and sauté for 1 or 2 minutes over low heat. Remove from heat when sugar begins to caramelize, and set aside.

Heat a small skillet coated with olive oil over medium heat. Add morels, shallots, garlic, black pepper, artichokes, tomatoes, and butter. Sauté for 6 to 8 minutes. Remove from heat and set aside.

Place salmon fillet in oven-proof dish and paint with reserved sauce. Cut salmon fillet into 3 pieces, and place cedar blocks next to and between between salmon pieces. Bake for 30 minutes. Remove salmon from oven and take out cedar blocks.

Place portions of salmon fillet on plates. Add some mushrooms and sauce to each, and serve with a bit of black pepper. This dish works well with Pisto's mushroom potatoes (page 102).

BROILED SWORDFISH WITH MUSHROOMS

BROILED SWORDFISH, JUICY & TASTY—SERVES 6

6 (8-oz)	swordfish steaks, ½" to ¾" thick
1 lb	white matsutake, wood ear, giant cypress, king bolete mushrooms (or your favorite mushrooms), sliced
¾ cup	chardonnay wine
¼ cup	olive oil, extra virgin
4 Tbs	Plugrá, European-style sweet butter
1 Tbs	Pisto's Sensational Seasoning
1 Tbs	basil, fresh chopped
4 Tbs	oregano, fresh chopped
4 Tbs	capers, chopped
2	lemons

salt & pepper to taste

Preheat broiler for 5 minutes or more.

In a large nonstick skillet over medium heat, sauté mushrooms in ¼ cup wine, 2 tablespoons olive oil, and 2 tablespoons butter for 5 to 6 minutes. Put aside.

Paint swordfish steaks lightly with olive oil. Season both sides of steaks with Sensational Seasoning (see spice substitutes page 126), basil, oregano, salt, and pepper.

Place swordfish steaks in a baking dish (single layer). Add ½ cup wine and capers. Place swordfish in broiler for 2 minutes, then baste with juices and remaining butter. Return to broiler for 5 to 6 minutes. Surface of swordfish steaks should be golden brown and meat slightly springy. Take care not to burn

Serve swordfish in baking dish or on platter with mushrooms placed around steaks. Squeeze juice of 1 lemon over steaks and garnish with lemon wedges.

MONK FISH WITH LOBSTER MUSHROOMS

SERVES 2

1 lb	monk fish (boned & skinned), sliced thin
1 oz	lobster mushrooms, dried
½ cup	heavy cream
½ cup	olive oil, extra virgin
2 Tbs	butter, unsalted
2 cloves	garlic, chopped
2	shallots, chopped
2 Tbs	basil, fresh chopped
1 tsp	rosemary, fresh chopped
1 oz	pernod liquor (or other pastis)
1 pinch	saffron
1 tsp	Pisto's Sensational Seasoning
4 sprigs	parsley, Italian flat-leaf
1	lemon, quartered

salt & fresh cracked black pepper

Reconstitute mushrooms for 20 minutes in cream. Gently squeeze excess cream from mushrooms, and chop mushrooms coarsely. Set both cream and mushrooms aside.

In a clean well-oiled saucepan, add butter, garlic, and shallots. Sauté for 3 minutes over medium heat. Add mushrooms, basil, rosemary, salt, and pepper. Sauté for 5 to 6 minutes, stirring continuously. Add pernod, saffron, and cream (from mushrooms), and allow to reduce by about half. Sauce is done when it coats the back of a wooden spoon.

Paint monk fish medallions with olive oil. Lightly season with Pisto's Sensational Seasoning (see spice substitutes page 126), salt, and pepper. Preheat a medium-size skillet containing ⅛ cup of olive oil. Carefully add monk fish medallions and sauté over medium-high heat for 4 to 6 minutes on each side. Remove from skillet and set aside. Do not over cook.

Place medallions on serving plates, and pour a bit of sauce over each one. Garnish with parsley and lemon wedges.

THE FEAST BEGINS With a basket full of fresh morels

Mushrooms not only taste good, they are good for you! High in valuable protein, they are also good sources of vitamins and minerals.

PISTO'S MUSHROOM POTATOES Recipe on page 102

FAVORITE MEDITERRANEAN DISHES WITH
MUSHROOMS

Vegetable Polenta Tower • Grilled Vegetables with Morels • Risotto allá Porcini • Pisto's Mushroom Potatoes • Italian Sausage with Polenta • Sautéed Veal Scallops & Mushrooms • Potato Gateau

VEGETABLE POLENTA TOWER

WONDERFUL & HEALTHY, FROM CHEF KURT GRASSING—SERVES 4

1 pkg	polenta (corn meal)	½ cup	marinara sauce (page 57)
1 head	garlic	4 Tbs	olive oil, extra virgin
1 cup	porcini, thinly sliced	1	eggplant, ¼" slices
1	summer squash, thinly sliced	1	zucchini, ¼" slices
1	white onions. thinly sliced	½ cup	cream
¼ cup	Madeira wine	1 tsp	white pepper
½ cup	Reggiano parmesan cheese, grated	2 sprigs	basil
salt & pepper to taste		2 sprigs	thyme

Preheat oven to 350°.

Prepare polenta according to instructions on package. Place cooked polenta in a large baking dish, forming an even layer approximately ½ inch thick. Place in refrigerator for 1 hour, or until firm.

Paint garlic with olive oil and roast in oven for one hour. When garlic has cooled, chop 2 cloves and set aside.

Coat both sides of vegetables with olive oil, and season lighlty with salt and pepper. Place vegetables in a preheated cast iron grill or skillet over high heat. Grill for 3 to 5 minutes on each side.

In a small saucepan over medium-low heat, add cream and chopped garlic. Stir continuously. Add Madeira wine and white pepper. Allow liquid to reduce by about a third. Remove from heat when it coats the back of a wooden spoon.

Remove polenta from refrigerator. Cut polenta and egg-plant into circles 3 inches in diameter (use plastic cup as a cutter). Place a round of polenta on serving plate, add a tablespoon of marinara sauce to top, then add a layer of vegetables. Drizzle a bit of the cream sauce and sprinkle with cheese. Repeat process with vegetable varieties. Stack as high as you dare!

Add some of each sauce decoratively to dish; garnish with basil and thyme.

THE LONE HUNTRESS Cheryl Pisto is oblivious to all that goes on around her as she keeps her eye on the ground.

Mushroom hunting offers everyone his or her own unique experience. For Cheryl Pisto, it is one of quiet serenity, a time of contemplation and dreamy thought. When this experience is especially moving, you can hear singing deep in the forest.

Cheryl respects nature and is careful to leave the forest as she found it. On spotting a shrump under a large oak, she gently kneels and begins unearthing her find—a family of Chanterelle mushrooms! She harvests the largest of the mushrooms by slicing at the bottom of the stem. She then carefully sprinkles ground cover over the remaining smaller mushrooms, with the hope they will have an opportunity to mature and release their spores for next season.

Cheryl Pisto recommends wearing a strong, large-brimmed hat when hunting. It not only protects you from falling debris, it also warns you of low-hanging branches when your eyes are fixed on the ground.

GRILLED VEGETABLES WITH MORELS

SERVES 4

1 cup	morels, sliced
1 cup	olive oil, extra virgin
2 Tbs	oregano, fresh chopped
5 cloves	garlic, chopped
1 Tbs	Pisto's Sensational Seasoning
4–6	asparagus (or other vegetables of your choice)
1 bulb	fennel, sliced
1	eggplant, 1" slices, skin on
1	red onion, sliced thick
2	bell peppers, cleaned & quartered
3 Tbs	balsamic vinegar
1	lemon, quartered

salt & fresh cracked black pepper to taste

Preheat well-oiled, cast iron, stovetop grill or skillet over medium-high heat.

In a small mixing bowl, add olive oil, oregano, garlic, salt, and pepper; toss well.

Brush vegetables on both sides with olive oil mixture. Sprinkle a bit of Sensational Seasoning on vegetables (see spice substitutes page 126). Place asparagus and fennel on the grill, and cook for 3 to 4 minutes on each side, or until done. Remove from grill and cook remaining vegetables accordingly.

Pour the remaining olive oil mixture into a small saucepan. Add vinegar, salt, and pepper to taste. Mix well and heat over medium–low heat, until warm.

Place vegetables on plate and spoon over sauce. Garnish with quartered lemons and sprinkle with cracked black pepper.

RISOTTO ALLÁ PORCINI

SERVES 4

1 cup	king bolete (porcini) mushrooms, chopped			
2 cups	short-grain (arborio) rice			
¼ cup	sherry	2 ears	sweet white corn, cobbed
2 Tbs	olive oil, extra virgin	1 cup	sweet peas, shelled
3 Tbs	butter, unsalted	½ cup	red wine
3 cloves	garlic, chopped	½ tsp	saffron (optional)
1 med.	onion, chopped	2–3 cups	chicken stock (page 40)
½ bunch	parsley, Italian flat-leaf, chopped	2–3 cups	beef stock (page 38)
½ bunch	basil, fresh chopped	½ cup	heavy cream
¾ cup	fennel, chopped	1 cup	Reggiano parmesan cheese, grated
1	carrot, chopped	salt to taste	

Reconstitute king bolete mushrooms (porcini) in a small bowl with sherry (about 30 minutes).

Heat skillet over medium-high heat. Add olive oil and 2 tablespoons of butter. When butter has melted, add garlic, onion, parsley, basil, fennel, carrot, and rice, stirring occasionally. Sauté ingredients until they begin to lightly brown.

Add mushrooms, corn, peas, and wine, stirring occasionally until the wine reduces by about two-thirds.

Lower heat to medium and add saffron (optional). While rice mixture continues to simmer, add about ½ cup each of chicken and beef stock, and continue to simmer for about 10 minutes, stirring occasionally.

Add another ½ cup of each stock, and continue simmering. Add stock at least twice more every 10 minutes or so, allowing liquid to reduce in between. Stir occasionally.

Add cream and remaining butter. Allow to simmer for 5–10 minutes, stirring occasionally. Season lightly with salt. Dish is done when rice is al dente.

Serve on plates with grated cheese.

PISTO'S MUSHROOM POTATOES

SERVES 4

3	baking potatoes, peeled & cut into bite-size pieces
3 oz	morels, dried
6	baby artichokes
½ cup	olive oil, extra virgin
3 Tbs	butter, unsalted
½	onion, chopped
2	shallots, chopped
2 cloves	garlic, chopped
2	roma tomatoes, seeded & quartered
1 tsp	black pepper, fresh cracked
3 sprigs	parsley, Italian flat-leaf
2	lemons,

Reconstitute mushrooms in warm water for 20 minutes.

Prepare baby artichokes by cutting off stalks and top 15% of leaves. Remove outer leaves until you get down to soft yellow leaves. Quarter artichokes and place in bowl with juice of one lemon and water to cover. (With baby artichokes it is not necessary to remove core.)

In a large skillet, add ⅓ cup olive oil, 2 tablespoons butter, potatoes, ¾ of the chopped onion, 4 artichokes, and 1 shallot, and sauté over high heat for 10 to 15 minutes, turning occasionally. To tell if done, check thickest part of potatoes, which should be easily pierced with a fork or knife tip. When almost done, add tomatoes. Remove from heat.

Heat a small skillet coated with olive oil over medium heat. Add garlic, black pepper, mushrooms, remaining shallots, onions, artichokes, and remaining butter. Sauté for 6 to 8 minutes.

Serve on large platter, with mushrooms poured over potatoes. Garnish with sprigs of parsley and quartered lemon.

JOHN & GIA PISTO On the trail again

All parents hope to share interests with their children. In this I have been blessed! Not only do my children share my interest in the family restaurants, they also look forward to accompanying me on mushroom hunts. There's nothing like a hunt to bring the family together—into the forests, meadows, or mountains—spouse, siblings, children, grandchildren, and all.

ITALIAN SAUSAGE WITH POLENTA

SERVES 6–8

1 lb	Italian sausage, skin removed	½ lg	yellow onion, chopped
1 pkg	polenta (corn meal)	6 cloves	garlic, chopped
½ cup	king bolete mushrooms, dried	½ cup	dry red wine
1 qt	tomatoes, chopped, in puree	1 tsp	salt
½ tsp	crushed red pepper	2 Tbs	butter, unsalted
1 tsp	sugar	½ cup	petit pois (peas)
½ cup	Reggiano parmesan cheese, grated	4 Tbs	olive oil, extra virgin
1 tsp	black pepper, ground		

Reconstitute mushrooms in a cup of warm water for 20 minutes. Squeeze excess water from mushrooms and set aside.

Prepare polenta according to package instructions. When mixture is thick add butter and stir to melt; then add cheese and do the same.

Place cooked polenta on a lightly buttered baking dish to form an even layer approximately ½ inch thick. Place baking dish into refrigerator. When firm (after approximately 30 minutes), cut polenta into square or diamond shapes. Place polenta squares on a well-oiled stovetop grill or skillet and grill for 1 to 2 minutes on each side. Set aside.

Coat the bottom of a large saucepan with olive oil, and place over medium-high heat. Add onion, garlic, and sausage, breaking sausage into pieces as it cooks. Stir frequently while browning. When sausage begins to brown, add wine and mix well. Add tomatoes, red pepper, and sugar, stirring frequently. Lower heat to medium and add peas. Simmer for another ten minutes, then add mushrooms. Allow ingredients to simmer for another 10 to 15 minutes.

Place a grilled polenta square on plate, spoon sauce over polenta, and add a portion of sausage mixture to plate. Serve with cheese and black pepper.

SAUTÉED VEAL SCALLOPS & MUSHROOMS

SERVES 4

1 lb	veal scallops, ⅜" thick slices
1 lb	wild mushrooms—a mixture of wood ear, giant cypress, king bolete (or other available mushrooms), chopped
½ cup	flour
1 tsp	Pisto's Pepper & Garlic Blend
1 tsp	Pisto's Sensational Seasoning
2 Tbs	olive oil, extra virgin
3 Tbs	butter, unsalted
3 Tbs	shallots, chopped
2 Tbs	thyme, fresh chopped
4 strips	bacon, lightly cooked & cut into squares
⅓ cup	red wine, dry
2	lemons
2 sprigs	parsley, Italian, flat-leaf, chopped
salt & pepper to taste	

Place a sheet of butcher paper on cutting board with veal scallops on top. Cover veal with a sheet of wax paper or plastic wrap, and pound firmly with a wooden mallet. Move systematically up and down scallops, which will almost double in size.

In a pie pan, add flour, Pisto's Pepper & Garlic Blend, and Sensational Seasoning (see spice substitutes page 126). Mix well. Dredge veal scallops in seasoned flour.

Preheat a skillet over medium-high heat, add 2 tablespoons of olive oil and 2 tablespoons of butter. Place coated veal one layer thick on skillet, and sauté for 1 minute on each side. (Cook in more than one batch if necessary.) Season lightly with salt & pepper, and place on serving platter (covered in foil) in warm oven.

In same skillet (remove excess oil) add mushrooms, shallots, thyme, and bacon. Sauté for 6 minutes over medium heat. Deglaze pan with wine, 1 tablespoon of butter, and juice from one lemon .

Remove platter from oven. Remove foil, and pour mushroom sauce over scallops. Garnish with lemon wedges and sprigs of parsley.

POTATO GATEAU
WITH OREGON WHITE TRUFFLES, CODY'S FAVORITE—SERVES 4

| 8 | yellow potatoes, peeled | ½ cup | butter, unsalted |

2   Oregon white truffles (or substitute dried mushrooms as available)

salt & pepper to taste

Preheat oven to 400°.

Generously coat a 6" to 8" inch round metal or glass baking dish with butter, then place in coolest part of refrigerator for at least 1 hour. (The French prefer a métal dish to give the potato a golden hue.)

Slice the potatoes into very thin medallions. Use an adjustable slicer or food processor—the thinner, the better. Cutting the potatoes by hand is not recommended because it produces potatoes of different thicknesses.

Melt remaining butter in a medium-size nonstick skillet over low heat. When butter is melted, turn heat up to medium and add sliced potatoes. Cook potatoes 10–15 minutes, or until no longer translucent. Turn potatoes frequently. Try not to brown them.

When potatoes are cooked, take the baking dish from the refrigerator and line its bottom and sides with a thin layer of overlapping and interlocking potatoes. (Do not fill baking dish.)

Chop truffles thinly, fold mushrooms into remaining potatoes. Add this mixture to center of baking dish to form filling.

Cover dish with foil, and push down on foil to firm contents. Bake for 1 hour.

Remove from oven and let cool for 10 minutes. Loosen sides with a knife. Place dish upside down on serving platter. Tap top and sides of baking dish sharply. Remove baking dish. Slice potato gateau as you would a cake and serve.

RHEA & GIA (l to r) Still excited from the hunt, the girls show off their finds. (Rhea pictured before outbreak of poison oak)

When our daughter has friends over for the weekend, we don't jump in the minivan and head to Great America; we go mushroom hunting. The kids think its exciting, and what's more, they end up learning a great deal about the forest and its inhabitants.

I don't recommend taking other people's children into the forest without their permission. Always inform parents of the situation in detail. I know from experience that some parents do not appreciate it when their child comes home with a bad case of poison oak.

RISOTTO ALLÁ PORCINI Recipe on page 101

PISTO'S GOURMET
PRODUCTS

Gourmet Seasonings • Pisto's Signature Stovetop Grill • Gourmet Dried Mushrooms • Herb Infused Vinegars and Olive Oils • Gourmet Gift Packs • Books • Pisto Restaurants

PISTO'S OLD CALIFORNIA SEASONING

2.35 OZ. JARS

Inspired by the regional flavors of Old California, this blend includes sweet chili powder, onion, and garlic. It adds a sweet and spicy flavor to seafood and poultry dishes. Also an excellent ingredient for home-made barbeque sauces.

$6.95* EACH

PISTO'S PEPPER & GARLIC BLEND

2.3 OZ. JARS

Chef Pisto's special blend of eight different peppers, and garlic is a unique and flavorful choice for just about any dish calling for pepper.

Use generously on grilled steaks, fish, and poultry. If you like it hot, you'll love Pisto's Pepper & Garlic Blend.

$6.95* EACH

PISTO'S SENSATIONAL SEASONING

2.3 OZ. JARS

Pisto's famous Sensational Seasoning truly lives up to its name! This all-purpose gourmet seasoning is sensational for seafood dishes, pasta sauces, meat stews, grilled vegetables, or as a delicious blackening rub on meat, poultry, and fish.

$6.95* EACH

PISTO'S MOROCCAN SEASONING

2.35 OZ. JARS

This unusual blend of spices transforms seafood and poultry dishes into exciting entrees with an international flair. Use generously when grilling to create a flavorful crust. Add a few dashes to soups and sauces for an exotic flavor.

$6.95* EACH

* Shipping included within the continental United States

PISTO'S SIGNATURE STOVETOP GRILL

Chef Pisto has designed a heavy-duty, cast iron grill that is so versatile it will literally replace your frying pans and barbeque, never leaving your stovetop. Grill steaks, chicken, fish fillets, even mushrooms and vegetables!

It's easy to use, and the professional design gives you unequaled heating capacity, unmatched flavor, and a restaurant style presentation.

$49.95*

PISTO'S GOURMET DRIED MUSHROOMS

OYSTER MUSHROOMS *(Pleurotus ostreatus)* .5 OZ.   **$6.95***
This mushroom grows on trees, stumps, and logs during fall and winter along the California Coast. Its mild flavor will enhance soups and sauces made with meat and/or vegetables.

CHAMPIGNON MUSHROOMS *(Agaricus campestris)* .5 OZ.   **$6.95***
This popular mushroom is found in grassy areas throughout the Western United States. It offers a delicate, earthy flavor and is quite versatile in the kitchen.

PORCINI MUSHROOMS *(Boletus edulis)* .5 OZ.   **$6.95***
This mushroom, a long-time Italian favorite, is fast becoming one of California's most popular varieties. Its strong, woodsy flavor adds richness to pasta dishes, beef stews, sauces, and soups.

CANDY CAP MUSHROOMS *(Lactarius fragilis)* .5 OZ.   **$9.95***
This mushroom is found under oak and pine trees throughout Central California. Its rich maple flavor is perfect for cookies, pancakes, pork dishes, and pasta.

* Shipping Included within the continental United States

GOURMET SPRING HERB-INFUSED VINEGAR

16.9 FL. OZ.

White wine vinegar infused with parsley, dill, chives, bay leaves, dried peppers, black pepper, and garlic.

Add a dash of springtime to your seafood and poultry dishes and bring new life to green salads with this flavorful white vinegar.

$16.95* EACH

GOURMET HERB-INFUSED RED WINE VINEGAR

16.9 FL. OZ.

Chianti red wine vinegar infused with thyme, rosemary, allspice, and bay leaves.

This versatile red wine vinegar is an excellent marinade, and a wonderful flavoring agent for sauces, salads, and barbequed meats.

$16.95* EACH

* Shipping included within the continental United States

SICILIANO OLIVE OIL

16.9 FL. OZ.

This Italian extra virgin olive oil is infused with oregano, basil, thyme, chili peppers, and garlic.

Use it as a base for marinading steaks and poultry, as a dipping oil for French bread, or as a base for salad dressings. Try it in place of your generic olive oil in all your favorite recipes.

The decorative bottle makes a beautiful addition to any kitchen and a wonderful housewarming gift.

$16.95 EACH

GOURMET PEPPER OIL

16.9 FL. OZ.

Add a burst of flavor to your meals when you use this Italian extra virgin olive oil infused with whole chile peppers and hot red pepper flakes.

This hot olive oil spices up just about any dish. Ideal for barbequed meats, pasta, and salads.

$16.95 EACH

* Shipping included within the continental United States

CHEF PISTO'S GOURMET GIFT PACKS

Now, you can start cookin' Pisto Style with one of these fabulous gift packages.

GOURMET GIFT PACK #1

The perfect starter gift pack, complete with Chef Pisto's first cookbook and his two original seasonings.

INCLUDES:

- *Monterey's Cookin' Pisto Style*— cookbook
- 1 jar Pisto's Sensational Seasoning
- 1 jar Pisto's Moroccan Seasoning

($26.00 value)

ONLY $21.95*

GOURMET GIFT PACK #2

This gift package includes all the products in Gift Package #1 PLUS a specially selected bottle of Pisto's infused olive oil: all the ingredients to make an impressive housewarming gift.

INCLUDES:

- *Monterey's Cookin' Pisto Style*— cookbook
- 1 jar Pisto's Sensational Seasoning
- 1 jar Pisto's Moroccan Seasoning
- 1 bottle of Pisto's Olive Oil—

($42.00 value)

ONLY $29.95*

* Shipping included within the Continental United States

CHEF PISTO'S GOURMET GIFT PACKS

For serious gourmets consider Chef Pisto's more complete Gift Packs.

CHEF GIFT PACK #4

The complete gourmet gift pack for the serious chef.

INCLUDES:

- Pisto's Signature Cast Iron Grill
- *Monterey's Cookin' Pisto Style*— cookbook
- 1 jar Pisto's Sensational Seasoning
  - 1 jar Pisto's Moroccan Seasoning
  - 1 jar Old California Seasoning
  - 1 jar Pisto's Pepper & Garlic Blend
- 1 bottle of Pisto's Olive Oil
- 1 bottle of Pisto's Vinegar
- 1 package Dried Mushrooms
- 1 Year Subscription to Newsletter ($135.00 value)

ONLY $99.95*

GOURMET GIFT PACK #3

This gift package is the ideal survival kit for kids moving out on their own, or to complete your own kitchen supplies.

INCLUDES:

- Pisto's Signature Cast Iron Grill
- *Monterey's Cookin' Pisto Style*— cookbook
- 1 jar Pisto's Sensational Seasoning
- 1 jar Pisto's Moroccan Seasoning
- 1 bottle of Pisto's Olive Oil—
- 1 Year Subscription to Newsletter

($100.00 value)

ONLY $79.95*

* Shipping Included within the continental United States

MONTEREY'S COOKIN' PISTO STYLE

FROM SICILY TO MONTEREY

Chef Pisto's first cookbook showcases 70 recipes from his popular television show, "Monterey's Cookin' Pisto Style." Featuring a beautiful full-color cover and historical photos throughout, the book depicts life in Monterey, California, during the old sardine days of John Steinbeck. Meet Doc Rickets, Flora, and Steinbeck himself as Chef Pisto shares his personal view of Monterey's colorful past. Each chapter reflects the bounty of California's agricultural and fishing industries, with recipes such as blackened salmon, barbequed sardines, baby artichoke risotto, and old-fashioned tomato salad. Also included are recipes for meat, poultry, and wild game.

$14.95* EACH

"...the best single guidebook to American mushrooms"
Andrew Weil—Whole Earth Catalog.

MUSHROOMS DEMYSTIFIED

BY DAVID ARORA

The latest edition of the most comprehensive field guide to wild mushrooms—more than 2000 species and 800 photos. This comprehensive book celebrates the gathering, identifying, and study of mushrooms, with detailed descriptions, keys to identification, even advice on eating fungi. (Picture on page 71)

$39.95* EACH

ALL THAT THE RAIN PROMISES & MORE . . .

BY DAVID ARORA

A handy pocket guide to the West Coast's most prolific mushrooms. More than 200 mushrooms identified. Full color photos, detailed descriptions, and a handy identification chart. The perfect perfect companion for *Mushrooms Demystified.*

$19.95* EACH

* Shipping included within the continental United States

MONTEREY'S COOKIN PISTO STYLE NEWSLETTER

Your subscription to the *Monterey's Cookin' Pisto Style Newsletter* will deliver dozens of Chef Pisto's recipes right to your front door..

Learn about Chef Pisto's travels, important guests, and upcoming events, and take advantage of "subscribers only" special offers on Chef Pisto's products. (USA only)

$8.95—4 ISSUES

ORDERING INFORMATION

Pisto's Seasonings: Sensational (blackening spice, Moroccan (rub & marinade), Old California (all purpose), Pepper & Garlic Blend—each................$6.95
Pisto's Signature Stovetop Grill $49.95
Pisto's·Select Dried OYSTER Mushrooms $6.95
Pisto's Select Dried CHAMPIGNON Mushrooms............................$6.95
Pisto's Select Dried PORCINI (King Bolete) Mushrooms $6.95
Pisto's Select Dried CANDY CAP Mushrooms $9.95
Pisto's WHITE WINE Vinegar, 500ML (16.9 fl. oz. bottle)..............$16.95
Pisto's RED WINE Vinegar, 500ML (16.9 fl. oz. bottle)...................$16.95
Pisto's Infused SICILIANO Olive Oil, 500ML (16.9 fl. oz. bottle)........$16.95
Pisto's Infused PEPPER Olive Oil, 500ML (16.9 fl. oz. bottle)...........$16.95
Pisto's Gift Pack #1 ....$21.95
Pisto's Gift Pack #2 ....$29.95
Pisto's Gift Pack #3 ....$79.95
Pisto's "Chef" Gift Pack #4..$99.95
Monterey's Cookin' Pisto Style cookbook $14.95
Mushrooms Demystified, By David Arora $39.95
All That The Rain Promises & More. . ., By David Arora..................$19.95
Monterey's Cookin' Newsletter Subscription (1 Year).........................$8.95

Prices Include Shipping within the Continental United States
Send check or money order to:

PISTO'S KITCHEN

P.O. Box 51201, Pacific Grove, CA 93950 • 1 800 45 PISTO

All Prices Subject to change without notice.

DOMENICO'S ON THE WHARF 50 Fisherman's Wharf, Monterey, CA 93940 (408) 372-3655

A local favorite for more than a decade, Domenico's on the Wharf offers traditional Italian cuisine, featuring fresh seafood caught each morning and delivered to the private loading docks.

Enjoy spectacular views of Monterey's historic yacht harbor from every table. View the never-ending water show provided by playful sea lions, soaring seagulls, and even an occasional sea otter.

The restaurant is known for its formal yet friendly ambiance and impeccable service, as well as its one-of-a-kind menu.

Sample from the tantalizing oyster bar and the award-winning wine list while the staff pampers you.

One visit to Domenico's on the Wharf and you will become a regular guest too!

ABALONETTI'S SEAFOOD TRATTORIA 57 Fisherman's Wharf, Monterey, CA 93940 (408) 373-1851

Abalonetti Seafood Trattoria offers a new twist to wharfside dining. The trattoria's fun and casual atmosphere, with bright seascape colors, greets you as you enter the main dining room, where you are surrounded by views of the bay. Or if you prefer, you may dine outdoors on Abalonetti's private terrace.

Established in 1951, the trattoria is famous for Monterey Bay calamari and offers almost a dozen varieties of squid dishes—many found only at Abalonetti Seafood Trattoria!

The tantalizing menu also offers a bountiful antipasti bar, gourmet pizza from the wood-burning oven, and meat and poultry dishes, complemented by a fine selection of California wines and a full bar.

WHALING STATION
RESTAURANT

WHALING STATION 763 Wave St., Monterey, CA 93940 (408) 373-3778

An extraordinary regional restaurant with an international reputation, the award-winning Whaling Station is known for its prime steaks and fresh seafood, as well as exemplary service.

One of the finest dinner houses in existence, the Whaling Station promises both quality and quantity with every meal served.

Located in an historic building perched just above John Steinbeck's Cannery Row, the restaurant offers a timelessly elegant atmosphere perfect for those very special occasions.

The Whaling Station boasts an award-winning wine list and a full bar to complement your meal.

PARADISO TRATTORIA 654 Cannery Row., Monterey, CA 93940 (408) 375-4155

The latest addition to Chef Pisto's family of fine restaurants, Paradiso Trattoria showcases Pisto's California–Mediterranean cuisine in a paradise-like setting overlooking Monterey Bay. The restaurant offers spectacular beach-front views from every table.

Serving lunch and dinner seven days a week, Paradiso Trattoria also features a wood-burning pizza oven, a bountiful antipasti bar, and a children's menu.

A full bar and extensive wine list complement your meal.

JOHN & CODY With yet another fungi find

In Europe they have specially bred pigs that smell black truffles growing underground. Our family has our trusty canine friend Cody. While perhaps not as talented as the truffle-smelling pigs, Cody is quite capable of locating a variety of mushrooms, including king boletes, oysters, and candy caps.

FINIMÉNTO

John Pisto, "The Man Behind the Apron" • Substitutions
& Intuitions • Thank You! • A Few Definitions • Index •
Notes

JOHN PISTO
THE MAN BEHIND THE APRON

Chef Pisto's Italian heritage combined with his talent for creating and perfecting recipes made with fresh California ingredients has earned him the reputation of an innovator of California Italian cuisine.

With more than 30 years of culinary experience, John loves nothing more than cooking. Over the years, he has cooked for and with many of the world's finest chefs. To promote the culinary trade, John became a founding member of the International Institute of Food & Wine, along with friends Julia Child and Richard Graft.

As a children's advocate, John has created and hosted educational programs for elementary school children throughout the Monterey County area. He has also worked with the California Seafood Council and the Department of Education on audio/visual educational projects distributed nationwide.

Chef Pisto is host of the popular televised cooking show, "Monterey's Cookin' Pisto Style," available internationally via Nostalgia Television Network. During the half-hour show, Chef Pisto often takes viewers on culinary adventures throughout the world, then back to his home kitchen to prepare a tantalizing dish.

JOHN PISTO at home preparing a meal

Chef Pisto's gourmet products, which include a line of seasonings, olive oils, vinegars, and a signature cast iron grill, are sold nationwide under the Pisto's Kitchen brand name

Chef Pisto is also owner of four award-winning restaurants in Monterey, California: The Whaling Station Restaurant, Paradiso Trattoria, Abalonetti Seafood Trattoria, and Domenico's on the Wharf. Each offers its own unique flavors and atmosphere.

PISTO FAMILY Gia, John and Cheryl Pisto

The Pisto family lives in Monterey, California, near famed Pebble Beach and Carmel-by-the-Sea.

When John and his family are not traveling the world looking for exotic mushrooms and other culinary treats, they are usually entertaining guests.

The four Pisto Restaurants are a culmination of the family's personal goals and successes. Even today, in between filming his television show, developing new gourmet food products, and writing cookbooks, John is actively involved with each of his restaurants, including menu preparation, and planning. In any given week, John will alternate between his restaurants' kitchens, working with staff to assure that his patrons receive the very finest dining experience.

When his wife, Cheryl, is not mushroom hunting, she is involved in the family restaurant business and is actively involved in the community.

Gia Pisto, his youngest daughter, is a promising chef herself, as well as a mushroom afficionado in her own right.

SUBSTITUTIONS & INTUITIONS

Many of my recipes use my own special blend of spices, herbs, olive oil, and vinegars and sometimes my stovetop grill. We sell these products as a convenience; none of them are required to prepare and enjoy the recipes. Below is a list of simple substitutions for the various products.

SENSATIONAL SEASONING
Any good blackening spice will do. Depending on the particular spice, you may want to add a bit of salt.

MOROCCAN SEASONING
Substitute cumin and perhaps a bit of salt and pepper.

PISTO'S OLD CALIFORNIA SPICE
Substitute with of sweet chile powder (or paprika) and a bit of salt and dried garlic.

PISTO'S PEPPER & GARLIC BLEND
Substitute a variety of fresh ground peppers and a dash of garlic powder.

PISTO'S SIGNATURE STOVETOP GRILL
My cast iron grill is used in many of my recipes. In almost every case a cast iron skillet can be substituted. Of course, a BBQ would be fine also but usually is not as convenient.

BUTTER
I use butter for taste. When using butter, be careful not to burn it (unclarified butter burns easily). If you must, you can substitute a good-quality olive oil for butter. Most often my recipes call for Plugrá, which is a good-quality, European-style sweet butter that adds flavor to any dish. If you are sautéing in butter, use a nonstick pan with 50% butter and 50% olive oil.

PISTO'S OLIVE OIL & VINEGARS
Of course I use my own oils and vinegars that I have had specially prepared. Any good quality extra virgin olive oil will work just fine, as would any quality vinegar. One caution though: olive oils vary in taste as much as wines. Taste your ingredients before using them in recipes.

ONE MORE NOTE ABOUT OLIVE OILS
Seems like the latest reports on olive oil practically claim it's a health food. Who knows? My family has been using olive oil for generations, without any noticeable adverse effects. I use extra virgin olive oil that is unrefined, because in my opinion it tastes the best. You can substitute other oils at your discretion— they just don't taste as good.

FRESH VS FROZEN OR DRIED
When it comes to meat and vegetables, fresh is better. That doesn't mean I stop cooking with ingredients as soon as they are out of season. It means that I prefer fresh to frozen.

The one possible exception is that of dried mushrooms. Many reconstitute, with a stronger more intense flavor than when fresh.

GIANT CYPRESS AGARICUS Make a beautiful still life

THANK YOU!

This page is dedicated to the many wonderful people who have made this mushroom cookbook possible.

To my lovely wife Cheryl, whose enthusiasm for the hunt rivals my own.

To my darling daughter Gia, my favorite mushroom hunting partner

To my daughter Kim, her husband Lee, and my little porcini, Aston, who went on his first hunt at the age of 8 months.

To my friend, David Arora, who, through his fascinating and informative books, is responsible for furthering my passion for mushrooms.

To Tony and Barbara Ricciardi, my dear friends and ever-present entourage, who help make my life experiences much more memorable.

To Dr. Roy Thomas and his wife Mary Ellen, for great times we have spent together and all the wine that was poured.

To Diane Ramistella, for her genuine enthusiasm and her determination to steal my best mushroom-hunting grounds.

To my recent converts, Myles Williams, connoisseur, and his charming wife, Rhonda.

To my children Michelle, Tawni & Dana and my grandson little John who are all I can hope for.

To Dr. Ben Ichinose & Mayon for being such good friends and advisors.

To my friend Tom Verga, who calls right after the first rain with new hunting locations.

To my co-defendant, Bob Zampatti, for our exciting, remotely dangerous, and rather expensive mushroom hunt.

To John Rowly, my Seattle mushroom connection.

To Sal and Linda Balesteri, who have never gone mushroom hunting yet will listen to me babble about mushrooms for hours on end.

To Steve Davis and the guys at TCI for their tremendous efforts and talents.

To Julia Child, for her patience and confidence in my newly found passion.

To Ronnie Aliotti, for his unfailing appetite, and his wife, Francesca, for putting up with us.

To the Hyman's for providing such cordial company on our culinary odysseys

To Nate Udomsri, my restaurant chef and partner in good food.

To Devin McGilloway, the best partner a man could have: Thanks for manning the fort while I'm off following my passions.

A FEW DEFINITIONS

blanch: to briefly precook or preheat food in either boiling water or steam

blackening: process of heavily coating meat or fish with spices and seasoning and then grilling or barbecuing over high heat to seal the juices in

braise: to cook food in a small amount of liquid or steam, in a covered container, so that it cooks slowly

breaded: food covered with crumbs of bread or other food

cast Iron grill: used for grilling food indoors on top of the stove

al dente: foods prepared to a point of *just done,* when foods retain a high level of texture, flavor and vitamins.

garnish: to decorate the dish with ingredients that add color or flavor—traditional garnishes include paprika, lemons, parsley, radish, carrots, and olives

grill: to cook food with direct heat (also an appliance used for cooking)

roast: to cook uncovered with heated air such as in an oven

shell: to remove the outer shell from crabs, mussels, clams, etc. to access the inside meat

simmer: to cook in liquid just below the boiling point

INDEX—RECIPES BY MUSHROOMS

GENERAL INDEX

LOUIS CANEPA A good friend and one of the first to take me mushroom hunting

Contents

Contents

Contents

Contents

Contents

Introduction

The impetus for the book came from a desire to share the knowledge gained while developing applications for the TiVo HME platform, and to help others gain access to the market created by TiVo HME applications. TiVo HME (Java applications for TiVo) are a new development, and one of the first set-top box platforms to allow user-written code to run on an unmodified system.

Who This Book Is For

The target readers for this book are TiVo users with some programming expertise who are interested in creating a TiVo HME application. The book covers the fundamentals of building applications for TiVo, and the process of building an application that is user friendly. This book is ideal for readers looking to bring their vision of a TiVo application to users.

What This Book Covers

The main goal of this book is to get you started writing polished applications using the TiVo HME SDK. TiVo users have grown accustomed to a powerful, friendly user interface that is intuitive and simple to use. This book walks you through writing applications, utilizing the basic and more advanced features of HME to build new and exciting applications to extend the TiVo experience.

The key features this book covers are

- ❑ Configuring and getting comfortable in your development environment
- ❑ The HME Event model
- ❑ Displaying images and text
- ❑ Playing audio files and streams
- ❑ Optimizing the behavior of your application
- ❑ Packaging your application for deployment

You should take from this book a solid understanding of the way the TiVo HME SDK functions, and an understanding of how to build applications that will be responsive and intuitive for the user as well as set up a solid development process for producing quality applications.

How This Book Is Structured

This book is designed to guide you through setting up a development environment for writing TiVo HME applications. The book starts by describing software development for the TiVo platform. You will learn the basic building blocks of designing applications for TiVo and how to respond to events. Exercises and examples illustrate the concepts throughout the book.

After covering the basics of developing applications for TiVo, you will read about a component library from TiVo that makes developing advanced applications easier. The end of the book covers information regarding polishing the final product and packaging applications for your users.

What You Need to Use This Book

The book contains many programming examples. Applications for TiVo boxes are written in Java, so a basic understanding of the Java language and syntax will be needed. The installation of software needed for developing TiVo HME applications is covered in the book.

A TiVo box (Series 2 or Series 3) is also needed for certain examples and sections of the book. The book does cover configuration that needs to take place on the TiVo box itself.

Conventions

To help you get the most from the text and keep track of what's happening, we've used a number of conventions throughout the book.

Try It Out

The *Try It Out* is an exercise you should work through, following the text in the book.

1. It usually consists of a set of steps.
2. Each step has a number.
3. Follow the steps through with your copy of the database.

How It Works

After each *Try It Out*, the code you've typed will be explained in detail.

> **Boxes like this one hold important, not-to-be-forgotten information that is directly relevant to the surrounding text.**

Tips, hints, tricks, and asides to the current discussion are offset and placed in italics like this.

As for styles in the text:

- ❏ We *highlight* new terms and important words when we introduce them.
- ❏ We show keyboard strokes like this: Ctrl+A.
- ❏ We show file names, URLs, and code within the text like so: `persistence.properties`.
- ❏ We present code in two different ways:

```
In code examples we highlight new and important code with a gray background.
```

```
The gray highlighting is not used for code that's less important in the present
context, or has been shown before.
```

Source Code

As you work through the examples in this book, you may choose either to type in all the code manually or to use the source code files that accompany the book. All of the source code used in this book is available for download at `http://www.wrox.com`. Once at the site, simply locate the book's title (either by using the Search box or by using one of the title lists) and click the Download Code link on the book's detail page to obtain all the source code for the book.

Because many books have similar titles, you may find it easiest to search by ISBN; this book's ISBN is 978-0-470-05427-7

Once you download the code, just decompress it with your favorite compression tool. Alternatively, you can go to the main Wrox code download page at `http://www.wrox.com/dynamic/books/download .aspx` to see the code available for this book and all other Wrox books.

Errata

We make every effort to ensure that there are no errors in the text or in the code. However, no one is perfect, and mistakes do occur. If you find an error in one of our books, like a spelling mistake or faulty piece of code, we would be very grateful for your feedback. By sending in errata you may save another reader hours of frustration and at the same time you will be helping us provide even higher quality information.

To find the errata page for this book, go to `http://www.wrox.com` and locate the title using the Search box or one of the title lists. Then, on the book details page, click the Book Errata link. On this page you can view all errata that has been submitted for this book and posted by Wrox editors. A complete book list including links to each book's errata is also available at `www.wrox.com/misc-pages/booklist.shtml`.

If you don't spot "your" error on the Book Errata page, go to `www.wrox.com/contact/techsupport .shtml` and complete the form there to send us the error you have found. We'll check the information and, if appropriate, post a message to the book's errata page and fix the problem in subsequent editions of the book.

p2p.wrox.com

For author and peer discussion, join the P2P forums at p2p.wrox.com. The forums are a Web-based system for you to post messages relating to Wrox books and related technologies and interact with other readers and technology users. The forums offer a subscription feature to e-mail you topics of interest of your choosing when new posts are made to the forums. Wrox authors, editors, other industry experts, and your fellow readers are present on these forums.

At http://p2p.wrox.com you will find a number of different forums that will help you not only as you read this book, but also as you develop your own applications. To join the forums, just follow these steps:

1. Go to p2p.wrox.com and click the Register link.

2. Read the terms of use and click Agree.

3. Complete the required information to join as well as any optional information you wish to provide and click Submit.

4. You will receive an e-mail with information describing how to verify your account and complete the joining process.

You can read messages in the forums without joining P2P, but in order to post your own messages, you must join.

Once you join, you can post new messages and respond to messages other users post. You can read messages at any time on the Web. If you would like to have new messages from a particular forum e-mailed to you, click the Subscribe to this Forum icon by the forum name in the forum listing.

For more information about how to use the Wrox P2P, be sure to read the P2P FAQs for answers to questions about how the forum software works as well as many common questions specific to P2P and Wrox books. To read the FAQs, click the FAQ link on any P2P page.

Beginning
TiVo® Programming

Introduction to TiVo Applications

What is TiVo? If you need an answer to that question, most likely this book isn't going to be of much interest to you. However, if you are looking for a fun way to create new and exciting living room multimedia experiences leveraging the TiVo platform, you've found the right place to get you well on your way. This chapter introduces you to the TiVo platform and provides a good foundation before you begin writing applications for yourself.

In this chapter, you learn about the following:

- ❑ Home Media Option
- ❑ Home Media Engine
- ❑ TiVo HME SDK

The TiVo Platform

Essentially, the TiVo platform is a small personal computer that up until recently was dressed as an easy to use, yet powerful, alternative to the household VCR. The current generation of TiVo hardware contains a low-powered MIPS CPU, a high-capacity internal hard drive, a modem for connecting to the TiVo servers over dial-up, a few USB ports for expansion opportunities, a small amount of video and system RAM, a video output system to connect to televisions, and a simple input system that uses the fantastic TiVo Remote. Though that might not seem like a powerful platform for providing DVR (digital video recorder) functionality (especially compared to the horsepower needed for running a Windows Media Center PC), TiVo has also included a hardware-based MPEG-2 Encoder/Decoder chip to handle all of the heavy tasks like video encoding and decoding.

When they designed the TiVo hardware platform, the wizards at TiVo decided to use Linux as the base operating system. Naturally, this made a good portion of the technical community quite pleased, because under the GPL (GNU General Public License) that covers Linux distributions, TiVo had an obligation to freely distribute the full source code for any changes that it makes to optimize the core OS to run its software. Almost immediately after getting their hands on the source code of the TiVo Linux distribution, a TiVo hacking community was born. It came as a surprise to many that for the most part, TiVo didn't interfere with people tinkering with the software powering their box, unless of course the tinkerer's goal was to avoid continuing to pay for TiVo's subscription service.

The first wave of TiVo hacks included simply growing the hard drive space, allowing users to add more recording capacity to their DVR. Following shortly thereafter, some brilliant hardware engineers outside of TiVo started devising a way to include the TiVo box in their home networks. Inside the TiVo box was a diagnostic slot that allowed the fabrication of an expansion board that would allow users to install a card, load some Linux drivers, and be on their way to a network-connected TiVo box. However, loading the Linux drivers proved difficult for the average end user. Shortly thereafter, engineers internal to TiVo embraced the idea of allowing users to have a network connected to their unit, and started to build an optimized driver set for the expansion cards directly into their software. This made TiVo discover a new set of inter-networked features that could be available to its users. This freed users of using their phone line to get software updates and electronic programming guide data.

TiVo soon started working on a set of drivers and a TV-based user interface for configuring and controlling external USB adapters. These can connect to both Ethernet and Wi-Fi networks. These drivers, along with some great software, allow users to make TiVo part of their life beyond avoiding the drama of missing their favorite television show. Proving its commitment of transitioning TiVo boxes from a DVR to a digital lifestyle device, TiVo's newest generation of hardware includes a physical Ethernet port, allowing TiVo boxes to connect directly to household networks out of the box without the need to consider external USB network adapters. To connect to Wi-Fi networks, TiVo created its own TiVo-branded Wi-Fi adapter, optimized to integrate with TiVo boxes and speed up communication by offloading encryption and other network overhead to specialized hardware on the adapter.

Brief History of Software Development for TiVo

It's always good to start with a bit of history before diving into new application-building technology. TiVo HME offers a fairly rich environment for building end-user applications; however, it isn't the first attempt that TiVo has made at entering the applications delivery market. TiVo created a set of rudimentary tools called TiVo HMO, which is targeted specifically to solve the problem of delivering personal music and photo content to the television through the TiVo box.

Home Media Option and TiVo Desktop

Home Media Option (HMO) was the first digital lifestyle software solution introduced by TiVo. HMO runs two basic types of applications: audio streaming to TiVo boxes over a home network and displaying digital photo slideshows. The user interface on the television used to select and view photos or to choose music to play was a simple set of templates that, for the most part, followed the standard TiVo user interface guidelines. The templates were then populated by the TiVo box itself after requesting the information from TiVo Desktop server software running on a desktop machine located on the household network.

Originally TiVo charged an activation fee for Home Media Option on top of your normal subscription costs per TiVo box in your home. In order to show users the value in using a sidecar TiVo platform versus just renting a DVR directly from your video provider, TiVo subsequently dropped the activation fee for HMO features and now it comes standard with every TiVo subscription.

In addition to allowing access to music and photos (Figure 1-1 and Figure 1-2) on the user's desktop, TiVo also added a web-based interface for users to send program requests to their TiVo boxes via TiVo Central Online, hosted at TiVo.com. It also added Multi-Room Viewing, which brought the ability to stream or copy recordings from one TiVo box to another, provided both TiVo boxes were listed under the same account and on the same home network. This drove many users into adopting multiple networked TiVo boxes throughout their home and made the Photo and Music streaming services available in many more rooms in a household, all from a single TiVo Desktop server.

Figure 1-1

Figure 1-2

TiVo Desktop as a Server

Although HMO is limited to the capabilities of the display template frameworks that TiVo provides, it was the first time TiVo allowed end users to send their own personal content to TiVo boxes throughout their home and was a step in the right direction. In order to facilitate trafficking all of this foreign information into the TiVo world, a small software server called TiVo Desktop was released. As mentioned earlier, the TiVo Desktop runs on a Windows PC (Figure 1-3) or Macintosh (Figure 1-4) to serve music and photos to TiVo boxes throughout the household network. It is basically a simple web server that you can browse to with any browser if you know the specific URL format you need to use. The server is responsible for converting the audio and graphic content into a compatible MP3 or JPEG format and also for including the XML-based meta-data required to describe the content appropriately so the TiVo box will know the proper views to display on the television.

Though the TiVo Desktop software continues to provide the photo and music browsing services today, the latest generation of applications are largely unconstrained in terms of the user interface that is displayed, and the types of information that are accessed.

TiVo Desktop successfully set the stage for TiVo users to have independent software running on their personal computers within a home network to bring new functionality to their beloved TiVo boxes.

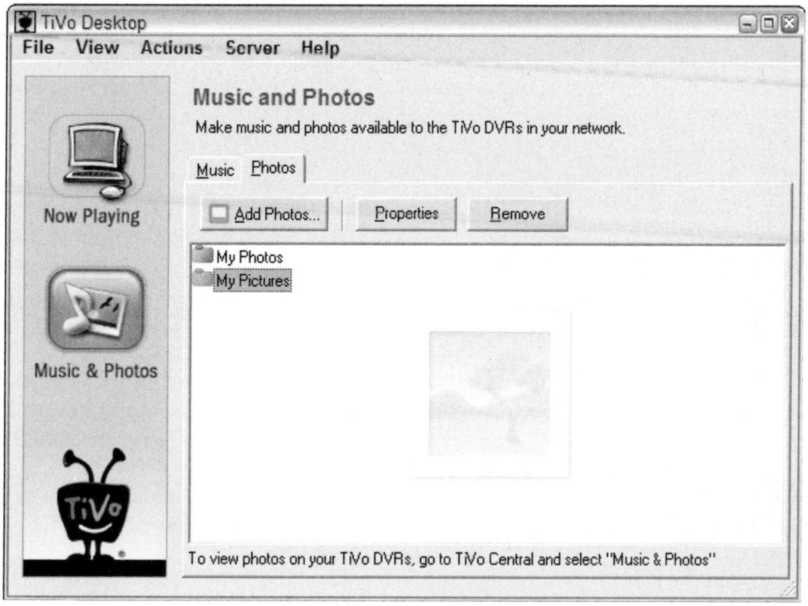

Figure 1-3

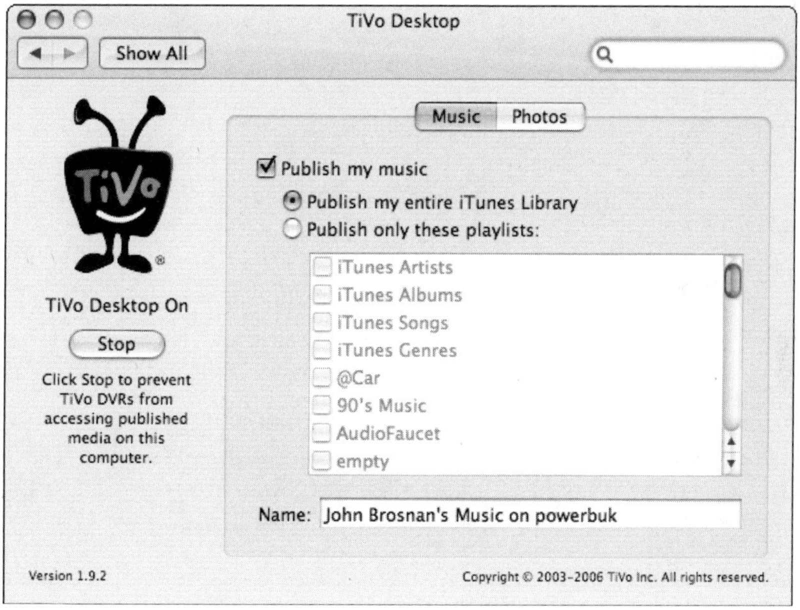

Figure 1-4

HMO Protocol

TiVo opened the HMO protocol to developers to extend their existing software offerings or to create new music and photo applications that could leverage the TiVo box's ability to display information on televisions throughout the household. The documentation for the HMO protocol is available at `http://www.tivo.com/developer`.

The protocol itself consists mainly of HTTP requests from the TiVo box to the computer. In effect, the desktop machine becomes a mini web server in the HMO system, serving content in the way the TiVo box knows how to display. The most interesting thing about this is that any application on any computer can extend its functionality by simply adding a very thin web server layer and talking to TiVo's specific XML and URL schemes.

The main thing that makes HMO applications so easy to use from an end-user perspective is an auto discovery technology called TiVo Connect. Applications can register with a machine's local beacon service to periodically broadcast information about the current suite of applications available that TiVo boxes on the household network can connect to. TiVo boxes would pick up these broadcast messages to automatically detect and alert users to the availability of expired or newly announced content that was available for use within the household. In Figure 1-5, the local HMO services on the Music, Photos & More screen is shown.

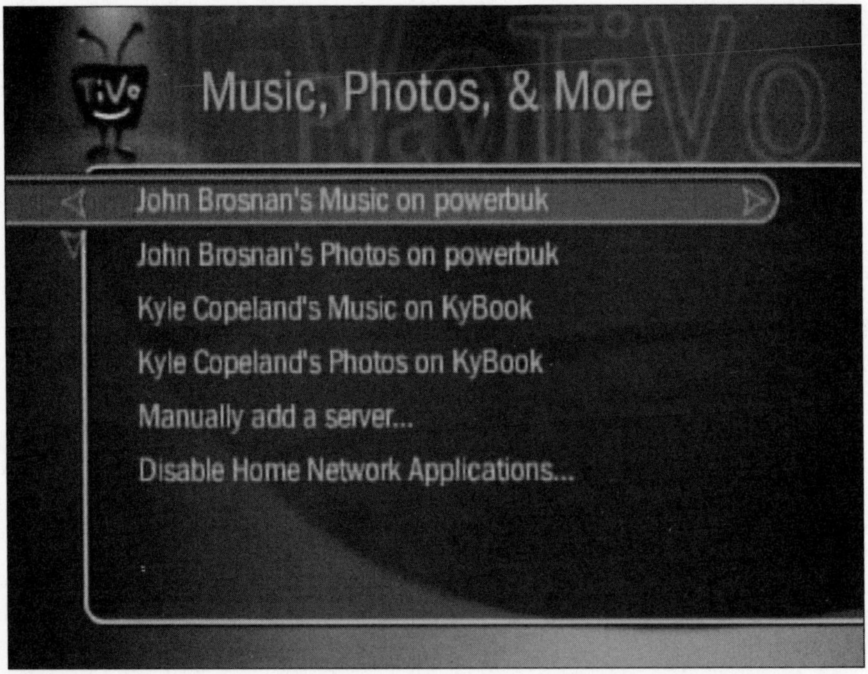

Figure 1-5

HMO Applications

There are two flavors of HMO applications: applications running on a personal computer locally within the user's household network extending the functionality of TiVo Desktop, and server-hosted applications mostly used for promotional purposes.

TiVo Server-Hosted Applications

HMO also brought the ability for TiVo to publish hosted services to the Music, Photos, Products, & More menu on any TiVo box connected to the global Internet. TiVo used the new network push opportunity to land two large advertising partners.

On the music side, Universal Music and later Best Buy signed on to push New Music Tuesday content, which was periodically updated when artists or labels wanted to promote new works as they became available. For photos, TiVo inked a deal with Nikon to promote artsy samples of the world's greatest photographers that used Nikon digital cameras. The Nikon Photo application is still available through the Music, Photos, Products, & More menu today.

Desktop Applications

Initially there were several applications available for TiVo box owners to run on their desktops that leveraged HMO's ability to display and interact with audio and visual content, but the main application that was born of the opening of the HMO protocol was the very popular JavaHMO. JavaHMO is a Java-based program that conveniently provides weather, movie listings, and a menagerie of other useful information via the photo album browsing interface frameworks of HMO.

JavaHMO was a completely open source replacement for TiVo Desktop, allowing users to collect personal and web content and push it to the TiVo boxes throughout their home in a more innovative way than even TiVo had intended. It cleverly took advantage of the hooks that TiVo provided in its API for HMO, with the end result of the JavaHMO server being more aware of the type of content that was being collected and aggregated throughout the home. Due to the constraints of the TiVo-provided template frameworks for HMO, the screens simply referred to themselves as Music or Photos depending on what type of information was being pushed. Despite this, many users still found the applications created using the new Java-based server to be well worth the aggravation of learning how to interact with the UI on the TiVo.

The initial intent of the open API from TiVo was to allow application providers to extend their existing applications to include new ways of pushing their existing content to networked TiVo boxes throughout a home network. This prompted a few media jukebox and photo shoebox software creators to extend their software to share user libraries with TiVo boxes on the household network while their programs were running.

The first to enter the fray was JRiver Media Center, a media organization jukebox, which allowed users to enhance their Home Media Option experience by allowing them to share music playlists and browse photo slideshows already categorized within JRiver's rich media organization environment. Many others soon followed. MoodLogic released a TiVo HMO music interface for its active music-mixing software that dynamically categorizes an entire music library based on the mood you are in at any given moment. Adobe added a "Publish to TiVo DVR" option in its Photoshop Album and Photoshop Elements photo organization and editing software, and soon thereafter Picasa followed suit adding similar functionality to its Digital Picture Organizer product.

HMO fell short in gaining developer excitement, hampered by the inability to create truly unique and valuable applications for the TiVo platform because of the limitations of the template framework environment. However, all of this changed dramatically in early 2004 when TiVo purchased a small company called Strangeberry, which, led by Arthur Van Hoff, a seasoned software engineer from Sun's Java labs, created a robust platform for delivering broadband content to low-powered television-connected devices. TiVo feverishly began work to merge the Strangeberry technology into its Series2 TiVo boxes, and by November of 2004, TiVo delivered the first early release version of a flexible and completely open source Java SDK initiative for creating network-powered applications for TiVo boxes, and dubbed it the Home Media Engine.

Home Media Engine

Home Media Engine (HME) is truly designed to allow full-fledged applications to display on the TiVo box. Though Home Media Option gave birth to networking and access to music and photos on a desktop machine, the interface on the TiVo box remained constrained, and all events (such as pressing a button on the remote) were handled by software on the TiVo box.

The basic model in Home Media Option, to make a directory structure of information available via HTTP for access from the TiVo, is extended in HME to create a full event processing system so HME applications can process remote control key presses, display custom interfaces, control sound effects and audio streams, and launch complex animations and screen transitions. This brought forth the ability to write and run truly custom network-powered applications on the TiVo box for the first time. As you can see in Figures 1-6 and 1-7, the user interface is far more flexible than the HMO interface (shown in Figures 1-1 and 1-2).

HME builds on several components that were originally introduced in HMO:

❑ **Network access:** TiVo HME applications don't actually run on the TiVo box itself — they typically run on a local desktop machine or on a server over the Internet.

❑ **Auto Discovery:** TiVo HME applications announce their availability similar to the way HMO announcements function through ZeroConf. ("ZeroConf" describes a set of technologies that provide some level of automated network addressing and discovery.)

HME introduces a new protocol for communication with the TiVo box that allows you as the developer to lay out the graphics and play sounds on the TiVo box in almost any way you can think of, as long as you bear in mind that the TiVo box has limited resources and processing power to create the display. Despite the limitations of the TiVo hardware platform, you can create very sophisticated applications, and you can take steps when writing your applications to ensure what they intend to display onscreen survives.

The variety of applications for TiVo HME is far greater than what is available for HMO. The new generation of applications includes access to information in your Yahoo account such as local weather, movies in the area, and traffic information. Live 365 has a radio station application that streams audio from the Internet to the TiVo box and provides a great selection of music. Users of Fandango can use Fandango's TiVo HME application to browse and purchase movie tickets.

TiVo has produced applications that range from games to podcasting players to an application to predict who will be voted off of *American Idol*. Independent software developers have written applications, such as AudioFaucet (shown in Figure 1-6 and written by the authors of this book), to play audio from your music library. Open source applications such as Galleon (Figure 1-7, the rebirth of JavaHMO as an HME application) do everything the original JavaHMO did, but offer a more elegant user interface. Apps.tv, located at `http://www.apps.tv`, is a web site that hosts many HME applications that can run over the Internet. Like the applications that TiVo hosts, apps.tv-hosted applications run over the Internet and range in functionality from a browser for Flickr photo galleries to fun family games written by independent developers using the HME software development kit.

Figure 1-6

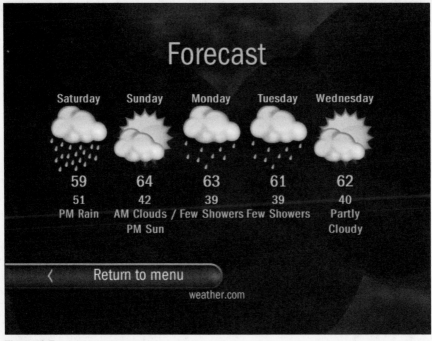

Figure 1-7

Software Development Kit

One of the reasons HME development has grown so quickly is because of the software development kit (SDK) that TiVo released along with HME. With all the plumbing for managing events from the TiVo box and built-in capabilities for displaying images and playing sounds through the TiVo box, the creation of an SDK for HME was a huge step forward in making development of HME applications simpler, faster, and more powerful. Applications that before had to rely on processing HTTP requests could now implement event models in the SDK and the application lifecycle, allowing much more sophisticated applications to be developed.

The SDK for HME was released in November of 2004 as an open source project, and is available from http://tivohme.sourceforge.net. Developed in Java, the HME SDK allows developers to leverage a wide variety of other open source and free libraries available, as well as mature Java development tools such as Ant, NetBeans, and Eclipse.

Along with the Java SDK, TiVo also introduced a library called "Bananas," which has tools for displaying standard TiVo interface widgets such as lists, screens, and buttons and providing an application the ability to easily have the familiar look and feel of a built-in TiVo screen. As every TiVo user knows, a highly intuitive and responsive interface is one of the great successes of the TiVo experience.

The documentation for the protocol that HME uses to communicate with the TiVo box is also available in the HME documentation. This is significant because it means that programming languages other than Java can be used with the HME protocol. Although the official TiVo HME SDK is in Java, applications have been written in other languages using the open protocol for HME. This book covers the Java SDK, because it is the official SDK from TiVo and because the concepts of handling events and working with the processing limitations of the TiVo hardware to create an application are applicable to any HME development.

How HME Interacts with TiVo

As mentioned earlier, the HME application runs either hosted on a server on the Internet or on a desktop machine within your home network. The TiVo box acts as a client, and displays the user interface as directed by the server, collecting input via remote control keys and sending the key press data back to the server for processing, as shown in Figure 1-8.

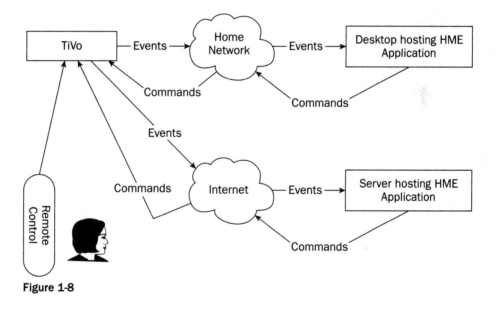

Figure 1-8

What HME Is and Isn't

HME, at the time of this writing, is a separate runtime environment on the TiVo box to run applications that provide access to information, games, and pretty much anything a creative developer can imagine. Access to internal information and other functions on the TiVo box outside of the HME subsystem and display model are not possible at this time. That is, HME does not allow access to any DVR functionality on the TiVo box, nor access to any of the local resources (such as recordings) that are stored on the TiVo boxes.

If you run the sample applications again (using the `runsamples` script) after starting the Simulator, you see that the sample applications appear on the Applications menu. From this menu, you can choose an application and run it in the Simulator just as you would on the TiVo box (Figure 3-10).

Figure 3-10

The Simulator command line can also take arguments to direct it to run an application without having to select the application. This mode is particularly useful when debugging applications.

Command-Line Option	Description
-d	Turn on debugging.
-mute	Disable sound.
-s	Disable application discovery using mdns.
url or class	When started with a url, the Simulator will connect to that url at startup. If the first argument is not a url, the Simulator will pass all arguments to a Factory and connect to it.

You can simulate TiVo remote control commands in the Simulator by using keyboard keys. For a list of these, select Help ➪ Keyboard Shortcuts in the Simulator.

Limitations of the Simulator

Although the Simulator application is great for testing functionality of an application, there are areas in which the Simulator may give misleading results.

For instance, the Simulator doesn't have the resource limitations that the normal TiVo box would. In fact, because the Simulator is running on your computer, it has access to all the resources available on your machine. How does this affect the application? The most common problem you can run into is using too many graphics or too much animation. These may work great in the Simulator, but when running on a TiVo box, the resource limitations prevent different graphics in your interface from being displayed, or the time it takes to send information over the network to the TiVo box can affect the performance of your application.

The Simulator also cannot display MPEGs the same way that the TiVo box can. Single-frame MPEGs can be used as a background image, primarily to save graphics memory on the TiVo box for image elements in an application's interface. Because the Simulator does not have access to the MPEG background layer, only image backgrounds can be displayed.

In short, the HME Simulator is great for quickly testing an application or for testing when you don't have access to a TiVo box, but because of the need to accurately test the effects of communicating over a network and appropriately size graphic elements to manage the limited graphic resources on the TiVo effectively, it shouldn't be the only thing relied on to test an application.

Summary

After this chapter, you should be familiar with how to run TiVo HME applications, and how to access them both through the TiVo box and from the Simulator application.

The requirements for developing and running HME applications should also be installed and configured on your system, and you should have a familiarity with the files included in the HME SDK.

You should be able to use the HME libraries and run the HME sample applications from within Eclipse as well as create HME projects in Eclipse.

Questions

1. What jars are needed to run TiVo HME applications?

2. What is the purpose of setting the network interface when running a TiVo HME application (using the `--inf` flag in the application)?

3. What does the output about MDNS mean? What does it signify?

Your First TiVo HME Application

The TiVo HME SDK provides a great amount of functionality for creating applications. The SDK does have a few requirements of the application in terms of the way it is written. An HME application must extend the Application class provided in the SDK; the Application superclass provides lifecycle methods and event-handling hooks to process events from the TiVo box and from other threads in the application. The lifecycle of an application takes place while the application is running through the TiVo box itself. That is, a new application is created and destroyed each time the application is launched from the TiVo box.

Hello World

Let's start with the classic Hello World example. Although a simple start, this application is a good way to examine the classes that must be extended in order to write an HME application, and a great opportunity to explore the hosting environment used to run applications.

Creating Hello World

To create a new HME application in Eclipse, select File ⇨ New Project. Select Java Project as the project type. Name the project "Ch4-01" and add the HME jars as you did in Chapter 3.

To create the main Application class:

1. Right-click your project in the Package Explorer tab.
2. Select New ⇨ Class.
3. Fill in the New Java Class form as shown in Figure 4-1.
4. Click Finish.

You now have a Java file open in Eclipse named Example1Ch4.java that contains the start of your TiVo HME application.

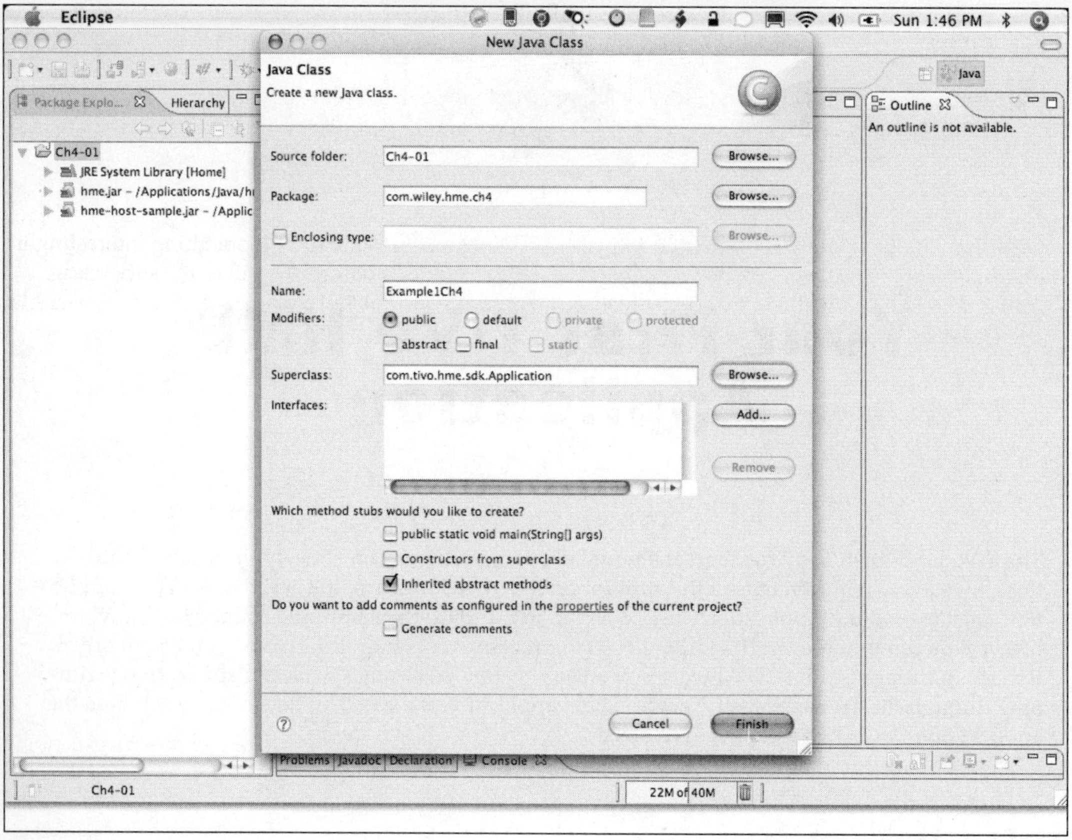

Figure 4-1

Eclipse Shortcut: When making a new class that you intend to extend from another class, clicking the Browse button next to the Superclass field will list all the classes you can extend from. The list is also searchable; in this case, you would search for "Application" and select the one from com.tivo.hme.sdk.

The code that is generated is just the framework for the class. To really do anything, you need to implement at least the init(...) method from Application, which is the method called when the application is run on the TiVo box:

```
package com.wiley.hme.ch4;

import com.tivo.hme.interfaces.IContext;
import com.tivo.hme.sdk.Application;

public class Example1Ch4 extends Application {

    public void init(IContext arg0) throws Exception {
        // TODO Auto-generated method stub
        super.init(arg0);
    }

}
```

The highlighted code shows the function that must be added to override the `init()` method in your application.

Eclipse Shortcut: To override methods, you can select Override/Implement Methods... from the Source menu and select methods to override by checking the box next to them. This ensures that you are overriding the correct method and makes it easier to get the method signature correct. Eclipse will also handle any additional import statements that are required because of the new method.

Now that you have the `init()` method in your Application, it is time to put something interesting in there. At the moment, you are just calling `super.init()`, which passed the call to the superclass, Application. This will allow the application to run on the TiVo box, but the screen will just appear black. Let's add some text so you know it is working correctly:

```java
package com.wiley.hme.ch4;

import java.awt.Color;

import com.tivo.hme.interfaces.IContext;
import com.tivo.hme.sdk.Application;
import com.tivo.hme.sdk.Resource;
import com.tivo.hme.sdk.View;

public class Example1Ch4 extends Application {

  public void init(IContext arg0) throws Exception {
    super.init(arg0);
    View root = getRoot();
    Resource text = createText("default-36.font", Color.red,  "Hello World");
    root.setResource( text );

  }
}
```

In this listing, you added three lines to produce the text "Hello World" on the screen. The first line retrieves the root View object. The root view is the base layer for drawing on the display. The second line creates a Resource, which holds the text "Hello World." The simplest explanation of Resources is that they are the "stuff" that is displayed in a view. Views are containers that define areas of the screen that can hold Resources. Resources are the data that is displayed (or played in the case of sound resources) on the TiVo box. In this case, you are using text, but Resources also describe images, sounds, and streams (such as an MP3 stream). Because Resources are the data that is shown on the screen, and Views are the boxes, to display the text you just created you must add it to a View in order to be seen. Because the text object is the only thing you are going to add to the View, you add it to the root view as shown in the third line. Even though the application is overriding the `init()` method, you still want to make sure to call `super.init()` to ensure that any initialization is performed in the parent Application class.

When adding code that uses libraries you have not yet imported, you can select Source ⇨ Organize Imports, and Eclipse will attempt to add the correct import statements for you (in this example, the ones for Resource and View). If there's more than one available, Eclipse will present you with a choice for each one. This command will also remove any unnecessary import statements and keep your code clean.

Running the Example in the Simulator

The HME SDK contains an HME Simulator, which is contained in the jar file `simulator.jar` that is in the HME SDK main folder. This program shows how an application will display on the actual TiVo box, and is a quick way to get started testing an application without having to run it on the TiVo box each time.

The Simulator can run your application one of two ways. You can run your HME application through the hosting environment and run the Simulator separately. The Simulator will then discover your application just like the TiVo box would, listening for MDNS announcements that an application is available for use. The other method, well suited for testing out an application as it is developed, is to run the application directly in the Simulator without any discovery.

Simulator in Discovery Mode

There are two steps to running in discovery mode:

❏   Set up the run configuration in Eclipse for the application and start the application.

❏   Run the Simulator.

Setting up the run configuration is similar to the steps in Chapter 3 for running the sample applications from within Eclipse:

1.   From the Run menu, select Run....

2.   Select Java Application in the options on the left and click the New icon near the top of the options (it has a document with a + on it), or the New button on the Windows version of Eclipse.

3.   On the Main tab, enter the main class name as `com.tivo.hme.host.sample.Main`.

4.   On the Arguments tab, in the Program Arguments box, type `com.wiley.hme.ch4.Example1Ch4` — you need to provide the name of the application for the HME host environment to run.

5.   Click Apply and then click Run. Eclipse may ask you if you wish to save the file before launching if the file that was just edited changed. Eclipse will ask this, and you probably want to save to make sure any changes are compiled into the code about to be run.

The application is now running from within Eclipse. In the Console tab inside Eclipse, you should see output similar to the following:

```
HME SDK 1.4 (TiVo, Inc.)
LOG: added factory
MDNS: http://192.168.1.107:7288/ch4/
```

If the output does not match this, or reports errors, check the run configuration created in the previous steps. Also, the Problems tab at the bottom of the Eclipse window will report any problems in the code that must be fixed before the application can run.

In Windows and Mac OS X, double-clicking the simulator.jar file should launch the Simulator application. It can also be started from the command line using the command java -jar simulator.jar. (Tip: adding a shortcut to simulator.jar onto your Windows desktop or Quick Launch menu is very handy.)

The Simulator will start up with a black screen. From the Network menu in the Simulator, choose your IP address, then from the Applications, choose the example, ch4 (see Figure 4-2). You may also need to choose the correct interface under the Network menu if you have not already done so.

Figure 4-2

The application will start up and display the text "Hello World" (Figure 4-3).

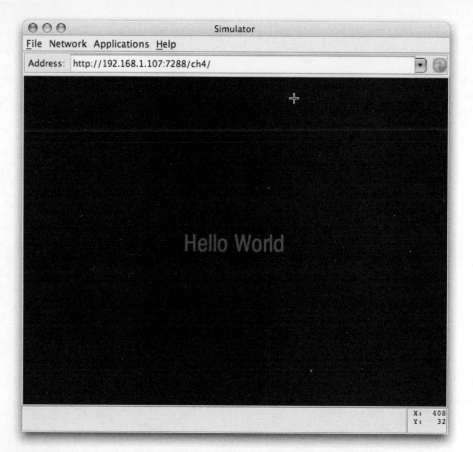

Figure 4-3

Simulator in Direct Mode

The `simulator.jar` program can also take as an argument the name of the application to run. Just as you set up `com.tivo.hme.host.sample.Main` to take the argument `com.wiley.hme.ch4.Example1Ch4`, you can set up a run configuration where the Simulator program takes the same argument. There is no discovery in this method, and it is quicker for running the application without additional steps in the Simulator.

To set up this configuration, first the `simulator.jar` file must be in the "build path" of the project. To add the `simulator.jar` or any other jar file you need in the future to your build path:

1. Right-click the main project in the Package Explorer tab in Eclipse and select Properties.

2. Select the Java Build Path option in the list on the left, and then select the Libraries tab.

3. Click Add External Jar... to locate the `simulator.jar` file and add it to the build path. The list of libraries should match Figure 4-4.

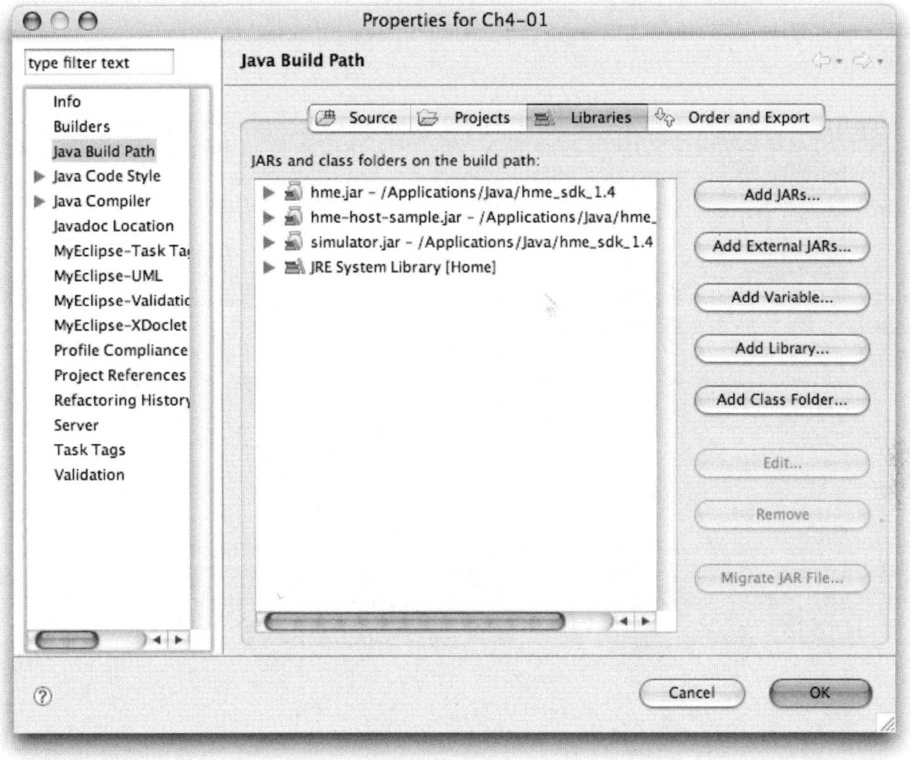

Figure 4-4

To set up the run configuration:

1. From the Run menu, select Run....

2. Select Java Application in the options on the left and click the New icon or New button.

3. On the Main tab, enter the main class name as com.tivo.hme.sim.Simulator.

4. On the Arguments tab, in the Program Arguments box, type com.wiley.hme.ch4 .Example1Ch4 — you need to provide the name of the application for the HME host environment to run.

5. Click Apply and then click Run.

The Simulator will now start and automatically run the example application, and will look like Figure 4-3. You may need to select the application under the Application menu to launch it.

Starting Hello World on the TiVo Box

The Simulator application is a great tool for quickly testing changes in an application, but ultimately all applications have to be tested on the TiVo box. The Simulator provides capabilities in terms of processing power and graphic resources that the TiVo box simply does not possess. Because an HME application runs over a network link and maintains a persistent connection, network latencies and communications are also not tested using the Simulator.

To run the application on the TiVo, start the "Run..." target you created for using the Simulator in discovery mode by selecting Run... from the Run menu, locating the name of the configuration in the box on the left (under Java Application), and clicking the Run button. The TiVo box discovers applications on the local network the same way the Simulator does.

On the TiVo box, navigate to the Music, Photos, & More menu and locate the application—applications running on local machines are generally at the bottom of the list of applications, so if you don't see it at first, scroll all the way down (see Figure 4-5).

Figure 4-5

The "Hello World" example, when running on the TiVo box, appears the same as in the Simulator, with red text on a black background (Figure 4-3). When using the other applications in the Music, Photos, & More menu, you probably noticed that applications are exited by pressing the left directional key on the remote control. Pressing the left key in the Hello World application, however, doesn't seem to have the same effect. The Hello World application can be exited using the TiVo button on the remote. This is because the other applications exit gracefully by handling the event for the left key. The TiVo button exits the application because it is a key that HME applications cannot override—it will always bring the user to the main TiVo screen so that the user experience when using HME applications is not completely different than using the other functionalities on the TiVo box.

Try It Out   Setting a Custom Icon and Name for the Application

When browsing through the Music, Photos, & More menu, the example application does not have an icon or title like the rest of the TiVo-hosted applications.

Setting a custom icon and name for the application is pretty simple. The TiVo receiver will check for a file named `icon.png` at the base URL published by the application, therefore an icon file would need to be in the base of the Java `CLASSPATH`. To add an icon, create a PNG graphic file named `icon.png` that is 34 pixels wide by 26 pixels high. Place the graphic file in the main project directory in Eclipse. (For this example, you can also drag and drop the `icon.png` file onto the package named `com.wiley.hme.ch4` in the Package Explorer, and Eclipse will copy it to the right place.)

To set the title for the application, add the highlighted line shown in the following code with the name of the application:

```java
public class Example1Ch4 extends Application {

    public final static String TITLE = "Hello World Example";

    .
    .
    .
}
```

If you run the application now and check out the Music, Photos, & More menu, you will see the name and icon (Figure 4-6).

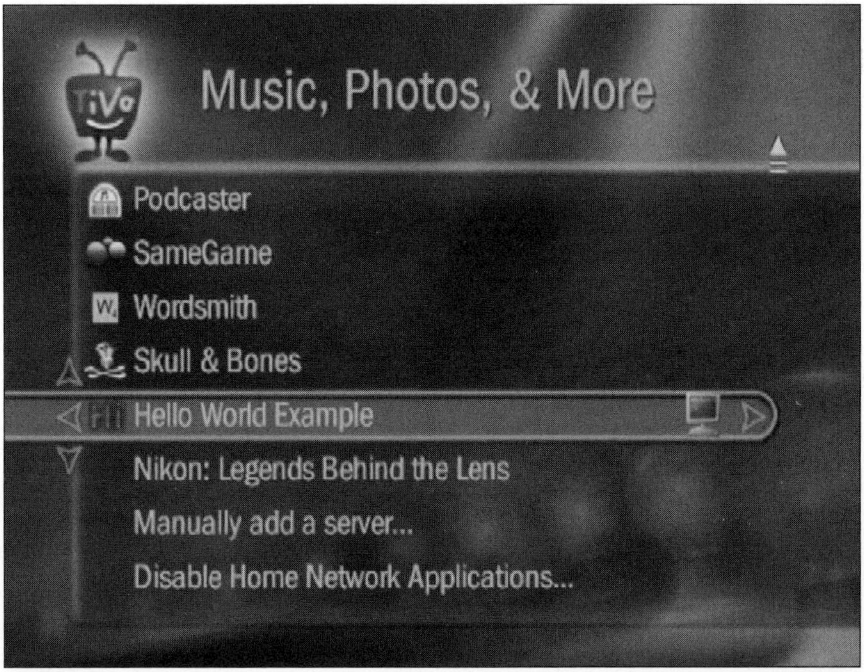

Figure 4-6

How It Works

When the TiVo box loads the Music, Photos, & More menu, the TiVo box knows of the applications that are running because of the MDNS announcements the application makes. The MDNS announcements are made by the hosting environment, which uses the string TITLE for the name of the application that is announced.

The TiVo box then asks each application for which it has received an announcement for the file icon.png. The TiVo box then uses this file as the icon displayed in the Music, Photos, & More menu.

Handling Events

How would the "Hello World" application be modified to handle HME events and exit gracefully? All the key press events that come from the TiVo box to the application are handled in the handleKeyPress() method. The following code shows how to handle a "left key" event from the TiVo box:

```java
package com.wiley.hme.ch4;

import java.awt.Color;

import com.tivo.hme.interfaces.IContext;
import com.tivo.hme.sdk.Application;
import com.tivo.hme.sdk.Resource;
import com.tivo.hme.sdk.View;

public class Example1Ch4 extends Application {
 public final static String TITLE = "Hello World Example";

  public void init(IContext arg0) throws Exception {
    super.init(arg0);
    View root = getRoot();
    Resource text = createText("default-36.font", Color.red,  "Hello World");
    root.setResource( text );

  }

    public boolean handleKeyPress(int code, long rawcode) {
      if (code == KEY_LEFT) {
        this.setActive(false);
        return true;
      }
      return super.handleKeyPress(code, rawcode);
    }
}
```

You added the method handleKeyPress(), which has been overridden from the HmeObject class. The first line determines if the key code is the key that matches the one you wish to react to, in this case the left key. When the left key is pressed (either on your remote, if you're running this from your TiVo, or on your keyboard, if running in the Simulator), you set the application to inactive mode and return true to indicate that you handled the event.

All other events that do not match KEY_LEFT are passed along. Although passing events along doesn't matter in this case, as more views and objects are added to the display, passing events along so that another object can handle them becomes increasingly important.

Exiting the application with setActive(false) may seem an unintuitive way to exit an application, but this exit isn't quite the same as quitting a normal program. In this case, the instance of the application that is communicating with the TiVo box is shut down, but it can be run again from the Music, Photos, & More menu — exiting the application on the TiVo box does not quit it on the PC desktop.

You can find a complete list of the keys you can watch for in handleKeyPress() in the HME documentation. See hme-devguide.pdf in the doc directory of the HME SDK and search for "KEY_LEFT."

Application Lifecycle

By way of examining how the "Hello World" application runs and handles events, you have started to look at the application lifecycle. The lifecycle is really just a description of how the process of starting an application, communicating with the TiVo box, reacting to events, and exiting the application takes place.

Startup

In any HME application, there are really two major stages involved in starting an application on the TiVo box. First, the host system must be running the application that will communicate with the TiVo box. After the host is running the application, the URL of the application will be broadcast to the TiVo box. This informs the TiVo box of how to locate the application.

When a TiVo receiver accesses the application, the Factory for the application creates a new instance of the application. After the application instance has been created, the init() method is called. As shown in the "Hello World" example, the superclass's (Application's) init() method should be called to make sure any initialization in the superclass is performed correctly.

Running Events

When an HME application is running, it is responsible for handling events from the TiVo receiver and sending commands to the receiver.

Events are first processed using the dispatchEvent(HmeEvent event) method of the Application. This method will determine which HmeObject the event is for, and will call the handleEvent(HmeEvent event) method for the HmeObject. Events that should be handled in the Application's handleEvent handler are events such as the idle event, an event indicating a key press has not been sent to the application for a period of time.

In the "Hello World" application, the specific handler for key press events, handleKeyPress(), is used.

Specific handlers are the best way to handle key press events. The specific handlers are

- ❑   handleKeyPress
- ❑   handleKeyRelease
- ❑   handleKeyRepeat

For only handling key events, the specific handlers are the proper way to handle these events. If the key events are unhandled, the handleEvent() method in Application will eventually receive the event. In "Hello World," the key press event could have been processed in handleEvent(); however, the correct way to process key presses is via one of the specific handlers.

Errors

Errors that are not fatal that occur while the HME application is running are sent to the application using the handler handleApplicationError(). These errors can include problems loading resources or warnings from the receiver.

Shutdown

Application shutdown can really take place in two ways. Either it can be initiated by the user of the application as in the "Hello World" example, where the left key is handled via the handleKeyPress() method and the application is cleanly exited. In this case, the application exits itself by calling setActive(false). The lifecycle method handleActive(boolean active) is called, followed by the destroy() method to notify the application to completely clean up any resources being held (that is, Threads and so on).

The other method of exiting an application occurs when the user uses a "warp key" (a key that immediately brings the user to another screen without any event handling by the HME application), the handleActive(boolean active) method will not be called, and only the destroy() method will be called.

Therefore, to ensure that the application's resources are always cleaned up, any thread or resource cleanup should be handled in destroy. Later, in the discussion on storing user preferences, you will see that you use the Context object. The context is created and destroyed by the Factory and is still available to the HME application when the destroy() method is called; in other words, it is still possible to store user preferences at this point.

Summary

This chapter started with a sample TiVo HME application for displaying simple text on a TiVo box. This simple example illustrated the lifecycle of an HME application and how to process events from an application.

The detailed information about the application lifecycle will be important in upcoming chapters as well as for managing and cleaning up the resources your application uses.

This chapter also covered details in Eclipse in terms of running an HME application as well as using the Simulator included with the SDK to test changes quickly without testing on a TiVo box.

Questions

1. How does an application respond to a key press?

2. What are the methods called when exiting an application? Are these always called?

3. How do you set a custom icon and name for an application?

5

Displaying Resources

In this chapter, you create an application that collects weather information based on a geographical location and display it on a TiVo box. The chapter provides a solid understanding of how your applications will use resources to present and organize information on the screen and also how sounds can be used throughout your applications. Resources are, in short, any graphic, text, or sound that your application displays or plays. Everything that is displayed to the user is transmitted to the TiVo box as a Resource object.

Understanding Views

Views are the primary building block for laying out the graphics, text, and other drawing items that can be displayed in an HME application. Everything that is displayed in an HME application is contained in a View, and the placement on the screen is defined by the coordinate system used with Views.

Introduction to Views

The `View` class extends the `HmeObject` class, inheriting the ability to create resources and to handle HME events. The View class also implements the `IHmeProtocol` interface and the `IHmeEvent Handler` interface. The `IHmeProtocol` interface is just a set of constants that are used in the HME protocol. The example in the previous chapter used the constant `KEY_LEFT` when processing events from the TiVo box. These constants and others are part of the IHmeProtocol. The `IHmeEvent Handler` is the interface that is a hook into the event-processing chain. The events that an HME application can receive and the chain of events are covered in more detail in the next chapter.

View Hierarchy

Views are arranged in a hierarchy. A view is always contained by another view, and may be the parent of other views. When creating views, the View constructor takes as its first argument another View object, which will be the parent of the new View. When an HME application starts up, the Application class (which all applications extend) will create the root view — the top-level view that can act as a parent to views. The first few views created in an application, therefore, may look like this:

```
View view1 = new View(this.getRoot(), 50, 50, 300, 300);
View view2 = new View(view1, 50, 50, 100, 100);
```

The first view, view1, is created with the root view as its parent view. The next four parameters specify the x and y coordinates and the width and height, respectively. The second view is created with view1 as the parent. This makes all the coordinates specified when creating view2 relative to the 0,0 coordinate system defined in the parent view, view1. So even though view1 and view2 contain the same x and y coordinates for the top/left placement of the box, the coordinates are always relative to the parent view. The root view derives its size from the maximum possible visible screen on a standard definition television. The root view is 640 pixels wide by 480 pixels high. Views may have coordinates that are beyond the viewable area of the root view, however, the views will not be visible. Visit www.wrox.com to view example Ch5-01, which contains a working application that draws these two views.

The views created in the preceding code would appear on the TiVo box as depicted in the following diagram (Figure 5-1).

Figure 5-1

Drawing Order and Hiding Views

Views are drawn based on where they lie in the view hierarchy. The root view is drawn first, then the children of the root view, then the children of the children of the root view, and so on. If a view contains multiple children, the children will be painted in the order in which they were created.

If views contain no resources, there is nothing to draw, so they are omitted until a Resource is set for the view. Drawing can be turned off for a view by setting the view to be invisible:

```
view2.setVisible(false);
```

This will in turn hide any views that have view2 as their parent view. Painting of a view can also be suspended. Suspending painting will not hide the view as setVisible(false) will, but will pause updates to the view until painting is resumed. The following code suspends painting, changes the color of a view, waits ten seconds, and then resumes painting:

```
    view1 = new View(this.getRoot(), 50, 50, 300, 300);
    view2 = new View(view1, 50, 50, 100, 100);

    view1.setResource(Color.red);
    view2.setResource(Color.gray);

    new Thread() {
      public void run() {

        view2.setPainting(false);
        view2.setResource(Color.blue);
// the flush is necessary because these instructions are in a separate thread
// than normal event processing. This flush forces updates to be transmitted to the
// TiVo Box, showing that the box color is not updated until
// painting is turned back on.
        flush();
        try {
          sleep(10000);
        } catch (InterruptedException e) {
          e.printStackTrace();
        }
        view2.setPainting(true);
        flush();
      }
    }.start();
```

The full code for this application is Ch5, example 2, and is available on the web site for the book at www.wrox.com.

Properties of Views

The x and y coordinates along with the width and height determine the size of the View that is displayed in the application. Although these must be initially set in the constructor, along with the parent view, these parameters may be altered after the view has been created using the following calls:

Method	Description
setLocation(int x, int y)	Sets the x and y coordinate of where a View should draw, relative to its parent View. The changes take place immediately.
setLocation(int x, int y, Resource animation)	Sets the x and y coordinate of where a View should draw, relative to its parent View. Changes take place over the period of time specified in the animation. Animations are covered in Chapter 12.
setSize(int width, int height)	Sets the width and height of the View; changes take place immediately.
setSize(int width, int height, Resource aninimation)	Sets the width and height of the view. Changes take place over the period of time specified in the animation.
setBounds(int x, int y, int width, int height)	Sets the x and y location of the View and the width and height. All changes take place immediately.
setBounds(int x, int y, int width, int height, Resource animation)	Sets the x and y location of the View and the width and height. Changes take place over the period of time specified in the animation. Animations are covered in Chapter 12.
getLocation()	Retrieves the location of the view.
getSize()	Retrieves the size of the view.
getBounds()	Retrieves the bounds of the view.
getX()	Retrieves the x coordinate of the view.
getY()	Retrieves the y coordinate of the view.
getHeight()	Retrieves the height of the view.
getWidth()	Retrieves the width of the view.

All measurements are in pixels for these methods, and the location is always set relative to the parent view.

Translation

Translation of a view will move the contents of the view an amount relative to the x and y coordinates that define where a view is drawn onscreen. The difference between translation and merely changing the location of the view is that a translated view will move the contents of the view.

The parameters for setting the translation of a view are relative to the current translated location, instead of absolute values, which they would be when changing the bounds. The translate methods would be useful, for instance, when moving a cursor around the screen. Instead of recalculating the position of the cursor each time, the translate method could be used to move it a defined distance.

The translate methods, however, do not move the view itself, only the contents of the view. If there is a view that is 100px by 100px and `my_view.translate(200,200)` is called, the contents of the view will be translated outside the viewable area, so they will seem to have disappeared. The contents have only been translated outside the bounds of the view, and can be translated back again by calling `my_view.translate(-200,-200)`.

Method	Description
`translate(int xAmount, int yAmount)` `setTranslation(int xAmount, int yAmount)`	Both of these methods set the amounts in the x and y directions that the view should move.
`translate(int xAmount, int yAmount, Resource animation)` `setTranslation(int xAmount, int yAmount, Resource animation)`	Both of these methods set the amounts in the x and y directions that the view should move. Changes take place over the period of time specified in the animation. Animations are covered in Chapter 12.
`getTranslation()`	Gets the currently set translation of the View.
`getTranslationX()`	Gets the x value of the currently set translation of the View.
`getTranslationY()`	Gets the y value of the currently set translation of the View.

Scaling

Views can also be scaled relative to the bounds set for a view. Scaling a view will also scale all the child views and resources of all child views.

Method	Description
`setScale(float xAmount, float yAmount)`	This method sets the scaling factor for the view. Changes take place immediately.
`setScale(float xAmount, float yAmount, Resource animation)`	This method sets the scaling factor for the view. Changes take place over the period of time specified in the animation. Animations are covered in Chapter 12.
	Animation with scaling should probably not be used because it causes performance problems when rendering on the TiVo box.
`getScaleX()`	Gets the x scaling factor for this view.
`getScaleY()`	Gets the y scaling factor for this view.

Visibility, Transparency, and Focus

Visibility has many uses in HME application development. From hiding certain elements at different times in the application lifecycle to showing different views based on events, view visibility is probably one of the more frequent actions taken on a view after it has been created.

Turning off painting (as you saw earlier) can be used to "queue" several updates to a view without some of the update commands displaying a view before all the updates have been made.

Method	Description
setVisible(boolean visible)	This method sets the visibility for the view. Changes take place immediately.
setVisible(boolean visible, Resource animation)	This method sets the visibility for the view. Changes take place over the period of time specified in the animation.
setPainting(boolean painting)	This method sets the flag indicating that updates should be suspended or enabled for the view. Changes take place immediately.
getVisible()	Determines if this view is currently visible.
getPainting()	Determines if painting has been turned off for this view.

Method	Description
setTransparency(float transparency)	This method sets the transparency for the view. Changes take place immediately. 0.0 is opaque, 1.0 is fully transparent.
setTransparency(float transparency, Resource animation)	This method sets the transparency for the view. Changes take place over the period of time specified in the animation.
getTransparency()	Gets the currently set transparency for this view.

Method	Description
setFocus()	This method sets the view on which it is called as having focus.
hasFocus()	Determines if this view has focus or not.

Extending Views

The View class works great by itself for placing items on the screen and moving them, even for animating objects onscreen.

Subclassing views is required if the view needs to process events. Events will eventually propagate to the Application class if they are not handled by the individual views, but processing all events in the application leads quickly to unmanageable code, as well as very tightly coupled objects.

The following example subclasses View in order to receive events for the view:

```java
package com.wiley.hme.ch5;

import java.awt.Color;

import com.tivo.hme.interfaces.IContext;
import com.tivo.hme.sdk.Application;
import com.tivo.hme.sdk.IHmeProtocol;
import com.tivo.hme.sdk.View;

public class TwoViews extends Application {

  myView view1;
  myView view2;
  myView focusedView;

  public void init(IContext context) throws Exception {
    super.init(context);

    view1 = new myView(this.getRoot(), 10, 10, 150, 150);
    view2 = new myView(view1, 10, 10, 50, 50);

    view1.setFocus();
    focusedView = view1;

    view1.setResource(Color.red);
    view2.setResource(Color.gray);

  }

  public boolean handleKeyPress(int code, long rawcode) {
    //
    // This code is to cleanly exit the application
    //
    switch(code) {
    case KEY_LEFT:
      this.setActive(false);
      return true;
    case KEY_RIGHT:
      if (focusedView == view1) {
```

```
        view2.setFocus();
      } else {
        view1.setFocus();
      }
      return true;
    }
    // keypresses that we don't handle, we pass along.
    return super.handleKeyPress(code, rawcode);
  }


  public class myView extends View {
    String name;

    public myView(View parent, int x, int y, int w, int h) {
      super(parent, x,y,w,h);
    }

    public myView(View arg0, int arg1, int arg2, int arg3, int arg4, boolean arg5)
{
      super(arg0, arg1, arg2, arg3, arg4, arg5);
    }

    public boolean handleKeyPress(int key, long rawcode) {
      switch (key) {
      case IHmeProtocol.KEY_SELECT:
        this.setResource(Color.blue);
        return true;
      case IHmeProtocol.KEY_PLAY:
        this.setResource(Color.cyan);
        return true;
      }
      return super.handleKeyPress(key, rawcode);
    }


  }

}
```

In this example, a new class, myView, extends the View class and overrides the `handleKeyPress()` method in order to receive key press events from the TiVo box. The Application class also handles a few keys to "switch" focus between the views. To see this in action, press the Select key when running this application on your TiVo (or Enter on the Simulator), the Right key, and the Play key (or "p" on the simulator).

When the focus is switched, the View on which `setFocus()` was last called will be the View in the event-processing path. The code for this example is in Ch5-03.

Code Example

The following code is a simple layout of an application to show the current weather. In this example, the views have been set up on the screen. In the coming sections, this application will be enhanced with graphics, text, and sound.

```java
package com.wiley.hme.ch5;

import java.awt.Color;

import com.tivo.hme.interfaces.IContext;
import com.tivo.hme.sdk.Application;
import com.tivo.hme.sdk.View;

public class WeatherApplication extends Application {

  View dayView;
  View weatherIconView;
  View hiView;
  View lowView;
  View currentTempView;
  View forcastView;

  public static final String TITLE="Weather";

  public void init(IContext context) throws Exception {
     super.init(context);
     getRoot().setResource(Color.white);

     int dvWidth=250,
      dvHeight=150,
      wivWidth=250,
      wivHeight=200,
      hlcvWidth=200,
      hlcvHeight=60,
      fvWidth=250,
      fvHeight=120;

     dayView         = new View(getRoot(),    0,    0, 0, 0);
     weatherIconView = new View(getRoot(),    0,    0, 0, 0);
     hiView          = new View(getRoot(),    0,    0, 0, 0);
     lowView         = new View(getRoot(),    0,    0, 0, 0);
     currentTempView = new View(getRoot(),    0,    0, 0, 0);
     forcastView     = new View(getRoot(),    0,    0, 0, 0);

     // set up the location of the views
     dayView.setLocation(          SAFE_TITLE_H,            SAFE_TITLE_V);
     weatherIconView.setLocation(  SAFE_TITLE_H+dvWidth+10, SAFE_TITLE_V);
```

```
        hiView.setLocation(          SAFE_TITLE_H+20,
SAFE_TITLE_V+dvHeight+10);
        lowView.setLocation(         SAFE_TITLE_H+20,
SAFE_TITLE_V+dvHeight+10+hlcvHeight+10);
      currentTempView .setLocation(  SAFE_TITLE_H+20,
SAFE_TITLE_V+dvHeight+10+(hlcvHeight+10)*2);
        forcastView.setLocation(     SAFE_TITLE_H+10+wivWidth,
SAFE_TITLE_V+wivHeight+10);

    // set up the width and height of the views
    dayView.setSize(          dvWidth,      dvHeight);
    weatherIconView.setSize(  wivWidth,     wivHeight);
    hiView.setSize(           hlcvWidth,    hlcvHeight);
    lowView.setSize(          hlcvWidth,    hlcvHeight);
    currentTempView.setSize(  hlcvWidth,    hlcvHeight);
    forcastView.setSize(      fvWidth,      fvHeight);
    dayView.setResource( Color.black);
    weatherIconView.setResource( Color.black);
    hiView.setResource( Color.black);
    lowView.setResource( Color.black);
    currentTempView.setResource( Color.black);
    forcastView.setResource( Color.black);


}

public boolean handleKeyPress(int key, long longcode) {
  switch (key) {
  case KEY_LEFT:
    this.setActive(false);
     return true;
  }
  return super.handleKeyPress(key, longcode);
}

}
```

In this example, you use SAFE_TITLE_V and SAFE_TITLE_H to place the views on the screen. These constants define the safe area that will display on most televisions.

Although the root view is 640px by 480px, most televisions will not be able to display the full 640 x 480 image, and will cut off pixels from the outer edges. The constants define buffers on the sides and top so that views and resources can be placed so that they will appear as intended.

Constant	Description
SAFE_TITLE_V	The recommended vertical buffer for any text to be displayed onscreen.
SAFE_TITLE_H	The recommended horizontal buffer for any text to be displayed onscreen.

Constant	Description
SAFE_ACTION_V	The recommended vertical buffer for any active item on the screen. Items using this buffer may be clipped on some televisions.
SAFE_ACTION_H	The recommended horizontal buffer for any active item on the screen. Items using this buffer may be clipped on some televisions.

Running the preceding application in the Simulator would generate a display as seen in Figure 5-2. It seems like there is a large amount of space on the edges of the screen, but the Simulator shows all 640 by 480 pixels. Selecting File ⇨ Show Safe Action in the Simulator will show the application with the clipping of borders like a TV would display the application (Figure 5-2).

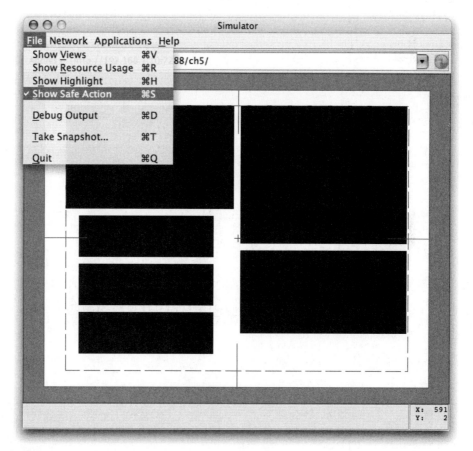

Figure 5-2

Chapter 5

Text

Text resources are one of the major components of any application. All text that is displayed onscreen must be made into a resource and assigned to a view in order to be displayed.

Creating Text Resources

Whereas views define the placement of Resources in the application, and sit in the path of events, resources are the actual items displayed onscreen for the application. Text is the simplest resource to create because the TiVo box is capable of rendering text quickly. Considerations that apply to images which would affect performance of the application on the TiVo don't apply to text, so it is a good place to begin learning about resources.

The TiVo HME SDK also supports font resources, which can be used to display text in TrueType fonts. TrueType fonts, like images, do require resources on the TiVo box. The default and system fonts, however, are already provided on the TiVo, so additional memory is not taken on the TiVo box when using the default or system fonts.

Try It Out

The following example uses the default font to display a message on the TiVo box (Figure 5-3).

Figure 5-3

```java
package com.wiley.hme.ch5;

import java.awt.Color;

import com.tivo.hme.interfaces.IContext;
import com.tivo.hme.sdk.Application;
import com.tivo.hme.sdk.Resource;
import com.tivo.hme.sdk.View;

public class Fonts extends Application {

  public void init(IContext arg0) throws Exception {
    super.init(arg0);
    getRoot().setResource(Color.darkGray);

    View view1 = new View( getRoot(), SAFE_TITLE_H, SAFE_TITLE_V, 200, 200);
    Resource text = createText("default-24.font", Color.white, "Learning About
Text...");

    view1.setResource(text);
    view1.setVisible(true);

  }

  public boolean handleKeyPress(int code, long rawcode) {
    switch(code) {
    case KEY_LEFT:
      this.setActive(false);
      return true;
    }
    return super.handleKeyPress(code, rawcode);
  }
}
```

How It Works

In the `init()` method, first you create a view. Resources can't be placed directly on the screen. As discussed in the first section of this chapter, to be placed on the screen, resources must be assigned to views, because views define the placement, size, and visibility of Resources.

After creating the view, you create the Resource. The resource is then assigned to the view to place it onscreen in the application, and the view is set to visible.

To create the resource, you use the helper method `createText(...)`. The parameters given to `createText()` are described in the following table. The example uses the default font in size 24 (`default-24.font`) in white (using the `java.awt.Color` class). The text to display is the first parameter to `createText()`. This method is part of the HMEObject class. Because the Application class extends HMEObject, and the application, Fonts, extends Application, all the methods of HMEObject are available for the application to use. HMEObject contains the helper methods to create all the types of resources in the HME SDK.

```
        }

        strBuff.append( string.substring(segments*sliceSize, length));

        return strBuff.toString();
    }

    public void init(IContext context) throws Exception {
        super.init(context);
        getRoot().setResource(Color.white);

        AppInfoView    = new TitledView ("AppEvent", getRoot(), 50,50,200,100);
        DeviceInfoView = new TitledView("DeviceInfo", getRoot(), 260, 50, 200,
100);
        eView          = new TitledView("key event", getRoot(), 50, 260, 200,
100);
        InitInfoView   = new TitledView("InitInfo", getRoot(), 260, 260, 200,
100);
        FontInfoView   = new TitledView("FontInfo", getRoot(), 400, 50, 200, 100);
        ResourceView   = new TitledView("ResourceView", getRoot(), 260, 350, 200,
100);

        Resource f = createFont("geodesic.ttf", 10, 10);
        f.addHandler(this);

        text = createText(f, Color.black, "Waiting for Event");
        text.addHandler(this);
        eView.setResource(text);
    }
}
```

The `handleEvent()` method receives all events in this example. All unhandled events will eventually be sent to the application's `handleEvent()` method. The preceding application shows how to process the different events that HME applications receive (Figure 6-1).

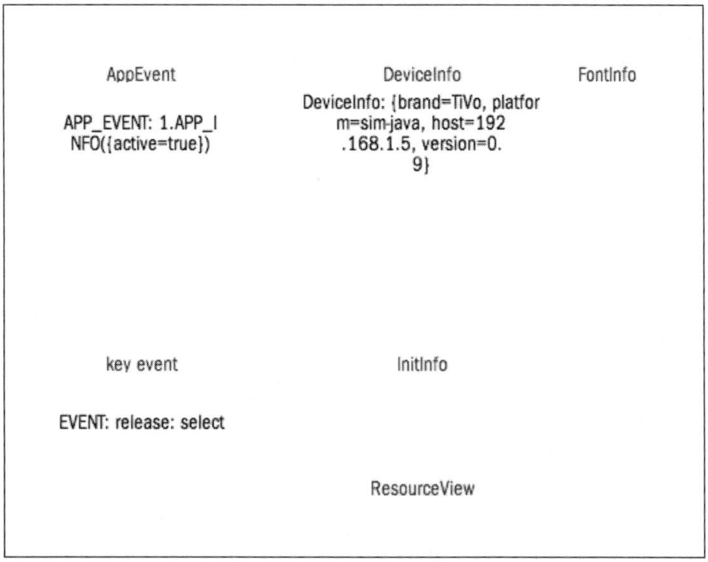

Figure 6-1

The event processing flow is shown in Figure 6-2. The postEvent() methods, although public, are probably not something you would want to override, because doing so could have unexpected effects on the processing of events.

The handle*() methods are the methods in which event processing should take place. The handle Event() and other handle*() methods all return a boolean. The boolean indicates whether or not the event has been processed. Returning false indicates to the event processing system that the event has not been handled; returning true indicates that the event has been handled properly.

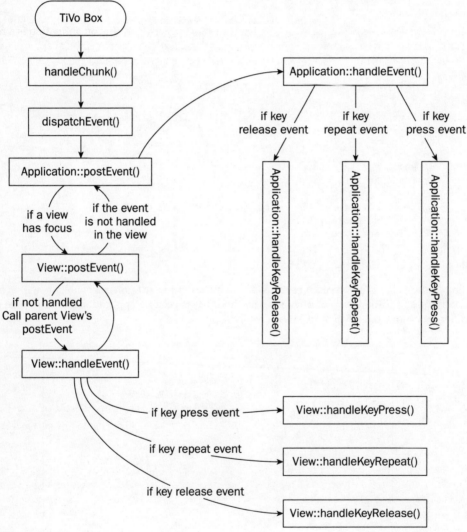

Figure 6-2

Sending Custom Events

In most cases, an HME application will be responding to events that are sent to the application from the TiVo box based on input from the user. The application is also able to queue events for delivery.

This method sends events to the TiVo box, and then the TiVo box sends the event back to the application. The two forms of sendEvent() are

```
sendEvent(HmeEvent event);
sendEvent(HmeEvent event, Resource animation);
```

Animations are discussed later in the book, but for now, suffice it to say that an animation is a resource that defines a period of time. If sendEvent() is passed an animation resource, the event will be sent back to the application after the period of time described by the animation.

For example, the following code excerpt will send an event to the current application with the TIVO_KEY immediately (no animation). Although the TIVO_KEY cannot be sent by the TiVo box, because it is a reserved key, it can be sent by the application to itself. This makes the TIVO_KEY a good way to send events from the application back to the application, without any doubt that the event is not being sent because of a user remote control key press.

```
HmeEvent event = new HmeEvent.Key(getID(), 0, KEY_TIVO, 1000);
sendEvent(event);
```

The code to handle this event looks like this:

```
public boolean handleKeyPress(int keyCode, long rawCode) {
        switch (keyCode) {
        case KEY_TIVO:
            if (rawCode == 1000) {
                ...
            }
        }
        .
        .
        .
}
```

The rawcode in handleEvent() will match the code that is the last argument when creating a new HmeEvent.Key object. This can be used as a small token of data to communicate information back to the application.

The sendEvent() method is defined in the Resource class, so it is available for any object that extends the Resource class. In this case, you have used the Application class's inheritance from Resource to send the event. This is probably the most common way to queue events, because the Application class is the most readily available.

Ticker Events

The Ticker class is provided in the SDK as a means of receiving timed callbacks. It really does not communicate with the TiVo box at all, like sending events does.

Ticker can be useful if there is something that is a re-occurring event that must happen repeatedly. To be able to use the Ticker, you must import the Ticker class:

```
import com.tivo.hme.sdk.util.Ticker;
```

The Ticker uses a thread to manage callbacks to different clients on a schedule. To register for Ticker callbacks, the class to receive the callback must implement the `Ticker.Client` interface:

```
public class SimonSays extends Application implements Ticker.Client { ...
```

In this case an application called SimonSays implements the `Ticker.Client` interface. This interface forces the class to have the method:

```
public long tick(long tm, Object arg) {
```

This is the method that is invoked when the Ticker times out. The return value of this method will set the next time the Ticker will invoke this method. To invoke the method again in 1.1 seconds, for example, the `tick()` method would return:

```
return System.currentTimeMillis()+1100;
```

The return value is the absolute time to invoke the `tick()` method again, so you take the current time and add on the additional time for the callback to wait.

Returning -1 from the `tick()` method will cancel the calls to the `tick()` method.

To set up an object to receive a callback, you would write:

```
Ticker.master.add(this, System.currentTimeMillis()+2000, null);
```

This would register the current class to receive a callback in 2000 milliseconds (2 seconds) from the current time. There is also a similar call to remove a Ticker callback from an object:

```
Ticker.master.remove(this, null);
```

The final object to `Ticker.master.add()` is an argument to pass to the `tick()` method. In the following example application, you do not use the argument, although it could be used to pass data along with the `tick()` call. This would be most useful if one object was registering a Ticker for another object and needed to pass data:

```
Ticker.master.add(updatingViewObject, System.currentTimeMillis()+2000, "String to
Display");
```

The following example application makes use of the Ticker and of `handleEvent()` to play a Simon Says game with the user and the remote control. As you can see, using the Ticker for constantly updating data can require careful control of the application state (Figure 6-3).

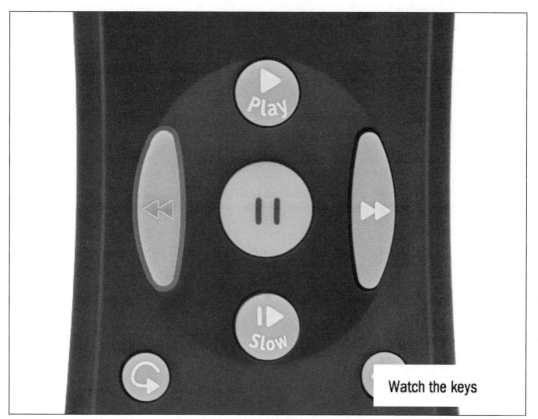

Watch the keys

Figure 6-3

```
package com.wiley.hme.ch6;

import java.awt.Color;
import java.awt.Rectangle;
import java.util.Hashtable;
import java.util.Random;

import com.tivo.hme.interfaces.IContext;
import com.tivo.hme.sdk.Application;
import com.tivo.hme.sdk.Resource;
import com.tivo.hme.sdk.View;
import com.tivo.hme.sdk.util.Ticker;

public class SimonSays extends Application implements Ticker.Client {

    private static final int PLAY_MODE = 40;
```

```
        private static final int LISTEN_MODE = 50;

    int mode;
    View onView;
    View textView;
    View textBg;
    View modeView;
    View modeViewBg;

    Hashtable locations = new Hashtable();

    Resource onImage;

    int keySeqArray[];
    int keyCounter=1;
    int currentKeyCounter=0;
    int replayKeyCounter=0;
    int keyNewPlace=0;

    Random rand;
    private String strInstructions = "Press the same\nkeys in the sequence\nthey
are displayed\non screen.\nPress Select\nto start.";
    private String strWatch = "Watch the keys";
    private String strRepeat = "Repeat the keys";

    private static int KEY_SEQUENCE_SIZE=20;

    private static Integer REVERSE_KEY  =  new Integer(0) ;
    private static Integer FORWARD_KEY  =  new Integer(1) ;
    private static Integer PLAY_KEY     =  new Integer(2) ;
    private static Integer SLOW_KEY     =  new Integer(3) ;
    private static Integer PAUSE_KEY    =  new Integer(4) ;
    private static Integer HIDDEN       =  new Integer(-1);

    private int[] KEYVAL = { KEY_REVERSE, KEY_FORWARD, KEY_PLAY, KEY_SLOW,
KEY_PAUSE };
    private boolean displayNow=true;


    public void init(IContext context) throws Exception {
        super.init(context);
        // create a new random number generator and seed it with the current time.
        rand = new Random(System.currentTimeMillis());
        mode = PLAY_MODE;
        setup();

        keySeqArray = new int[KEY_SEQUENCE_SIZE];
        onView = new View(getRoot(), 0,0,5,5);
        onImage = createImage("ThumbsAway-on.gif");
        onView.setResource(onImage, RSRC_HALIGN_LEFT|RSRC_VALIGN_TOP);

        textBg = new View(getRoot(), 160,  90, 300, 300);
        textView = new View(getRoot(), 160,90, 300, 300);
        textBg.setResource(Color.DARK_GRAY);

        modeViewBg = new View(getRoot(), 450, 420, 150, 50);
```

```
        modeViewBg.setResource(Color.white);

        modeView = new View(getRoot(), 450, 420, 150, 50);

        displayPlay(strInstructions);


        getRoot().setResource(this.createImage("ThumbsAway-off.gif"));

        setPlacement(HIDDEN);
        onView.setVisible(true);
}

public boolean handleKeyPress(int keyCode, long rawCode) {
    switch (keyCode) {
    case KEY_ENTER:
        setActive(false);
        return true;

    case KEY_SELECT:
        textView.setVisible(false);
        textBg.setVisible(false);
        if (mode == PLAY_MODE) {
            displayMode(strWatch);
            Ticker.master.add(this, System.currentTimeMillis()+2000, null);
        }
        return true;

    case KEY_REVERSE:
    case KEY_FORWARD:
    case KEY_PLAY:
    case KEY_PAUSE:
    case KEY_SLOW:
        this.textView.setVisible(false);
        textBg.setVisible(false);

        if(mode == PLAY_MODE) {
            break;
        }
        if (keyCode == KEYVAL[keySeqArray[replayKeyCounter]]) {
            this.setPlacement(new Integer(keySeqArray[replayKeyCounter]));
            play("thumbsup.snd");
            replayKeyCounter++;
            if ((replayKeyCounter-1) == this.KEY_SEQUENCE_SIZE) {
                play("thumbsup.snd");
                play("thumbsup.snd");
                play("thumbsup.snd");
                play("thumbsup.snd");
                play("thumbsup.snd");
                play("thumbsup.snd");
                displayPlay("You Win!");
            } else if (replayKeyCounter >= this.keyCounter) {
                play("thumbsup.snd");
                play("thumbsup.snd");
                play("thumbsup.snd");
                keyCounter++;
```

```
                        //this.displayPlay(strContinue);
                        replayKeyCounter=0;
                        currentKeyCounter=0;
                        setPlacement(HIDDEN);
                        mode = PLAY_MODE;
                        displayMode(strWatch);
                        Ticker.master.add(this, System.currentTimeMillis()+2000, null);

                    }
            } else {
                play("thumbsdown.snd");
            }
            return true;
        }
        return super.handleKeyPress(keyCode, rawCode);
}

public long tick(long tm, Object arg) {
        if (!displayNow) {
            setPlacement(HIDDEN);
            flush();

            displayNow=!displayNow;
            if (currentKeyCounter < keyCounter ) {
                return System.currentTimeMillis()+500;
            } else {
                mode = LISTEN_MODE;
                return System.currentTimeMillis()+500;
            }

        }

        if (mode == LISTEN_MODE) {
            //displayPlay(strPlay);
            setPlacement(HIDDEN);
            displayMode(this.strRepeat);
            flush();
            return -1;
        }

        if (isApplicationClosing()) {
            return -11;
        }
        int key = rand.nextInt();

        if (currentKeyCounter <= keyNewPlace) {
            key = keySeqArray[currentKeyCounter];
        } else {
            key = Math.abs(key%5);
            if (key == 0)
                key++;
            keyNewPlace = currentKeyCounter;
        }

        setPlacement(new Integer(key));

        keySeqArray[currentKeyCounter] = key;
```

```
        currentKeyCounter++;
        flush();
        displayNow=!displayNow;
        return System.currentTimeMillis()+1100;

    }

    private void displayMode(String str) {
        modeView.setResource(createText("default-20.font", Color.black, str));
        modeView.setVisible(true);
        modeViewBg.setVisible(true);
    }

    private void displayPlay(String str) {
        textView.setResource(createText("default-30.font", Color.white, str));
        textView.setVisible(true);
        textBg.setVisible(true);
    }

    private void setPlacement(Integer placement) {
        Rectangle curr = (Rectangle) locations.get(placement);
        setLocation(onView, curr);
        setTranslation(onView, curr);
        setSize(onView, curr);
    }

    private void setSize(View view, Rectangle r) {

        Double dx = new Double(r.getWidth());
        Double dy = new Double(r.getHeight());
        int ix = dx.intValue();
        int iy = dy.intValue();
        System.out.println("setting size: " + ix + "," + iy);
        view.setSize(ix, iy);
    }

    private void setTranslation(View view,Rectangle r) {
        Double dx = new Double(r.getX());
        Double dy = new Double(r.getY());
        int ix = dx.intValue();
        int iy = dy.intValue();
        System.out.println("setTranslation: " + ix + "," + iy);
        view.setTranslation(-ix, -iy);
    }

    private void setLocation(View view, Rectangle r) {
        Double dx = new Double(r.getX());
        Double dy = new Double(r.getY());
        int ix = dx.intValue();
        int iy = dy.intValue();
        System.out.println("setLocation: " + ix + "," + iy);
        view.setLocation(ix, iy);
    }

    private void setup() {
        locations.put(REVERSE_KEY, new Rectangle(137, 130, 96, 217));
```

```
            locations.put(FORWARD_KEY, new Rectangle(395, 133, 105, 217));
            locations.put(PLAY_KEY, new Rectangle(261, 38, 111, 114));
            locations.put(SLOW_KEY, new Rectangle(262, 324, 111, 116));
            locations.put(PAUSE_KEY, new Rectangle(234, 152, 161, 169));
            //locations.put(REPLAY_KEY, new Rectangle(125, 391, 86, 91));
            //locations.put(KEY_ADVANCE, new Rectangle(424, 392, 86, 91));
            locations.put(HIDDEN, new Rectangle(0,0,5,5));
    }
}
```

How It Works

The application's use of Ticker enables the periodic changing of the display. The `tick()` method is called when the Ticker timeout occurs. The return value from the `tick()` method is the timeout used before the next call to the `tick()` method.

The SimonSays application is a good review of using Views and Resources. The application makes use of some of the interesting features of Views, such as changing the size and translating the contents in order to display the "pressed button" image. The built-in sounds are also used to provide feedback to the user.

Focus Events

Another pseudo event, similar to the Ticker events, are focus events. The HME SDK has callbacks for views when focus changes.

These callbacks are most useful for views that want to change their state depending on if they have focus or not. A prime example of this would be a button that would have a highlighted state, so the user knew which button onscreen was active.

The callback for focus pseudo events is

```
handleFocus(boolean hasFocus)
```

Implementing this function in a View subclass will provide feedback to the View on whether it has focus or has lost focus.

Try It Out   Listening for Focus Events

The following example has a View subclass called buttonView, which will highlight the selected button. Try out the following code for listening for focus in an application. Focus is an important part of giving the user feedback on what item in the application he or she is interacting with.

Try adding a listener for the select button and changing the text of the button when the select key is pressed.

```
package com.wiley.hme.ch6;

import java.awt.Color;

import com.tivo.hme.interfaces.IContext;
```

```
import com.tivo.hme.sdk.Application;
import com.tivo.hme.sdk.Resource;
import com.tivo.hme.sdk.View;

public class hiliteExample extends Application {


    ButtonView bv1;
    ButtonView bv2;


    public void init(IContext context) throws Exception {
        super.init(context);
        bv1 = new ButtonView(getRoot(), 50,50, 200,50, Color.cyan,
Color.LIGHT_GRAY, "Button 1");
        bv2 = new ButtonView(getRoot(), 50,125, 200,50, Color.cyan,
Color.LIGHT_GRAY, "Button 2");
        getRoot().setResource(Color.white);

        bv1.setVisible(true);
        bv2.setVisible(true);

        setFocus(bv1);
    }

    public boolean handleKeyPress(int key, long rawcode) {

        switch(key) {

        case KEY_UP:
        case KEY_DOWN:
            if (bv1.hasFocus()) {
                setFocus(bv2);
            } else {
                setFocus(bv1);
            }
            return true;
        case KEY_LEFT:
            setActive(false);
            return true;
        }

        return super.handleKeyPress(key, rawcode);
    }

    public class ButtonView extends View {

        View textView;
        Resource text;
        Color highlight;
        Color normal;

        public ButtonView(View parent, int xCoord, int ycoord, int width, int
height, Color highlight, Color normal, String text) {
            super(parent, xCoord, ycoord, width, height);
            this.highlight = highlight;
```

```
            this.normal = normal;

            this.text = this.getApp().createText("default-20.font", Color.black,
    text);

            textView = new View(this,0,0,width,height);
            textView.setResource(this.text);
            textView.setVisible(true);
            this.setResource(this.normal);

        }

        public boolean handleFocus(boolean isFocused) {
            if (isFocused) {
                setResource(highlight);
            } else {
                setResource(normal);
            }

            return super.handleFocus(isFocused);
        }
    }
}
```

How It Works

The application basically performs two actions. In the `handleKeyPress()` method, the application listens for keys, changing the focus based on the up and down keys from one of the views to the other.

The `handleFocus()` method is called when processing the change in focus because changing focus generates events. The `handleFocus()` method changes the colors of the views in order to signal to the user the "highlighted" view.

Application Event Handling

The main application-level event that requires handling is the Idle event. The Idle event is sent by the TiVo box to the application after 15 minutes of inactivity in a TiVo HME application that has been started on the TiVo box.

The event is designed to protect the television against burn-in. Static images that are left on the screen for an extended period of time can cause burn-in on the television set, leaving a ghost image on the screen, or degrading picture quality over time.

The TiVo interface uses this same timeout mechanism for the built-in TiVo interface. A TiVo box, left at the main menu screen with no input, will eventually time out and show the live TV feed. This is exactly the same action that the TiVo box will take with HME applications.

Handling the Idle event should be done only if the application is able to mitigate the risk of screen burn-in. The authors' application, AudioFaucet, is an application that may expect to receive an idle event and may want to handle it. The application plays music from the user's home computer, so it is possible that a user may start a playlist, and not interact with the application until the playlist is done playing. In this case, the application will receive the Idle event after 15 minutes of inactivity; but the application doesn't want to quit, so it should display some sort of screensaver to prevent burn-in (see Figure 6-4).

Figure 6-4

To handle the Idle event, the application class must override the `handleIdle(boolean isIdle)` method from the Application class.

To handle the Idle event, the application must call the `acknowledgeIdle(true)` method to indicate to the HME application that it will handle the Idle event correctly.

```
public boolean handleIdle(boolean isIdle) {

    if (isIdle) {

        startScreenSaver(); // this method would do something to avoid burn in
        acknowledgeIdle(true);
        return true;
    }

    // if not idle, nothing to do
    return true;
}
```

Summary

Handling events is key to building an application that is not only responsive to user input, but manages TiVo box events such as the Idle event correctly. Processing events is the primary means of interacting with the user, and even the simplest applications must handle events properly to exit.

Using the Bananas library simplifies events surrounding focus and makes creating views simpler, but having a solid understanding of how events are processed is key to building user-friendly applications.

Questions

1. What is the difference between `sendEvent()` and the Ticker?

2. What is the purpose of `handleIdle()`?

3. In this example of the `handleKeyPress()` method, will the application ever see a key event? If so, which ones?

```
public boolean handleKeyPress(int keyCode, long rawCode) {
        switch (keyCode) {
            case KEY_FORWARD:
                return true;

            case KEY_REWIND:
                return true;

            case KEY_SELECT:
                return false;

        }
        return false;
}
```

4. There are two View subclass objects in an application. Both handle the KEY_SELECT event; how does the HME SDK determine which one will receive the event when KEY_SELECT is pressed? Could they both receive the event? Why?

Going Bananas

Until this point, you have been using the HME SDK for developing applications. There is another library that TiVo has made available called Bananas. Bananas is basically a user interface toolkit built on top of HME.

No doubt at some point in the past few chapters, you have wanted to define a TextView object that would combine the creation of the text resource object and the view for the text. Or perhaps you wanted to create a background color on a view that holds text. The SimonSays application does just that, but must create a second view in order to do so. Having to build up these widgets is a pretty time-consuming task; the Bananas widgets fill that need, and they provide for more quickly building HME applications.

Because Bananas is built on the HME SDK, the event and view knowledge from the past six chapters is very valuable. Bananas creates widget elements for use in an application, so the event and processing knowledge is still key to creating a great HME application.

Bananas builds on the HME base classes to deliver a framework for building and designing an application using widgets that preserve the look and feel of the TiVo interface, and provides standard tools for building HME interfaces such as sliding screens, buttons, and lists.

How to Include Bananas in Your Application

The Bananas library is available for download from `http://tivohme.sourceforge.net`. Inside the ZIP file that downloads is `bananas.jar`, the Java library that contains the Bananas classes. The current version of the Bananas library as of the writing of this book is version 1.3, which is the basis for the examples in this chapter.

To use the Bananas library in an application, add the `bananas.jar` file to the build path in Eclipse (Figure 7-1).

Chapter 7

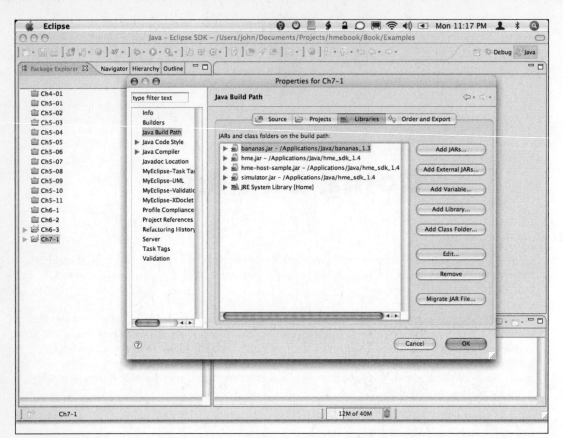

Figure 7-1

The Bananas library is in the package `com.tivo.hme.bananas`. To use the library in an application, import the Bananas library:

```
import com.tivo.hme.bananas.BApplication;
```

To use Bananas in an application, the application must extend the BApplication class. The BApplication class extends the HME Application class, and provides some of the basic services for a Bananas application.

```
import com.tivo.hme.bananas.BApplication;
import com.tivo.hme.interfaces.IContext;

public class BananasEx extends BApplication {
public void init(IContext arg0) throws Exception {
        super.init(arg0);
    }
}
```

Like the HME SDK, the Bananas libraries are open source as well. The source is available for download, and includes sample applications and documentation.

Reasons to Use Bananas

The HME APIs covered in the past few chapters provide the facility for transmitting resources to the TiVo box, arranging views in the HME application, and setting up an event processing system for communication from the TiVo to the application. Extremely flexible applications can be written with HME, but it is a lot of work to develop classes for all the widgets that TiVo users are used to.

In the last chapter, there was an application that changed the focus between two different views. Changing the focus of the screen — navigating between buttons, for example — is a manual process in the HME SDK. All the applications created so far have only one screen, unlike the TiVo interface for the rest of the TiVo box, which separates data into different screens for particular tasks.

Bananas provides all these services as well as access to all the underlying HME APIs already discussed. Bananas strengthens the application model introduced in the HME SDK by adding frameworks for screens, transitioning, management of layers in the application, skinning of the widgets, and a set of widgets to build user interfaces that mimic the TiVo interface look and feel.

Bananas Sample Application

Running the sample applications included in the Bananas library gives a good example of the capabilities that Bananas includes, and the advantage of using the Bananas libraries to design the user interface of an application.

To start the examples, open a command line and change to the directory or folder where the Bananas library is stored. The environmental variable HME_HOME should be set to the location of the HME folder, so that the script for starting the Bananas samples can locate the hme.jar.

On Mac OS X or Linux:

```
~$ cd /Applications/Java/bananas_1.3/
/Applications/Java/bananas_1.3$ export HME_HOME=/Applications/Java/hme_sdk_1.4/
/Applications/Java/bananas_1.3$ cd samples/
/Applications/Java/bananas_1.3/samples$ ./runsample.sh
HME SDK 1.4 (TiVo, Inc.)
LOG: added factory
MDNS: http://10.113.20.63:7288/bananas/
```

On Windows:

Start the Simulator application to connect to the sample application:

1. Choose your network address from the Network menu.
2. Select the Bananas application from the Application menu.

The main menu that appears in the Simulator can be navigated with the arrow keys (Figure 7-2).

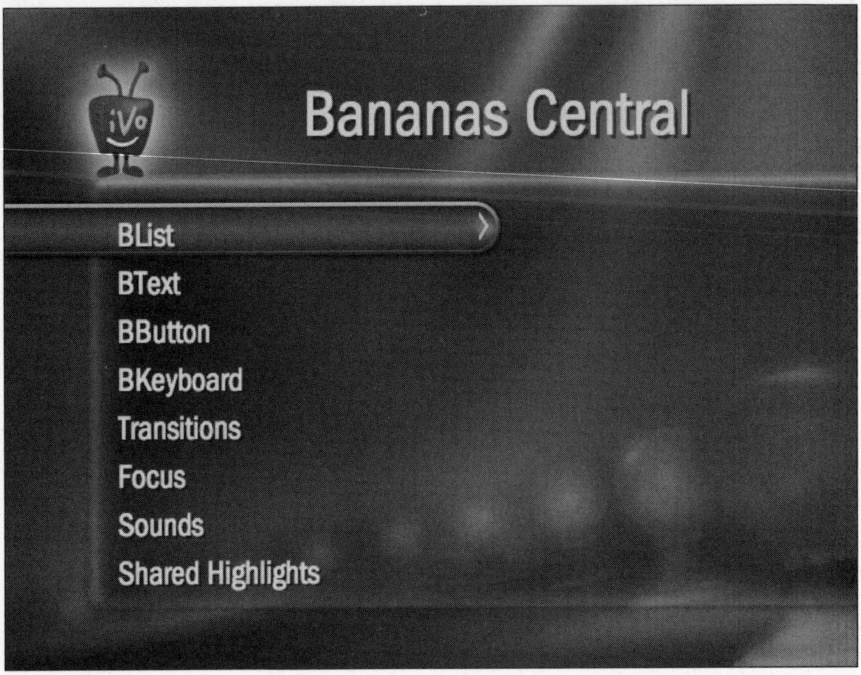

Figure 7-2

To get a list of the keys in the Simulator, and the mapping of keyboard keys to remote control, select Keyboard Shortcuts from the Help menu in the Simulator, as shown in Figure 7-3.

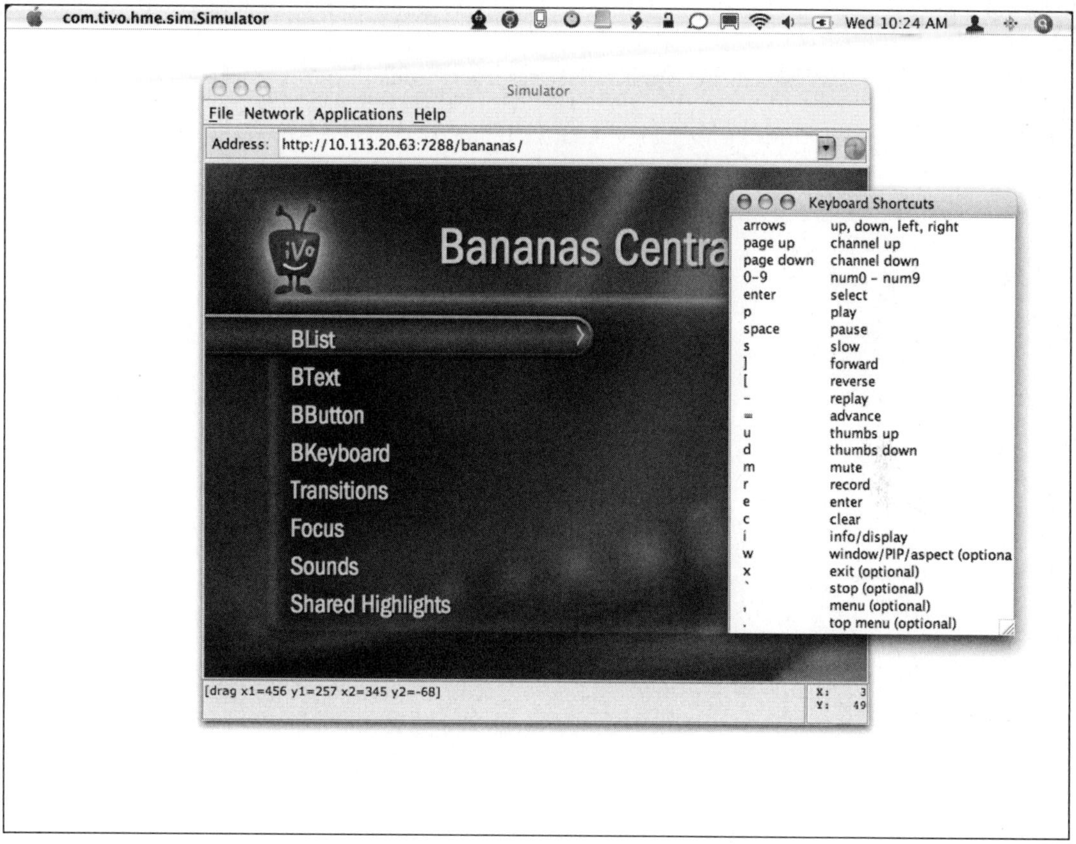

Figure 7-3

Navigating the example will provide a sense of the capabilities that Bananas affords an application that extends the Bananas classes.

BApplication

The BApplication class extends the Application class from HME.

The BApplication class adds the following methods on top of the HME Application class:

Method	Parameters	Description	Returns
getAbove		Gets the BView that contains views that appear in the above layer (that is, above all screens).	BView
getBelow		Gets the BView that contains views that appear in the below layer.	BView
getCurrentScreen		Gets the current screen.	BScreen
getNormal		Gets the BView that contains the screens.	BView
getSkin		Gets the current skin generator.	BSkin
getStackDepth		Gets the depth of the stack.	int
handleAction	BView view Object action	An action occurred.	boolean
pop		Pops back to the previous screen, no return argument.	
pop	Object arg	Pops back to the previous screen.	
push	BScreen screen int transition	Pushes a new screen onto the stack, no argument.	
push	BScreen screen int transition java.lang .Object arg	Pushes a new screen onto the stack. The BScreen parameter is the screen that is being pushed, the transition is a constant designating the type of transition, and the argument is any data for the "incoming screen." Normally args would be a String, but any object may be sent to the screen as an argument.	
setSkin	BSkin skin	Sets the skin generator.	

Some additional methods are implemented in BApplication, but they are either re-implementations of the corresponding Application class methods, or internal methods that aren't really useful for discussing how BApplication works.

Looking over the additions to Application that BApplication makes, the functionality offered is pretty clear. The BApplication class introduces a stack of screens that can be pushed and popped. Also introduced are three layers to the application: the "above" layer, which sits on top of the screens; the "below" layer, which sits below the screens; and the "normal" layer, which contains the screens themselves.

These layers are view objects (actually BView objects, but we'll get to that a little further on). Similar to the way you used getRoot() to hold other views in the HME examples earlier, the above, below, and normal views behave as containers for other views and resources.

The following example places an image in each layer of the application. If you remember from the *Understanding Views* references in Chapter 5, Views are normally stacked onscreen in the order in which they are created. In this case, the myAbove view is created before the myNormal and myBelow views. Because they are using the layers above, below, and normal created by BApplication, however, they are stacked accordingly.

```
package com.wiley.hme.ch7;

import com.tivo.hme.bananas.BApplication;
import com.tivo.hme.interfaces.IContext;
import com.tivo.hme.sdk.View;

public class LayersExample extends BApplication {

    /**
     * init is called on application startup, just like
     * in standard HME applications
     */
    public void init(IContext context) throws Exception {
        // always need to call this first.
        super.init(context);

        View myAbove  = new View(getAbove(), 50, 50, 200, 150);
        View myNormal = new View(getNormal(), 100, 100, 200, 150);
        View myBelow  = new View(getBelow(), 150, 150, 200, 150);

        myAbove.setResource(getResource("above.jpg"));
        myBelow.setResource(getResource("below.jpg"));
        myNormal.setResource(getResource("normal.jpg"));

        myAbove.setVisible(true);
        myBelow.setVisible(true);
        myNormal.setVisible(true);
    }


    /**
     * use this to cleanly exit the application
     */
    public boolean handleKeyPress(int key, long rawcode) {
        switch (key) {
        case KEY_LEFT:
            setActive(false);
            return true;
        }
        return super.handleKeyPress(key, rawcode);
    }
}
```

When running this application from Eclipse, don't forget to add the External jars for `hme.jar` and `hme-host-sample.jar`, as you have in previous examples, but also `bananas.jar`, as shown in Figure 7-1. You'll also need to add three image files: `above.jpg`, `below.jpg`, and `normal.jpg`, which can be found on the supplementary web site for this book.

Calling `super.init(context)` should always be the first step of any BApplication. The BApplication's `init()` method is the method that creates the layers.

If the `super.init(context)` method is moved to the end of the `init()` method as follows:

```
public void init(IContext context) throws Exception {
    // always need to call this first.

    View myAbove  = new View(this.getAbove(), 50, 50, 200, 150);
    View myNormal = new View(this.getNormal(), 100, 100, 200, 150);
    View myBelow  = new View(this.getBelow(), 150, 150, 200, 150);

    myAbove.setResource(getResource("above.jpg"));
    myBelow.setResource(getResource("below.jpg"));
    myNormal.setResource(getResource("normal.jpg"));

    myAbove.setVisible(true);
    myBelow.setVisible(true);
    myNormal.setVisible(true);

    // this will cause a problem!
    super.init(context);
}
```

The application will report an error like this:

```
LOG: added factory
MDNS: http://192.168.1.5:7288/ch7/
RUNNING: http://192.168.1.5:7288/ch7/
LOG: HME receiver disconnected
LOG: Unexpected error: java.lang.NullPointerException

CLOSING: SimApp[#1,http://192.168.1.5:7288/ch7/]
ERROR: Connection lost : java.net.SocketException: Connection reset [4]
```

This is because the LayersExample uses the above, below, and normal views before they are created by calling `BApplication.init()`.

Other Features of BApplication

The next section on BScreens discusses how the `push()` and `pop()` methods function. There are some additional capabilities that BApplication provides, which are convenient and worth mentioning.

One of these features is the default handling of sounds. The BApplication will handle playing default sounds for any key that is not handled by a screen. This feature can be a little confusing because the definition of "handled" is different from the definition previously used in HME applications. The BApplication will play a sound unless

❏ The screen itself plays a sound when responding to the key event (it must play the sound via BApplication's `play()` method)

The BApplication will play the key sound associated with "success" (it is the "thumbs up" noise from the TiVo DVR UI) on the TiVo if

❏ The active screen changes

❏ The object that has focus in the current screen changes

If BApplication does not detect one of these events, it will play the "bonk" (error) sound.

This can be confusing because previously key events were considered handled if they returned true. This is still the case in terms of taking additional action based on the key press event, but now for an event that was handled by a screen, the bonk (error) noise may still be played if the screen doesn't play a noise itself.

The other main feature that BApplication provides is skins. This is discussed further in the "BSkins" section, but the application is in charge of setting a look and feel for the application. The skin is usually a ZIP file containing graphics to replace the buttons, lists, and other elements in the Bananas toolkit with custom images.

BScreen

BScreen is the next major concept introduced by the Bananas toolkit. BScreens form the basis of the organization of the application. Most user interaction in an onscreen display will take place inside screens. Screens can be thought of as a deck of cards, only one of which can be displayed at a time.

All screens take up the entire viewable area in the application. Only one screen is considered active at a time, so while there is a screen stack that is managed in the BApplication, the stack can be thought of more like a web browser's history than transparent overlays. The browser knows what the previous web page visited was, and knows how to get back to that page. Similarly, the screen stack knows about previous screens that were displayed, and can go back to them by taking the current screen off the top of the stack by popping it.

BScreen's inheritance model is shown in Figure 7-4.

The inheritance diagram shows that a BScreen, used in the Bananas toolkit as something to hold a whole screen's worth of information, is derived from the HME View class. All the methods available in the View class are also available in BScreen. Creating resources using `createImage()` and `createText()` are all still usable in the BScreen class. Because the BScreen is a subclass of View, it can also receive events. The event model for Bananas is slightly different than normal HME applications. Events in Bananas are discussed in the next chapter.

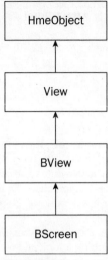

Figure 7-4

New Methods in BScreen

Method	Parameters	Description	Returns
getAbove		Gets the above layer in the screen above.	BView
getBelow		Gets the below layer in the screen above.	BView
getFocus		Retrieves the BView that currently has focus.	BView
getFocusDefault		Gets the default focus.	BView
getNormal		Gets the normal layer in this screen.	BView
handleAction	BView view Object action	Called when an action is to be processed by this screen.	boolean
handleEnter	Object arg boolean isReturn	Called when this screen is shown. isReturn indicates if the screen is being pushed or popped-to.	boolean
handleEvent	HmeEvent event	Called when an event should be processed by this screen.	boolean
handleExit		Called when this screen is exited.	boolean
handleFocus	boolean isGained BView gained BView lost	Called when focus is changed in the screen.	boolean

Method	Parameters	Description	Returns
setFocus	BView focus	Sets the focus to a new view.	void
setFocusDefault	BView focus Default	Sets which BView will get focus by default when entering the screen.	void

Pushing and Popping BScreens

The screen stack is automatically managed by the BApplication class via the BApplication's push() and pop() methods. Although the BScreen is what is displayed, the BApplication instance coordinates which BScreen should be displayed.

The following example pushes new screens when the "select" button (return/enter in the Simulator) is pressed. Hitting the left key will "pop" the current screen. When the first screen is reached, the "left" key will quit the application.

```java
package com.wiley.hme.ch7;

import java.awt.Color;

import com.tivo.hme.bananas.BApplication;
import com.tivo.hme.bananas.BScreen;
import com.tivo.hme.bananas.BText;
import com.tivo.hme.interfaces.IContext;
import com.tivo.hme.sdk.View;

public class LayersExample extends BApplication {

    /**
     * init is called on application startup, just like
     * in standard HME applications
     */
    public void init(IContext context) throws Exception {
        super.init(context);
        getRoot().setResource(Color.white);
        BScreen myScreen = new MessageScreen(this, "Screen", 1);

        push(myScreen, TRANSITION_FADE);
    }

    /**
     * use this to cleanly exit the application
     */
    public boolean handleKeyPress(int key, long rawcode) {
        switch (key) {
        case KEY_LEFT:
            setActive(false);
            return true;
        }
        return super.handleKeyPress(key, rawcode);
```

```
        }


        public class MessageScreen extends BScreen {

            private BText text;
            int counter = 0;
            String message;
            BApplication app;

            public MessageScreen(BApplication app, String message, int counter) {
                super(app);
                this.counter = counter;
                this.app = app;
                this.message = message;

                text = new BText(this, 270, 140, 150, 200);
                text.setColor(Color.blue);
                text.setValue(message + ": " + counter);
                text.setFont("default-30.font");
                text.setVisible(true);
            }


            public boolean handleKeyPress(int key, long rawcode) {
                switch (key) {
                case KEY_LEFT:
                    if (app.getStackDepth() == 1)
                        app.setActive(false);
                    pop(this);
                    return true;

                case KEY_SELECT:
                    app.push(new MessageScreen(app, message, 1+counter),
TRANSITION_LEFT);
                    return true;
                }
                return super.handleKeyPress(key, rawcode);
            }
        }
    }
```

In the example, the BScreen that is displayed is a subclass of BScreen. Like views, subclassing BScreen is the most common approach to creating a functional screen. Like with Views, methods like handleKeyPress are key to creating screens that respond to user input, and subclassing BScreen is the only way to provide customized instructions for key processing.

In the preceding example, the MessageScreen constructor creates the contents of the screen, which is typical for a subclass of BScreen. In handleKeyPress, you push a new MessageScreen instance with a new message when the select key is pressed. When the left key is pressed, the current screen is popped. The code for popping the screen also checks to see if the current screen is the last screen on the stack, and if it is, quits the application. The reason this is needed is because once a screen has been pushed, the stack cannot be emptied of screens again. The first screen pushed cannot be popped, so the first pushed screen (or some other screen) must handle exiting the application cleanly.

Transitions

In the preceding example, transitions from one screen to another are used when each screen is pushed. The first screen is pushed using a fade transition (the text Screen 1 fades onscreen). The rest of the screens are transitioned using the slide left transition.

The transitions that are provided are

- ❑ TRANSITION_NONE
- ❑ TRANSITION_FADE
- ❑ TRANSITION_LEFT

The TRANSITION_NONE transition is used to make the newly pushed screen just appear. An example of using TRANSITION_NONE in the preceding example would be

```
BScreen myScreen = new MessageScreen(this, "Screen", 1);
push(myScreen, TRANSITION_NONE);
```

This would push the first screen using no transition. In this case, the text Screen 1 would no longer fade on to the screen, it would just appear.

The TRANSITION_FADE is the transition that is used in the pushing/popping example code. The fade transition can be used as follows:

```
BScreen myScreen = new MessageScreen(this, "Screen", 1);
push(myScreen, TRANSITION_FADE);
```

Running the example should give you a good feel for what a transition fade looks like. The speed of the fade is controlled by the BApplication class, and is set to one second. This time period is *not* adjustable.

The TRANSITION_LEFT transition is the one used for the rest of the example application:

```
app.push(new MessageScreen(app, message, 1+counter), TRANSITION_LEFT);
```

Running the example should give you a good feel for how this transition looks as well. The speed of this transition is also controlled by the BApplication, and is not adjustable. The TRANSITION_LEFT transition takes 0.4 seconds.

If you have played with the screen push/pop example, you will notice that the screens not only transition when pushing a new screen, but when popping back to a previous screen as well. This happens even though the pop() method does not take a transition. This happens because when a screen is pushed onto the stack, the transition that is used for the push is also saved. The pop, therefore, simply reverses the transition.

The transitions are implemented by the BApplication class, which uses the normal view layer in the application to perform the transitions.

Creating Custom Transitions

Although the transitions built into the application are sufficient for most uses, it would be nice to add additional transitions. Unfortunately, because of the way the BApplication class is built, adding transitions is a little difficult. You could certainly re-compile the `bananas.jar` library with changes to the BApplication class to make it easier to add custom transitions, but mostly the same functionality can be accomplished by overriding certain methods in the base BApplication class.

The challenges in creating new transitions are

❑   push must be re-implemented with the new transitions

❑   pop must be re-implemented with the new transitions

❑   The BScreen stack must be managed in your class now:

❑   `push()` and `pop()` need to be able to modify the stack.

❑   The stack variable is private to BApplication, so you cannot access it.

❑   Because you are managing a new stack, you must also

❑   Override `getCurrentScreen()` because you have a new BScreen stack implementation

❑   Override `getStackDepth()` because of the new stack implementation

First, create a flag for the new transition:

```
public static final int TRANSITION_WIPE = 22;
```

Then you need to create the BScreen stack in your application:

```
public Vector myStack;

public void init(IContext arg0) throws Exception {
    super.init(arg0);
    myStack = new Vector();
    .
    .
    .
}
```

You use a Vector for the stack, though you could have just as easily used something else to implement the stack.

The two methods `getCurrentScreen()` and `getStackDepth()` must be implemented:

```
public BScreen getCurrentScreen() {
    if (getStackDepth() > 0)
        return (BScreen) ((StackFrame)myStack.lastElement()).screen;
    else
        return null;
```

```
    }

    public int getStackDepth() {
        return myStack.size();
    }
```

If you examine the BApplication source code, you will see that the stack actually stores a bit more information than just the BScreens in the order they were put onscreen. The transition is stored along with the screen.

The BApplication uses an object called StackFrame to store information on the stack. The implementation in BApplication works well, but subclasses do not have access to it, so in adding the custom transition, this can be copied to the BApplication subclass.

Though all this re-implementation sounds complicated, it is relatively straightforward, only requiring a few methods to be re-implemented. The following is a fully implemented BApplication class with a custom transition for a left to right wipe. The pop implementation for the reversal of the transition has also been implemented.

```
package com.wiley.hme.ch7;

import java.util.Vector;

import com.tivo.hme.bananas.BApplication;
import com.tivo.hme.bananas.BEvent;
import com.tivo.hme.bananas.BScreen;
import com.tivo.hme.bananas.BView;
import com.tivo.hme.interfaces.IContext;

public class CustomTransitions extends BApplication {

    public static final int TRANSITION_WIPE = 22;
    public Vector myStack;

    public void init(IContext arg0) throws Exception {
        super.init(arg0);
        myStack = new Vector();

        push(new ImageScreen(this, 1), TRANSITION_FADE);
    }

    public void pop(Object arg) {
        if (getStackDepth() <= 1) {
            return;
        }

        getRoot().setPainting(false);
        try {
// exit old screen

            StackFrame top = (StackFrame)myStack.lastElement();
            top.doExit();
```

```
            myStack.removeElementAt(myStack.size() - 1);

// enter new screen

            StackFrame previous = (StackFrame)myStack.lastElement();
            previous.doEnter(arg, true);

// perform the REVERSE transition

            switch (top.transition) {
            case TRANSITION_WIPE:
                previous.screen.setLocation(getNormal().getWidth(),
getNormal().getTranslationY());
                previous.screen.setSize(0, getNormal().getHeight());
                previous.screen.setTranslation(-getNormal().getWidth(),
getNormal().getTranslationY());

                previous.screen.setTranslation(0, 0, getResource(FADE_ANIM));
                previous.screen.setLocation(0, 0, getResource(FADE_ANIM));
                previous.screen.setSize(getNormal().getWidth(),
getNormal().getHeight(), getResource(FADE_ANIM));

                top.screen.setSize(0, getNormal().getHeight(),
getResource(FADE_ANIM));

                break;

            case TRANSITION_NONE:
                // the rest of this code is in the accompanying example
                break;

            case TRANSITION_FADE:
                // the rest of this code is in the accompanying example
                break;

            case TRANSITION_LEFT:
                                // the rest of this code is in the accompanying
example

                break;
            }
            //  By playing the sound below, BApplication will also be stopped from
            //  playing the error sound.
            //  screenChanged = true;
            play("pagedown.snd");
        } finally {
            getRoot().setPainting(true);
        }
    }

    public BScreen getCurrentScreen() {
        if (getStackDepth() > 0)
            return (BScreen) ((StackFrame)myStack.lastElement()).screen;
        else
            return null;
```

```
        }

    public int getStackDepth() {
        return myStack.size();
    }

    public void push(BScreen screen, int transition, Object arg) {

        getRoot().setPainting(false);
        try {
            //
            // exit old screen
            //

            StackFrame previous = null;
            if (myStack.size() > 0) {
                previous = (StackFrame)myStack.lastElement();
                previous.doExit();
            }

            //
            // enter new screen
            //

            StackFrame next = new StackFrame(screen, transition);
            myStack.addElement(next);
            next.doEnter(arg, false);

            //
            // perform the transition. for the new screen, always adjust:
            //    location
            //    transparency

            switch (transition) {
            case TRANSITION_WIPE:
                screen.setLocation(-getNormal().getTranslationX(),
getNormal().getTranslationY());
                screen.setSize(0, getNormal().getHeight());

                previous.screen.setTranslation(-getNormal().getWidth(), 0,
getResource(FADE_ANIM));
                previous.screen.setLocation(getNormal().getWidth(), 0,
getResource(FADE_ANIM));
                previous.screen.setSize(0, getNormal().getHeight(),
getResource(FADE_ANIM));

                screen.setSize(getNormal().getWidth(), getNormal().getHeight(),
getResource(FADE_ANIM));
                screen.setTransparency(0);
                break;
            case TRANSITION_NONE:
                // the rest of this code is in the accompanying example
                break;

            case TRANSITION_FADE:
                // the rest of this code is in the accompanying example
```

```
              break;

          case TRANSITION_LEFT:
             // the rest of this code is in the accompanying example
             break;
          }
          screen.setVisible(true);

             //  By playing the sound below, BApplication will also be stopped from
             //  playing the error sound.
             // screenChanged = true;

             play("pageup.snd");
          } finally {
             getRoot().setPainting(true);
          }
      }
   // The remainder of the source code accompanies the text.
   .
   .
   .
```

This application re-implements pop(), push(), and all the methods that interact with the StackFrame from BApplication. This *must* be done because the StackFrame is not accessible to subclasses of BApplication, so the StackFrame must be completely replaced by a local version.

The TRANSITION_WIPE, the new transition effect, must be added to the push() and pop() methods to draw the new transition.

The interdependence between BScreens and the BApplication class, which manages the BScreens, requires careful consideration when designing an application. Both BApplication and BScreen must be extended to create a functional Bananas application. Note that the full code can be found on the book's web site at www.wrox.com.

BView

BViews are the Bananas equivalent of HME View objects. In fact, they extend the HME View class from the HME SDK. The BView class fulfills the same role in Bananas as the View class in the HME SDK, allowing for placement of resources on the screen.

In addition to the normal functionality of the View class, BView also hooks into the advanced features of Bananas:

❑   For allowing a view to be used by the focus manager

❑   For allowing for the use of highlights (different state when the view has focus)

❑   As the basis for the other Bananas widgets

Try It Out

The following example is the same example as from Chapter 5, converted to using BApplication and BView (see Figure 7-5):

```java
package com.wiley.hme.ch7;


import com.tivo.hme.bananas.BApplication;
import com.tivo.hme.bananas.BView;
import com.tivo.hme.interfaces.IContext;
import com.tivo.hme.sdk.Application;
import com.tivo.hme.sdk.IHmeProtocol;
import com.tivo.hme.sdk.ImageResource;
import com.tivo.hme.sdk.View;

public class Images extends BApplication {

    public void init(IContext context) throws Exception {
        super.init(context);
        ImageResource picture = createImage("dog.jpg");

        BView picView  = new BView(getNormal(),  100,  100,  100,  100, true);
        BView picView2 = new BView(getNormal(),  210,  100,  100,  100, true);
        BView picView3 = new BView(getNormal(),  100,  210,  100,  100, true);
        BView picView4 = new BView(getNormal(),  210,  210,  100,  100, true);

        picView.setResource(picture, RSRC_IMAGE_BESTFIT);
        picView2.setResource(picture, RSRC_IMAGE_BESTFIT);
        picView3.setResource(picture, RSRC_IMAGE_BESTFIT);
        picView4.setResource(picture, RSRC_IMAGE_BESTFIT);

        picView.setResource(picture);
        picView2.setResource(picture);
        picView3.setResource(picture);
        picView4.setResource(picture);

    }


    public boolean handleKeyPress(int arg0, long arg1) {
        switch (arg0) {
        case IHmeProtocol.KEY_LEFT:
            this.setActive(false);
            return true;
        }
        return super.handleKeyPress(arg0, arg1);
    }


}
```

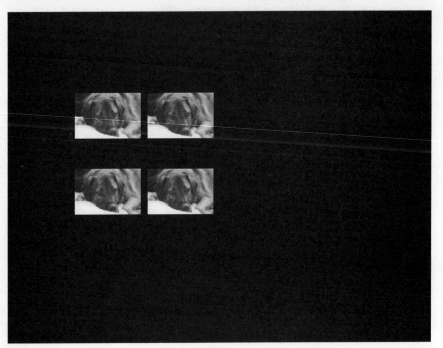

Figure 7-5

How It Works

BView is used in this example the same way that View was used in Chapter 5. In Bananas, BView is mainly used to contain images and as the base class for the other widgets. Because BView extends the View class, the same methods such as setResource(), covered in Chapter 5, still apply.

BList

BList is the first of the widgets in the Bananas toolkit. This widget helps build lists that have the look and feel of lists in the TiVo standard interface. BLists manage much of the events and processing that would be required to create a list, and so implementing a list is made far easier because of this class.

The following examples both use BList to create the lists that are displayed. Figure 7-6 is from the Bananas sample applications.

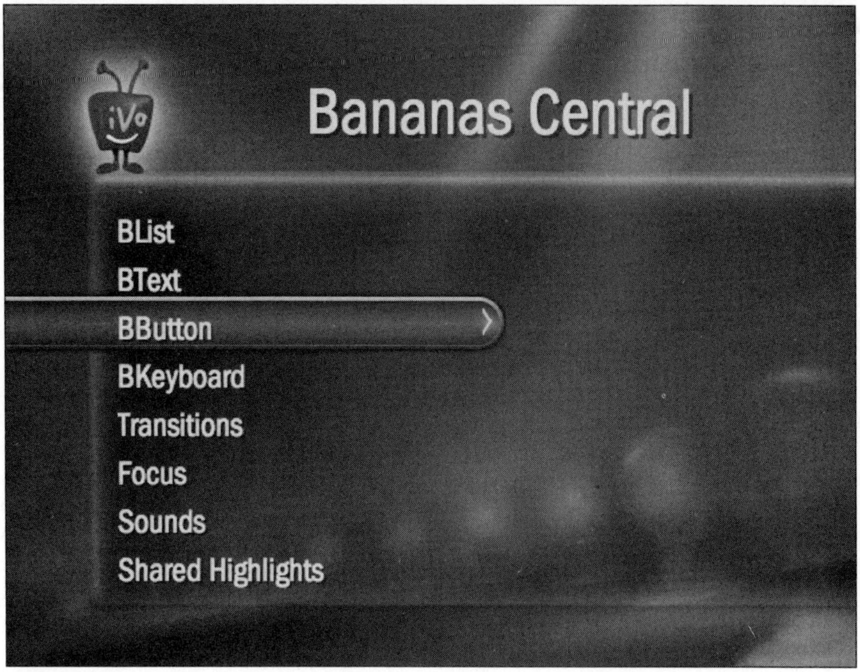

Figure 7-6

Figure 7-7 is from the AudioFaucet application (written by the authors).

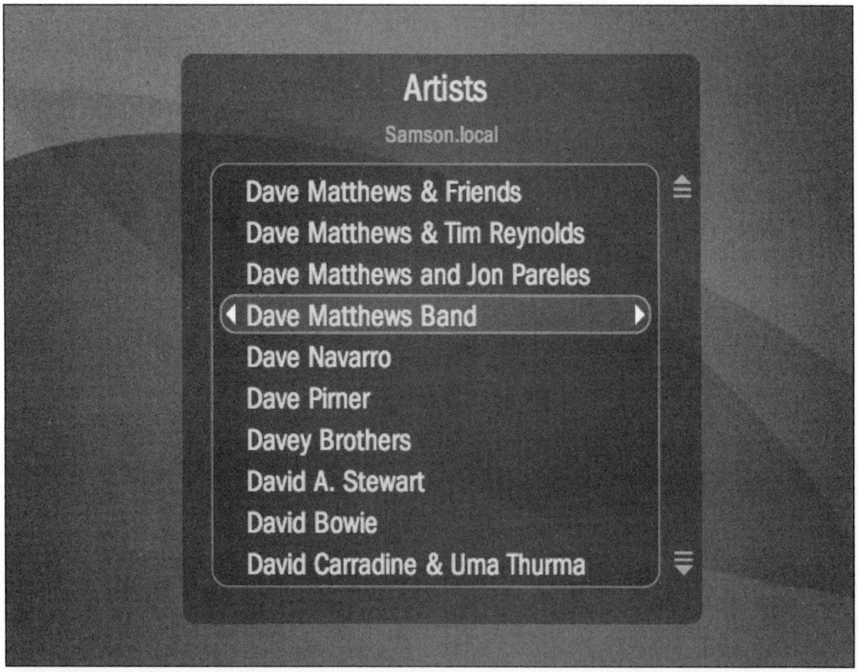

Figure 7-7

Using BLists

BLists are used very differently than the other widgets in the Bananas toolkit. The other widgets, which are discussed in the upcoming sections, can be created and used in BScreens. BList, however, is an abstract class. Abstract classes cannot be instantiated directly; the abstract designation means that the class has one or more methods that are declared, but not implemented.

When instantiating a class that implements BList, you provide as parameters the containing (parent) BView, the bounding box for the List (x/y/w/h), and a "row height." It is helpful to make the height of the bounding box a multiple of the row height. For example, if the row height is 35, making the height of the BList 350 will allow 10 rows to be displayed on the screen at the same time. If you add more rows than can visibly fit, the BList will automatically take care of adding them and scrolling the list properly when the user presses the appropriate key on the remote. BList contains one abstract method:

```
protected abstract void createRow(BView parent, int index);
```

In order to use BLists, this method must be overridden in a subclass, and the subclass may then be used in a BScreen. `createRow()` is called for each index that must be added to the list. The list of objects to be represented in the list is stored by BList as a java.util.Vector because, at least in Java 1.4, Vector does not possess information as to what type of object is stored in the Vector, forcing the user to re-implement BList to extract the proper type from the Vector and add a row to the list.

This is nice, though, because it allows your BLists to contain anything you want—simple text items, or more complex, custom objects you define yourself. Your BList row could contain an object with a number of fields (stock information, for example, with price, change, and high and low values).

To activate the selection pointer in the list, the screen that contains the list must give the list focus using the `setFocusDefault()` method. BLists automatically handle the KEY_UP, KEY_DOWN, KEY_CHANNELUP, and KEY_CHANNELDOWN keys to move around the list.

Styling the List

BLists automatically generate the highlight bar when focus is set on one of the rows. The highlights on the rows are styled using the `setBarAndArrows()` method in BList.

The selection bar can have rounded edges on one or both sides of the bar. Normally setting the bar drawing options would be done in the BList subclass constructor. The options that can be set for rounding or hanging (extending the bar all the way to the edge of the screen) have constants that can be used. The constants (from IBananas) are BAR_HANG and BAR_DEFAULT.

BLists Must Be Used in a BScreen

Some of the examples early in this chapter used BViews directly in a BApplication. Trying to use a BList (a class derived from BList, that is) directly in the BApplication, and attaching it to the normal layer, causes a NullPointerException.

This is because the BList code has an internal class that implements the IHightlightsLayout interface, which requires a BScreen.

The `setBarAndArrows()` call parameters are as follows:

Parameter	Type	Description
Left bar hang	Int	Whether the left side of the bar should hang offscreen (BAR_HANG) or be rounded (BAR_DEFAULT)
Right bar hang	Int	Whether the right side of the bar should hang offscreen or be rounded
Action for KEY_LEFT	Object	The action to send (actions are like Bananas events) when KEY_LEFT is received
Action for KEY_RIGHT	Object	The action to send when KEY_RIGHT is received

Managing the List

BList contains several add and remove methods for adding items to the list and for removing them. The add methods can add the following:

❑ A single element

❑ An array of elements

❑ A Vector of elements

There are two versions of each method, one for adding the elements to the end of the list, and one for adding them at a specific point in the list.

There are two `remove()` methods in BList. One removes an item based on the index in the list, and one takes an Object and removes that object from the list, if it is in the list.

BList Example

The following example is the minimum code needed to create a list and display it on a screen:

```
package com.wiley.hme.ch7;

import java.awt.Color;

import com.tivo.hme.bananas.BApplication;
import com.tivo.hme.bananas.BList;
import com.tivo.hme.bananas.BScreen;
import com.tivo.hme.bananas.BText;
import com.tivo.hme.bananas.BView;
import com.tivo.hme.interfaces.IContext;

public class BListExample1 extends BApplication {

    String listItems[] = {"one", "two", "three", "four" };

    public void init(IContext context) throws Exception {
```

```
        super.init(context);
        getRoot().setResource(Color.white);
        push(new simpleScreen(this), TRANSITION_LEFT);
    }

    public boolean handleKeyPress(int arg0, long arg1) {
        // TODO Auto-generated method stub
        return super.handleKeyPress(arg0, arg1);
    }


    public class SimpleBList extends BList {

        public SimpleBList(BView arg0, int arg1, int arg2, int arg3, int arg4, int
arg5) {
            super(arg0, arg1, arg2, arg3, arg4, arg5);
            this.setBarAndArrows(BAR_DEFAULT, BAR_HANG, "left", "right");
        }

        protected void createRow(BView parentView, int index) {
            if (get(index) != null) {
                BText text = new BText(parentView, 0 , 0 , parentView.getWidth(),
parentView.getHeight());
                text.setValue(get(index).toString());
            }
        }

    }

    public class simpleScreen extends BScreen {

        public simpleScreen(BApplication app) {
            super(app);
            BList list = new SimpleBList(getNormal(), 100, 100, 400, 300, 30);
            list.add(listItems);
            list.setVisible(true);
            setFocusDefault(list);
        }

    }

}
```

This example has two inner classes: one extending BScreen, because BLists must live inside a BScreen, and one extending BList to implement createRow() and draw the row (see Figure 7-8).

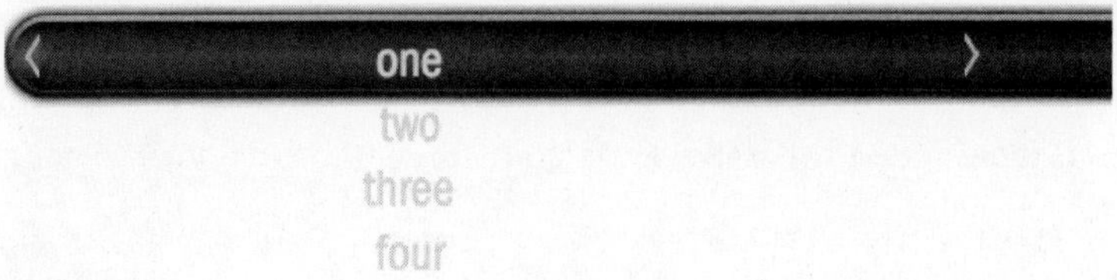

Figure 7-8

The following example uses images as the contents of rows to illustrate how to use and store other data in a list, and how createRow() would change to accommodate that data:

```java
package com.wiley.hme.ch7;

import java.awt.Color;

import com.tivo.hme.bananas.BApplication;
import com.tivo.hme.bananas.BList;
import com.tivo.hme.bananas.BScreen;
import com.tivo.hme.bananas.BView;
import com.tivo.hme.interfaces.IContext;
import com.tivo.hme.sdk.ImageResource;
import com.tivo.hme.sdk.Resource;

public class BListExample2 extends BApplication {

    public void init(IContext context) throws Exception {
        super.init(context);
        getRoot().setResource(Color.white);

        push(new simpleScreen(this), TRANSITION_LEFT);

    }

    public boolean handleAction(BView view, Object action) {
        if (action.toString().equals("pop")) {
            setActive(false);
            return true;
        }
        return super.handleAction(view, action);
    }



    public boolean handleKeyPress(int arg0, long arg1) {
        // TODO Auto-generated method stub
        return super.handleKeyPress(arg0, arg1);
    }


    public class SimpleBList extends BList {

        public SimpleBList(BView arg0, int arg1, int arg2, int arg3, int arg4, int
arg5) {
            super(arg0, arg1, arg2, arg3, arg4, arg5);
            this.setBarAndArrows(BAR_DEFAULT, BAR_DEFAULT, "left", "right");
        }

        protected void createRow(BView parentView, int index) {
            if (get(index) != null) {
                //BText text = new BText(parentView, 0 , 0 , parentView.getWidth(),
parentView.getHeight());
                //text.setValue(get(index).toString());
```

```
                BView image = new BView(parentView, 0, 0, parentView.getWidth(),
        parentView.getHeight());
                image.setResource( (Resource) get(index));
            }
        }

    }

    public class simpleScreen extends BScreen {
        ImageResource listItems[];

        public simpleScreen(BApplication app) {
            super(app);

            listItems = new ImageResource[5];

            listItems[0] = createImage("1.jpg");
            listItems[1] = createImage("2.jpg");
            listItems[2] = createImage("3.jpg");
            listItems[3] = createImage("4.jpg");
            listItems[4] = createImage("5.jpg");

            BList list = new SimpleBList(getNormal(), 100, 100, 120, 300, 100);
            list.add(listItems);
            list.setVisible(true);
            setFocusDefault(list);
        }

    }

}
```

BList Methods

BList contains several methods for retrieving information from the list, and for interacting with the list. Some of the important methods are listed in the following table. Notice that there are two add() methods; if you have a lot of items to add, you should first add them to an array, then add the whole array at once, rather than one by one, for performance reasons.

Returns	Method	Parameters	Description
void	add	int index Object element	Adds an item to the list at the given index.
void	add	int index Object[] a	Adds an array of items at the given index. The whole array is added at the index specified.
void	add	int index Vector v	Adds a Vector of items at the given index. The whole array is added at the index specified.
void	add	Object o	Adds this object to the end of the list.
void	add	Object[] a	Adds the array of Objects to the end of the list.

Returns	Method	Parameters	Description
void	add	Vector v	Adds the Vector to the end of the list.
void	clear		Removes all items from the list.
boolean	contains	Object o	Returns true if the list contains the object passed in.
java.lang.Object	get	int index	Gets the item at the provided index.
int	getFocus		Gets the index of the currently selected row.
int	getNVisible Rows		Given the size of the BList onscreen, gets how many rows are visible.
BView	getRow	int index	Gets the BView containing the row at the provided index.
int	getRow Height		Gets the row height.
int	getTop		Gets the index of the row that is currently at the top of the screen.
boolean	handle Focus	boolean isGained BView gained BView lost	Handles focus movement.
int	indexOf	Object o	Finds an object in the list.
int	lastIndexOf	Object o	Finds an object in the list, starting at the end.
void	refresh		If necessary, scrolls the list to show the currently focused row and creates new row views to wrap the elements that are currently visible.
java.lang.Object	remove	int index	Removes an element.
boolean	remove	Object o	Removes an object from the list. Returns true if the object was found and removed.
java.lang.Object	set	int index Object element	Sets an object in the list.
void	setBarAnd Arrows	int bar_left int bar_right Object action_left Object action_right	Sets up the hanging bars and the actions to send on the left and right keys. Actions are discussed in the next chapter.

Table continued on following page

143

Returns	Method	Parameters	Description
void	setFocus	int index boolean animate	Sets the focus to a particular row.
int	size		Returns the number of elements in the list.

Focus

Focus can be used in a list to change the display of other information onscreen — for instance, having a pane on the right side of the screen with more information about the selected item. Like the examples in Chapter 6, notification that focus has changed is sent via the handleFocus() callback method.

Implementing handleFocus() in a BList subclass, therefore, is a good way to display different information onscreen depending on which item in the list is selected. The handleFocus() method indicates that the focus has changed, but does not give an index into the list. A BList subclass can obtain this information by calling getFocus() to get the index and get(index) to retrieve the object at that index.

Try It Out   **handleFocus()**

The following example displays the image that is named by the current item in the list:

```
package com.wiley.hme.ch7;

import java.awt.Color;

import com.tivo.hme.bananas.BApplication;
import com.tivo.hme.bananas.BList;
import com.tivo.hme.bananas.BScreen;
import com.tivo.hme.bananas.BText;
import com.tivo.hme.bananas.BView;
import com.tivo.hme.interfaces.IContext;
import com.tivo.hme.sdk.ImageResource;
import com.tivo.hme.sdk.Resource;

public class BListExample3 extends BApplication {

    BView imageView;

    public void init(IContext context) throws Exception {
        super.init(context);
        getRoot().setResource("0x001166");
        push(new simpleScreen(this), TRANSITION_LEFT);

    }

    public boolean handleAction(BView view, Object action) {
        if (action.toString().equals("pop")) {
            setActive(false);
            return true;
        }
```

```
            return super.handleAction(view, action);
    }


    public class SimpleBList extends BList {

        public SimpleBList(BView arg0, int arg1, int arg2, int arg3, int arg4, int
arg5) {
            super(arg0, arg1, arg2, arg3, arg4, arg5);
            this.setBarAndArrows(BAR_DEFAULT, BAR_DEFAULT, "pop", "push");
        }

        protected void createRow(BView parentView, int index) {
            if (get(index) != null) {
                BText text = new BText(parentView, 0 , 0 , parentView.getWidth(),
parentView.getHeight());
                text.setValue(get(index).toString());
                text.setColor(Color.white);
                text.setFont("default-20.font");
            }
        }

        public boolean handleFocus(boolean isGained, BView gained, BView lost) {
            if (isGained) {
                String name = get(getFocus()).toString();
                imageView.setResource(getResource(name), RSRC_IMAGE_BESTFIT);
            }

            return super.handleFocus(isGained, gained, lost);
        }

    }

    public class simpleScreen extends BScreen {
        ImageResource listItems[];

        public simpleScreen(BApplication app) {
            super(app);

            imageView = new BView(getBelow(),250,100, 200,200);

            String listItems[] = {
                    "1.jpg",
                    "2.jpg",
                    "3.jpg",
                    "4.jpg",
                    "5.jpg"
            };

            BList list = new SimpleBList(getNormal(), 100, 100, 120, 300, 36);
            list.add(listItems);
            list.setVisible(true);
            setFocusDefault(list);
        }
    }
}
```

How It Works

The SimpleList class in the example has a `handleFocus()` method. This is the event handler for focus events. Because the handler is in the SimpleList class, it will be notified when the focus in the SimpleList class changes. In the case of this application, that occurs when the user moves to another item in the list. The image is then changed to reflect the new selection.

This technique is widely used in HME applications that TiVo makes available, and is an extremely useful method of displaying greater amounts of information in a single screen.

BText

The BText widget is a widget for displaying text. In Chapter 5, when covering how to create and use text resources, you saw that for every text resource being displayed, a View must be created, the text resource must be created, and then the resource must be assigned to the view. The process was always the same, and encapsulating the view and resource creation inside a single object seemed like an obvious choice.

BText does this encapsulation, and also provides text shadows and easier-to-use setter methods for configuring the text to be displayed. The following example sets up a BText with a shadow (see Figure 7-9):

```
package com.wiley.hme.ch7;

import java.awt.Color;

import com.tivo.hme.bananas.BApplication;
import com.tivo.hme.bananas.BScreen;
import com.tivo.hme.bananas.BText;
import com.tivo.hme.interfaces.IContext;

public class BTextExample extends BApplication {

    public void init(IContext context) throws Exception {
        super.init(context);
        getRoot().setResource("0x001166");
        push(new TextScreen(this), TRANSITION_FADE);
    }


    public class TextScreen extends BScreen {
        public TextScreen(BApplication app) {
            super(app);
            BText testText = new BText(this, 100,100,400,200);

            //set the font
            testText.setFont("default-50.font");
            testText.setValue("Example Text");
            testText.setColor(Color.white);
            testText.setShadow("0x888888", 2);
            testText.setVisible(true);
        }
    }
}
```

Figure 7-9

BButton

The BButton class is designed for creating a button object. Buttons participate in the focus manager that Bananas provides, so moving between buttons is mostly automatic.

Using BButtons

BButtons are created like most other BViews, with a parent view and the dimensions of the button:

```
BButton myButton = new BButton(this, 100, 100, 200, 50);
```

BButton objects possess an internal view that stores the label for the BButton. The view is accessed using `setResource()` the same way as in Chapter 5 when assigning resources to views. Because the BButton object is a descendant of BView, BButton can also be used as a parent view for other widgets. In particular, BText can use a BButton as a parent view in order to provide shadows and other text styling in the button.

After creating the button and assigning a label to the button, calling `setBarAndArrows()` is required to allow the buttons to have some sort of behavior. There are several variants of `setBarAndArrows()`. The one used in the next example sets up the following:

❑   Button hanging style

❑   Actions for the up/down/left/right key presses while the button is active

❑   The placement for the "hint" arrows

The button hanging style is set the same way as the BList hanging style: BAR_DEFAULT for a rounded end and BAR_HANG for a button that hangs all the way offscreen.

The first two parameters to setBarAndArrows are the left and right styles, respectively. The next four parameters indicate the actions that will be taken when the left, right, up, and down keys are pressed. Four constants exist that indicate that the press should be destined for the focus manager, which will automatically navigate to the next button closest in the direction of the button press. In the following example, the three buttons are placed in a vertical column, and the focus manager will manage traversing the set of buttons because the focus manager constants have been specified for the up and down keys.

The focus manager constants are as follows:

❑   H_UP

❑   H_DOWN

❑   H_RIGHT

❑   H_LEFT

In the example, the action "pop" is used in the left action field. Actions are discussed further in the next chapter, but you will see in the screen's handleAction() method that the application exits when the string "pop" is received as an action.

```
package com.wiley.hme.ch7;

import java.awt.Color;

import com.tivo.hme.bananas.BApplication;
import com.tivo.hme.bananas.BButton;
import com.tivo.hme.bananas.BScreen;
import com.tivo.hme.bananas.BText;
import com.tivo.hme.bananas.BView;
import com.tivo.hme.interfaces.IContext;

public class BButtonExample extends BApplication {

    public void init(IContext arg0) throws Exception {
        super.init(arg0);
        push(new ExampleScreen(this), TRANSITION_FADE);
        getRoot().setResource(Color.blue);
    }

    public class ExampleScreen extends BScreen {
        public boolean handleAction(BView arg0, Object arg1) {
            if ("pop".equals(arg1.toString())) {
```

```
                    getBApp().setActive(false);
                    getBApp().play("thumbsup.snd");
            }
            return super.handleAction(arg0, arg1);
        }

        public ExampleScreen(BApplication arg0) {
            super(arg0);
            BButton myButton = new BButton(this, 100, 100, 200, 50, true);
            myButton.setResource(createText("default-20.font", "0xFFFFFF", "Test
Button"));
            myButton.setBarAndArrows(BAR_DEFAULT, BAR_HANG, "pop", null, null,
H_DOWN, false);

            BButton myButton2 = new BButton(this, 100, 200, 200, 50, true);
            myButton2.setResource(createText("default-20.font", "0xFFFFFF", "Test
Button"));
            myButton2.setBarAndArrows( BAR_DEFAULT, BAR_DEFAULT, "pop", null, H_UP,
H_DOWN, true);

            BButton myButton3 = new BButton(this, 100, 300, 200, 50, true);
            myButton3.setBarAndArrows( BAR_HANG, BAR_DEFAULT, "pop", null, H_UP,
null, true);
            BText text = new BText(myButton3, 0, 0, myButton3.getWidth(),
myButton3.getHeight());
            text.setShadow("0x666666", 2);
            text.setValue("text 3");
            text.setFont("default-20.font");

            setFocusDefault(myButton);

        }
    }
}
```

BKeyboard

The keyboard widget that comes with Bananas is probably the most advanced widget in the toolkit, and simplifies retrieving data from the user that is not based on menus or buttons.

There are two basic types of keyboards built into the keyboard widget: the plain keyboard and the email keyboard. Figure 7-10 shows an example of a plain keyboard, and Figure 7-11 shows an example of an email keyboard.

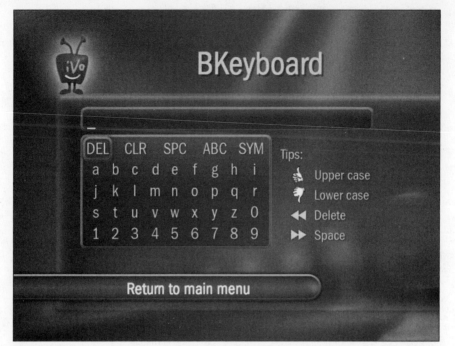

Figure 7-10

Figure 7-11

Using the Keyboard Widget

The keyboard is used like the button widget; there is no extension of classes required, and a new BKeyboard widget can be placed on a BScreen just like a button. The BKeyboard is created using one of the BKeyboard constructors:

```
new BKeyboard(BView parent, int x, int y, int width, int height)

new BKeyboard(BView parent, int x, int y, int width, int height, BKeyboard.Keyboard
keyboard, boolean tips, int textEntryWidth, boolean visible)

new BKeyboard(BView parent, int x, int y, int width, int height, int keyboardType,
boolean tips)
```

The first constructor takes the parent view (`getNormal()` on the BScreen containing the keyboard), the coordinates for the keyboard, and the width and height for the keyboard.

The second constructor also takes the same parameters as the first, and also additional parameters that indicate which Keyboard type to use, whether or not to show a tips area, the width of the text entry bar, and the visibility of the widget. The final constructor takes an integer instead of the BKeyboard.Keyboard type, but essentially performs the same task.

The following example sets up a keyboard and a button below the keyboard to exit the application. Like buttons, the whole keyboard widget participates in the focus manager.

```
package com.wiley.hme.ch7;

import java.awt.Color;
import java.awt.Point;

import com.tivo.hme.bananas.BApplication;
import com.tivo.hme.bananas.BButton;
import com.tivo.hme.bananas.BEvent;
import com.tivo.hme.bananas.BKeyboard;
import com.tivo.hme.bananas.BScreen;
import com.tivo.hme.bananas.BText;
import com.tivo.hme.bananas.BView;
import com.tivo.hme.interfaces.IContext;

public class ExampleKeyboard extends BApplication {

    public class BSelectButton extends BButton {

        private String selectAction;

        public BSelectButton(BView arg0, int arg1, int arg2, int arg3, int arg4) {
            super(arg0, arg1, arg2, arg3, arg4);
        }

        public void setSelectAction(String action) {
            this.selectAction = action;
        }

        public boolean handleKeyPress(int key, long arg1) {
```

```
                    if (key == KEY_SELECT) {
                        getParent().postEvent(new BEvent.Action(this, selectAction));
                    }
                    return super.handleKeyPress(key, arg1);
            }


    }

    public void init(IContext context) throws Exception {
        super.init(context);
        push ( new KeyboardScreen(this), TRANSITION_FADE);
    }

    public class KeyboardScreen extends BScreen {


        private BKeyboard kb;

        public boolean handleAction(BView arg0, Object arg1) {
            if ("pop".equals(arg1.toString())) {
                getBApp().setActive(false);
            } else if ("msg".equals(arg1)) {
                getBApp().push(new MessageScreen(getBApp(), kb.getValue()),
TRANSITION_LEFT);
            }

            return super.handleAction(arg0, arg1);
        }

        public KeyboardScreen(BApplication arg0) {
            super(arg0);
            Point p = BKeyboard.getKeyboardSize(BKeyboard.PLAIN_KEYBOARD, true);
            kb = new BKeyboard(getNormal(), 100, 100, p.x, p.y,
BKeyboard.PLAIN_KEYBOARD, true);
            kb.setFocusable(true);
            setFocusDefault(kb);

            BSelectButton b = new BSelectButton(getNormal(), 100, p.y+150, 100,
50);
            b.setSelectAction("pop");
            b.setResource(createText("default-20.font", "0xFFFFFF", "Quit"));
            b.setBarAndArrows(BAR_HANG, BAR_DEFAULT, "pop", H_RIGHT, H_UP, null,
true);

            BSelectButton b2 = new BSelectButton(getNormal(), 400, p.y+150, 100,
50);
            b2.setSelectAction("msg");
            b2.setResource(createText("default-20.font", "0xFFFFFF", "Okay"));
            b2.setBarAndArrows(BAR_DEFAULT,BAR_HANG, H_LEFT, "msg", H_UP, null,
true);
        }
```

```
        }

    public class MessageScreen extends BScreen {

        public boolean handleAction(BView arg0, Object arg1) {
            if ("pop".equals(arg1)) {
                getBApp().pop();
            }
            return super.handleAction(arg0, arg1);
        }

        public MessageScreen(BApplication arg0, String message) {
            super(arg0);
            BText bt = new BText(getNormal(), 100, 100, 400, 300);
            bt.setValue(message);
            bt.setFont("default-50.font");
            bt.setColor(Color.white);

            BSelectButton b = new BSelectButton(getNormal(), 100, 400, 100, 50);
            b.setSelectAction("pop");
            b.setResource(createText("default-20.font", "0xFFFFFF", "Back"));
            b.setBarAndArrows(BAR_HANG, BAR_DEFAULT, "pop", null, H_UP, null,
true);

            setFocusDefault(b);

        }

    }

}
```

In this example, the width of the widget is provided by the widget itself. The getKeyboardSize() call is a static method that provides the width and height of the keyboard widget. The dimensions are then used to create the widget in the next line of the sample code.

Try It Out   Use the Email Keyboard

How would you update the preceding example to use the email keyboard?

Both the plain keyboard and email keyboard are the same widget, essentially, only with a different type. Changing to the email keyboard would require changing the references from BKeyboard.PLAIN_KEY-BOARD to BKeyboard.EMAIL_KEYBOARD.

Changing the lines

```
Point p = BKeyboard.getKeyboardSize(BKeyboard.PLAIN_KEYBOARD, true);
        kb = new BKeyboard(getNormal(), 100, 100, p.x, p.y,
BKeyboard.PLAIN_KEYBOARD, true);
```

to

```
Point p = BKeyboard.getKeyboardSize(BKeyboard.EMAIL_KEYBOARD, true);
         kb = new BKeyboard(getNormal(), 100, 100, p.x, p.y,
BKeyboard.EMAIL_KEYBOARD, true);
```

will use the email keyboard instead.

BSkin

Bananas widgets are styled with a very TiVo UI look and feel. Of course, not all applications will want to have the exact look and feel of the TiVo user interface. The authors' application, AudioFaucet (Figure 7-12), for example, uses the Bananas toolkit but has custom graphics for all of the widgets it uses. Although this does create a somewhat different feel to the application, in this case, that was the intent.

The TiVo user interface is highly usable, but applications that are specific to a particular domain, or that have a style of their own, may want to override the default images with buttons or lists that match an established brand or user interface style.

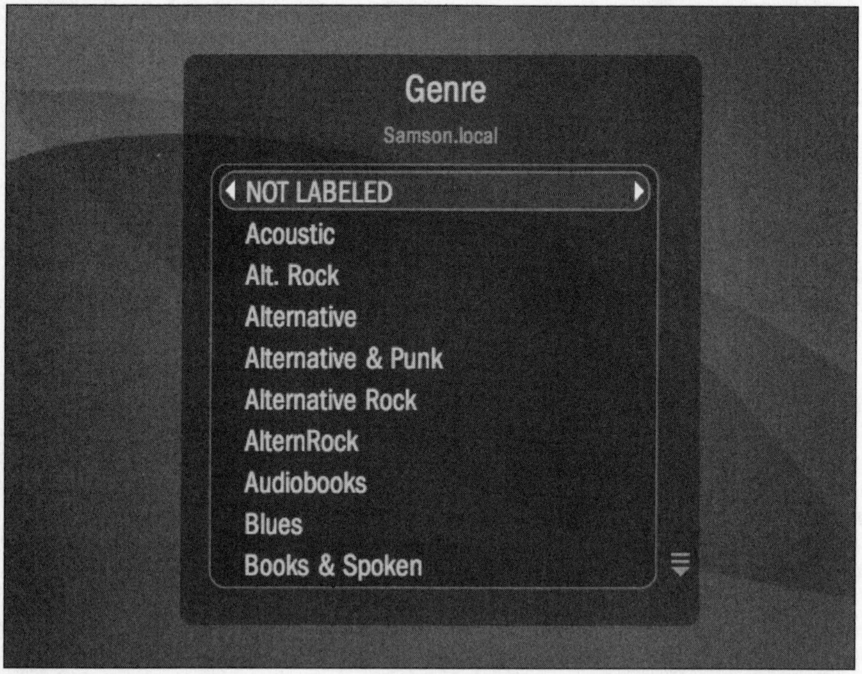

Figure 7-12

Bananas uses a class called BSkin to manage the graphics used for all the widgets, and it provides three different ways to override the default skin in order to customize an application. The widgets are all constructed of a few simple images:

Image File Name	Size of Image (pixels)
bar.png	640 Wide x 48 High
down.png	20 Wide x 7 High
left.png	8 Wide x 20 High
pagedown.png	14 Wide x 26 High
pageup.png	14 Wide x 26 High
right.png	8 Wide x 20 High
up.png	20 Wide x 7 High

The first task in creating a new skin is to create images with the file names listed in this table and the proper dimensions. There are three different BSkin subclasses. All these classes provide the same functionality, differing only in how the files that are used for the skin are located.

BDirSkin

BDirSkin uses a directory of images to locate the files for displaying the Bananas widget. The second argument in the constructor is the directory to find the skin files in:

```
BSkin skin = new BDirSkin(this, "skin/");
```

BZipSkin

BZipSkin uses a ZIP file of images to locate the files for displaying the Bananas widget. The second argument in the constructor is the ZIP file that contains the skin files:

```
BSkin skin = new BZipSkin(this, "skinFile.zip");
```

BResSkin

BResSkin uses the classpath to locate the files for displaying the Bananas widget. The second argument in the constructor is the path in the classpath to look for images. The images can either be inside a jar file or outside a jar file.

```
BSkin skin = new BResSkin(this, "com/wiley/hme/ch7/");
```

Example

The following shows how to set a skin for a user with Bananas. This example is using BResSkin. This example assumes that the required graphics listed in the preceding table—bar.png, up.png, and so on—reside in the `com/wiley/hme/ch7` directory. You can find an example set of these graphics in the `samples/skin-charcoal` directory of the Bananas toolkit (see Figure 7-13).

```
package com.wiley.hme.ch7;

import java.awt.Color;

import com.tivo.hme.bananas.BApplication;
import com.tivo.hme.bananas.BList;
import com.tivo.hme.bananas.BResSkin;
import com.tivo.hme.bananas.BScreen;
import com.tivo.hme.bananas.BSkin;
import com.tivo.hme.bananas.BText;
import com.tivo.hme.bananas.BView;
import com.tivo.hme.interfaces.IContext;

public class BSkinExample extends BApplication {

    String listItems[] = {"one", "two", "three", "four" };

    public void init(IContext context) throws Exception {
        super.init(context);
        getRoot().setResource(Color.black);
        BSkin skin = new BResSkin(this, "com/wiley/hme/ch7/");
        this.setSkin(skin);
        push(new simpleScreen(this), TRANSITION_LEFT);
    }

    public boolean handleKeyPress(int arg0, long arg1) {
        // TODO Auto-generated method stub
        return super.handleKeyPress(arg0, arg1);
    }


    public class SimpleBList extends BList {

        public SimpleBList(BView arg0, int arg1, int arg2, int arg3, int arg4, int
arg5) {
            super(arg0, arg1, arg2, arg3, arg4, arg5);
            this.setBarAndArrows(BAR_DEFAULT, BAR_HANG, "left", "right");
        }

        protected void createRow(BView parentView, int index) {
            if (get(index) != null) {
                BText text = new BText(parentView, 0 , 0 , parentView.getWidth(),
parentView.getHeight());
                text.setValue(get(index).toString());
            }
        }

    }

    public class simpleScreen extends BScreen {
        public simpleScreen(BApplication app) {
            super(app);
            BList list = new SimpleBList(getNormal(), 100, 100, 400, 300, 48);
```

```
        list.add(listItems);
        list.setVisible(true);
        setFocusDefault(list);
    }
}

}
```

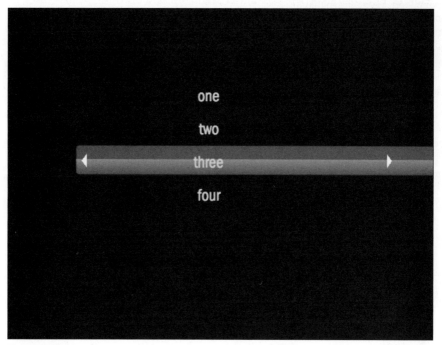

Figure 7-13

Summary

The Bananas widget toolkit provides the basic widget for imparting a TiVo look and feel on your application and inheriting key behaviors. The Bananas toolkit, like the base HME SDK, requires extension from the classes included in the library. Lists, buttons, and the keyboard widget provide enough basic functionality to create a high-quality interface, and the skinning capabilities allow for a custom look on top of the Bananas widgets.

Custom widgets may be built on top of the Bananas library, allowing for greater flexibility in developing an application with a unique user interface. Bananas has a slightly different event model, using actions for processing much of the interaction with the widgets. Bananas events and actions are the subject of the next chapter, which delves deeper into how to hook the widgets up to a functioning application.

Questions

1. What is wrong with the following code?

```
BList myList = new BList(getNormal(), 100, 100, 300, 400);
```

2. Should the BApplication's subclass call `super.init(context)`? When? Why?

3. How do BButtons know which of the left, right, up, and down keys can be used to move from the button to other items?

8

Using Bananas Events

Many of the examples in the previous chapter made use of Bananas event handling. Making HME applications is really all about interacting with the user, bringing data and an innovative interface to the television to allow for more complex tasks to be done from the living room or to extend the reach of a current application. Key to the success of all these types of applications is interaction with the user. Just as HME events made the applications from Chapter 6 more interesting than the static ones from Chapter 5, learning how events are processed in Bananas will greatly expand the range and level of complexity a Bananas application can handle and allow for more powerful user interaction.

The Bananas toolkit does not alter the underlying event processing system. If you recall from Chapter 6, events are sent by the TiVo and are processed by the application, which would normally take some sort of action, changing the display on the TiVo or playing a sound. The HME SDK contains the events for handling key presses, application events, and resource events. Bananas adds a few events for processing Bananas information using the HME event system. At the end of Chapter 6, there was an example of creating custom events in HME. This is precisely how Bananas manages to add events to the base set of HME events.

By the end of this chapter, you will learn

- ❑ The difference between HME events and Bananas actions
- ❑ How Bananas widgets send event data
- ❑ How to hook into the Bananas events flow

Event Model

The new Bananas classes introduce a different event model to handle the events that are introduced with Bananas. Event processing is still largely based on the event flow from Chapter 6. Some initial processing is done by the new BApplication class; BView relies heavily on the View subclass for event flow as well.

Chapter 8

The event flow in Bananas is shown in Figure 8-1.

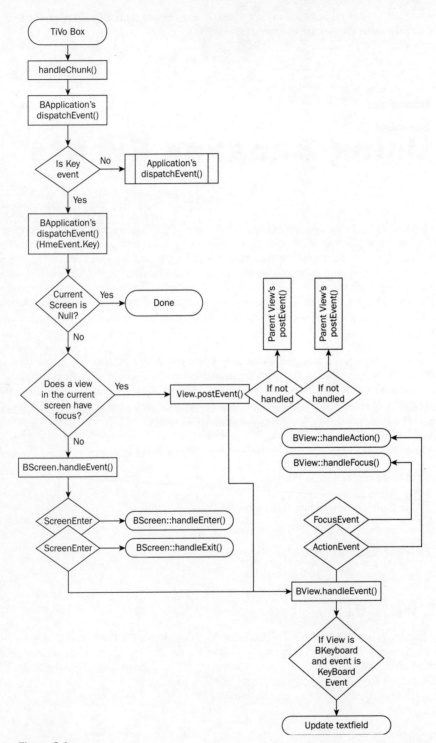

Figure 8-1

```
            return super.handleAction(view, action);
    }

    public void init(IContext context) throws Exception {
        super.init(context);
        getRoot().setResource(Color.white);

        push(new ZipScreen(this), TRANSITION_FADE);
    }

    public static class BWeatherAppFactory extends Factory {
        public InputStream getStream(String arg0) throws IOException {
            return super.getStream(arg0);
        }
    }

}
```

This example doesn't add any new functionality, but does add a custom factory. Because getAppFactory() is built into the Application superclass that BWeatherApp is descended from, the getAppFactory() method will return a new BWeatherAppFactory object when the hosting environment starts up. The factory object is located by the superclass (Application) because the Application class's getAppFactory() method will automatically locate a factory if the factory's name conforms to <application>Factory. In this case, the application is named BWeatherApp, and the factory is automatically located because it is named BWeatherAppFactory. The factory objects, unlike the application objects, which are created when the application is accessed on the TiVo box, are created when the hosting environment starts announcing the availability of the application. The factory is created in order to "manufacture" instances of the application.

To create a factory that does not conform to the coding scheme for auto-discovery (not inner-static inside the application), the application class must re-implement the getAppFactory() static method from Application to locate the correctly named Factory. Perhaps, for instance, there are different factories that the application wants to use depending on whether it is located on a server or installed locally.

Suppose the BWeatherAppFactory class was changed to be defined as:

```
public static class BWeatherAppFactory_NotFoundAutomatically extends Factory {
    public InputStream getStream(String arg0) throws IOException {
        return super.getStream(arg0);
    }
}
```

Even if it is a static inner class inside BWeatherApp, it will not be located because the naming scheme does not conform to the defaults the Application superclass can find (the name of the application, followed by "Factory"). In this case, the application class must re-implement getAppFactory() to locate the factory:

```
public static IFactory getAppFactory(String appClassName, ClassLoader loader,
IArgumentList args) {
    IFactory f = new BWeatherAppFactory_NotFoundAutomatically();
    f.initFactory(appClassName, loader, args);

    return f;
}
```

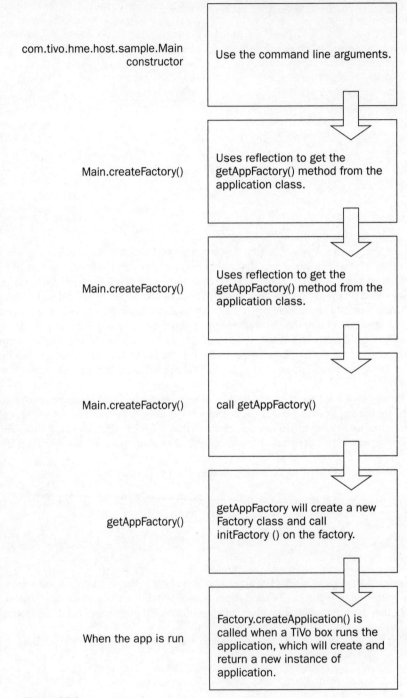

Figure 10-1

com.tivo.hme.host.sample.Main constructor	Use the command line arguments.
Main.createFactory()	Uses reflection to get the getAppFactory() method from the application class.
Main.createFactory()	Uses reflection to get the getAppFactory() method from the application class.
Main.createFactory()	call getAppFactory()
getAppFactory()	getAppFactory will create a new Factory class and call initFactory () on the factory.
When the app is run	Factory.createApplication() is called when a TiVo box runs the application, which will create and return a new instance of application.

In this case, the `getAppFactory()` method, which *must* be defined inside BWeatherApp, will create an instance of the correct factory, initialize it, and return it. The parameters to `getAppFactory()`, the name of the application class as a String, and the classloader are used by the default implementation of `getApp Factory()` to locate the factory. The classloader is a part of Java used to load and create objects in the Java Runtime. In the `getAppFactory()` method shown in the preceding code, there is no need to look up or dynamically load a Factory object, because you know that BWeatherApp will always be using the BWeatherAppFactory_NotFoundAutomatically class. The last argument, `args`, to `getAppFactory()` is the argument given to the application, typically on the command line. Normally these wouldn't be used in the `getAppFactory()` method. All of the parameters to `getAppFactory()` are required arguments to `initFactory()`. The `initFactory()` method *must* be called after the custom factory is created. Skipping the initialization will create difficulty when trying to track down problems when running the application.

Now that you can create custom factories, and integrate them into applications, you can explore some of the reasons that would prompt this sort of undertaking.

Accessing Files and Resources

The Factory object manages locating the files for images, fonts, sounds, and streaming audio to send to the TiVo box to display or play. The `getStream()` method in Factory is called from several places in the HME code, when an image, sound, or font must be transmitted to the TiVo box, or when the TiVo box is requesting another streamed resource from an application.

The default Factory's `getStream()` implementation handles the following cases:

❑ If the resource name starts with "http://", a URLConnection is opened to the web server, the file is read off the web server, and the data is passed to the TiVo box.

❑ If the resource is not an http resource, `getStream()` looks for a file with the resource name provided in the current package on the current classpath.

❑ If the resource is not found in the current package, `getStream()` looks for a file on the current classpath matching the resource name.

In the weather application in Chapter 8, the Yahoo RSS weather feed provided an image URL to describe the weather conditions. On the screen displaying the weather information, the application passes the URL of the image directly to `setResource()`:

```
icon.setResource(getResource(feed.getImageUrl()), RSRC_IMAGE_BESTFIT);
```

The default Factory will determine that the image URL is a URL by checking for the http:// prefix, and then retrieving the data and relaying it to the TiVo box.

Many of the other examples have made use of `getStream()`'s ability to locate files on the classpath:

```
onImage = createImage("ThumbsAway-on.gif");
```

This line of code (from the SimonSays game) will locate the image ThumbsAway-on.gif from the classpath and transmit it to the TiVo box.

These methods of locating files work for self-contained applications such as games where all the resources needed for the application can be predetermined or fetched from a web site. TiVo HME applications are often used to extend the user's desktop and the functionality of the desktop to the TiVo. A photo album viewer will need access to the user's photos, a music player will need access to the user's MP3 files, and both of these applications will need access to files outside the classpath.

If the `onImage` variable was using an image from a temp directory, for example, /tmp/Thumbs.gif on Mac OS X (probably in c:\windows\temp on Windows), the default `getStream()` would not be able to locate the file if the `createImage()` method was to be called with this:

```
onImage = createImage("/tmp/Thumbs.gif");
```

The application would fail with a resource not found error. To allow this file to be found, a custom factory would need to be written, and the `getStream()` method in the factory would have to read files from the filesystem, and return a java.io.InputStream to read the file.

```
public static class BWeatherAppFactory_NotFoundAutomatically extends Factory {
    public InputStream getStream(String uri) throws IOException {
        if (uri != null && uri.startsWith("/tmp/")) {
            File file = new File(uri);
            if (file.exists() && file.isFile()) {
                FileInputStream fis = new FileInputStream(file);
                return fis;
            }
        }
        return super.getStream(uri);
    }
}
```

In this code, the `getStream()` method looks for files in the local filesystem as long as they are under the "/tmp/" directory.

Some amount of security in terms of restricting the files that are streamed out to the TiVo is probably a decent precaution to take. In this case, you only want to provide access to /tmp. In other cases, you may want to make sure you can only access MP3 or image files from certain directories.

Changing the Application Name

When an application shows up on the TiVo box's Music, Photos, & More menu, the name of the application is determined by the string in the main application class named TITLE:

```
public final static String TITLE = "Weather Application";
```

If this was defined in BWeatherApp, the application would show up on the Music, Photos, & More menu as Weather Application. Because there is no TITLE variable defined, it normally shows up with the name of the application class, BWeatherApp.

Having a static title for an application may be quite acceptable. A game, for instance, will not change its name over time, nor will an application like the weather app. A music player or photo album view, or another application that relies on local data on the host machine it is running on, may want to indicate in its title which host system it is running on.

This is accomplished by overriding the `getAppTitle()` method in the Factory class. For instance, for the BWeatherApp application to be named "Weather from macbuk" (macbuk is the name of my laptop system), a `getAppTitle()` method like this could be added to the BWeatherAppFactory class:

```
public String getAppTitle() {
    String host = "";
    try {
        host = " on " + InetAddress.getLocalHost().getHostName();
    } catch (UnknownHostException e) {

    }
    return "Weather" + host;
}
```

This version of `getAppTitle()` is careful to ensure that the "Weather" title is returned correctly, even if there is a problem getting the host name for some reason.

Handling Arguments

Command-line arguments may also be handled in the factory via the `init()` method. The `init()` method receives as a parameter an IArgumentsList that contains the arguments sent to the application. If the BWeatherApp was run from the command line, assuming the classpath was set correctly, the command would look something like this:

```
java com.tivo.hme.host.sample.Main com.wiley.hme.ch10.BWeatherApp
```

In this case, the arguments passed to the factory's `init()` method would be empty. If the command was something more like

```
java com.tivo.hme.host.sample.Main com.wiley.hme.ch10.BWeatherApp -myTitle
MyWeather
```

where the `myTitle` parameter is intended to be used as the title of the application, the `init()` method would have to pick up the `myTitle` parameter from the IArgumentList using the `getValue()` method. Note that `getValue()` is a *destructive* operation on the IArgumentList. After a value has been retrieved, it is removed from the argument list, so make sure to save any values returned from `getValue()` immediately.

```
protected void init(IArgumentList args) {
    super.init(args);
    // get the title parameter, myTitle. Use a default of "Weather" if no
    // command line parameter is provided.
    myTitle = args.getValue("-myTitle", "Weather");
    System.out.println("Title will be: " + myTitle);
}
```

Additionally, any values on the command line intended for the application *must* be retrieved by the application. If the BWeatherApp does not call `args.getValue()` as shown in the preceding code, the hosting environment will display errors:

```
com.tivo.hme.interfaces.IArgumentList$BadArgumentException: don't understand -
myTitle
    at
com.tivo.hme.host.util.ArgumentList.checkForIllegalFlags(ArgumentList.java:208)
    at com.tivo.hme.host.sample.Main.createFactory(Main.java:392)
    at com.tivo.hme.host.sample.Main.<init>(Main.java:151)
    at com.tivo.hme.host.sample.Main.<init>(Main.java:60)
    at com.tivo.hme.sim.Simulator.main(Simulator.java:848)
error: don't understand -myTitle
usage: Main [options] class

Options:
  --port <port>         listen on a specific port
  --intf <interface>    listen on a specific interface
  --nomdns <interface>  listen on a specific interface, without mdns
  --launcher <file>     start factories listed in file
  --jars <dir>          scan directory for HME app jar files
  --jar <jarfile>       start factory for the given jar
```

When the -myTitle parameter is retrieved by the factory, the application starts as expected.

Common Actions

Factories have a completely different lifecycle from the applications that the factories produce. Factories start before any applications, and stick around between runs of the application. There are likely actions, parameters, or functions that affect all instances of a running application.

Using Factory for Shared Data

Suppose, for example, a user is running the BWeatherApp application on their desktop. If one TiVo has already run the application, and selected a location (Zip code), there is no reason to have another TiVo in the same house make the user re-select the Zip code. The Factory could store this data across all instances running in a household, and then reuse the data if a second TiVo box was to run the application.

First, in the factory, there would have to be setters and getters for the Zip code. This would go inside the BWeatherAppFactory class:

```
private String zipCode = "";

public String getZipCode() {
    return zipCode;
}

public synchronized void setZipCode(String zipCode) {
    this.zipCode = zipCode;
}
```

Notice that in this code, the setZipCode() method is declared synchronized. This is because while multiple instances of the application may be run, there is only one factory. Two application instances *must not* be allowed to set the Zip code at the same time, so you declare the setZipCode() method to be synchronized for this reason.

Now, in the application, you can check the factory to see if a Zip code has already been entered by another instance of the application, and if so, skip directly to the WeatherScreen. The init() method in BWeatherApp now looks like this:

```
public void init(IContext context) throws Exception {
    super.init(context);
    getRoot().setResource(Color.white);
    String zipString = ((BWeatherAppFactory)getFactory()).getZipCode();
    if ("".equals(zipString))
        push(new ZipScreen(this), TRANSITION_FADE);
    else
        push(new WeatherScreen(this, zipString), TRANSITION_FADE, "first");
}
```

In this example, a different form of push() is used to push the weather screen. This is because the Zip code screen normally comes before the weather screen. Now the weather screen has to know that it must be capable of quitting the application, and pushing the Zip code screen, if the Zip code needs to be changed.

The handleEnter() method in the WeatherScreen now sets up a button to quit the application or to configure the Zip code:

```
public boolean handleEnter(Object arg, boolean isReturn) {

    if ("first".equals(arg)) {
        BButton button = new BButton(getNormal(), 300, 400, 250, 48);
        button.setVisible(true);
        button.setResource(createText("default-20.font", "0xFFFFFF", "L to quit / R
to set zip"));
        button.setBarAndArrows(BAR_HANG, BAR_DEFAULT, "quit", "zip", H_UP, null,
false);
        setFocusDefault(button);
    }

    String titleStr = feed.getTitle();
    String forcastStr = join (feed.getForcast(), "\n");
    String currentlyStr = join (feed.getCurrentConditions(), "\n");

    title.setValue(titleStr);
    forcast.setValue(forcastStr);
    currently.setValue(currentlyStr);

    icon.setResource(getResource(feed.getImageUrl()), RSRC_IMAGE_BESTFIT);

    return super.handleEnter(arg, isReturn);
}
```

To handle the actions of the new button on the WeatherScreen, a handleAction() method must be added:

```
public boolean handleAction(BView view, Object action) {
    if ("quit".equals(action)) {
        getBApp().setActive(false);
        return true;
    }
```

```
      if ("zip".equals(action)) {
          getBApp().push(new ZipScreen(getBApp()), TRANSITION_LEFT, "second");
          return true;
      }
      return super.handleAction(view, action);
  }
```

The push() method is also used with arguments here to indicate to the ZipScreen that it is not the first screen in this case, so it will pop back to the WeatherScreen correctly, and will not quit the application. The handleEnter() method has to be updated in the ZipScreen now to handle the new argument and set up the screen correctly:

```
public boolean handleEnter(Object arg, boolean isReturn) {
    if (arg != null && arg instanceof WeatherScreen) {
        myWS = (WeatherScreen) arg;
        button.setResource(createText("default-20.font", "0xFFFFFF", "Continue"));
        button.setBarAndArrows( BAR_HANG, BAR_DEFAULT, "pop", null, H_UP, null,
false);
    }
    return super.handleEnter(arg, isReturn);
}
```

The complete source code for this example is available as project Ch10-2 on the accompanying web site at www.wrox.com.

This is really only one example of how to use the factory to perform actions that are common to all instances of the application. The authors' application, AudioFaucet, uses an overloaded factory to display a splash screen, start up communication with iTunes for obtaining data from iTunes, load user preferences, and various other tasks that take place once across all instances and runs of the application, or that must occur before any instances of the application are started.

Singletons

Each access to an application from a TiVo box results in a new instance of the application class generated by the Factory. If an application has particularly resource-intensive tasks that produce data that can be shared across applications, these tasks can be relocated to a common object in the code to avoid extremely high CPU usage when multiple instances of an application are running.

You have already seen one method of relocating code to a common area by using the factory to manage access to the shared data. However, relocating code to the factory imposes some restrictions. The shared object is likely created and maintained by the factory, and the factory has specific requirements around packaging and inheritance—namely, the factory must extend the Factory class, and must be a public static inner class inside the application itself. If the lifecycle of the shared object or any of the other factors require a shared object that lives outside the factory, the singleton design pattern is easily employed to manage the object.

The following code for the Zip code would turn the Zip code into a singleton instead of placing it inside the Factory:

```
package com.wiley.hme.ch10;

public class ZipCode {

    private static ZipCode ZC;
    private String value;

    private ZipCode() {

    }

    public static ZipCode getZipCode() {
        if (ZC == null) {
            ZC = new ZipCode();
            ZC.setValue("");
        }
        return ZC;
    }

    public String getValue() {
        return value;
    }

    public synchronized void setValue(String value) {
        this.value = value;
    }
}
```

Because the constructor for this class is private, the only way to access it is to call `getZipCode()`, which, if no Zip code object already exists, will create a new one, and if one already exists, will return the existing one. The ZipCode object accessed via the `getZipCode()` method will provide access to the same object as long as it is called from within the same JVM.

This also allows for shared access to the Zip code information, but the ZipCode object does not need to be stored in the factory — it can be set up when the Zip code is first entered, and allows for cleaner code by not cluttering the Factory with information that is really not needed for creating application instances, the main function of the application.

Threads

Threads are Java's main method of managing concurrent operations. Threads are useful for separating any task that will impede the application from being responsive to the user.

Tasks that take additional resource power, such as transferring and resizing images from the Internet before displaying them on the TiVo box, might well be put in a separate thread. Any output generated in separate threads from the main event handler should call the `flush()` method to make sure that changes to the user interface are sent to the TiVo box. The flush is done automatically when responding to an event, but in a separate thread, this must be done manually.

Using Threads

Concurrency was updated significantly between Java 4 and Java 5. Although Java 4 thread syntax will work in Java 5, it is worth looking at how threads are started and stopped in both Java 4 and 5 when running threads inside TiVo HME applications.

Java 4 Threads

Java 4 threads are classes that implement the Runnable interface or extend the Thread object. Take, for example, a thread used to fetch, parse, and present the data from the BWeatherApp.

In this case, the thread would live inside the WeatherScreen, and would fetch the data for the weather screen and update the screen. Though the BWeatherApp is not particularly slow to load, over a slow Internet connection it could take time to retrieve the Yahoo RSS feed, so a separate thread might be a wise design decision when relying on access to web-based resources.

The following code starts up a thread inside the WeatherScreen to grab the data. Notice the call to flush() to make sure the data is sent to the TiVo box.

```java
public void doZip(final String zip) {
    this.zip = zip;
    new Thread() {
        public void run() {
            try {
                feed = new WeatherFeedReader(zip);
            } catch (IllegalArgumentException e) {
                e.printStackTrace();
            } catch (FeedException e) {
                e.printStackTrace();
            } catch (IOException e) {
                e.printStackTrace();
            }
            feed.parse();

            String titleStr = feed.getTitle();
            String forcastStr = WeatherScreen.this.join (feed.getForcast(), "\n");
            String currentlyStr = WeatherScreen.this.join
(feed.getCurrentConditions(), "\n");

            title.setValue(titleStr);
            forcast.setValue(forcastStr);
            currently.setValue(currentlyStr);

            icon.setResource(getResource(feed.getImageUrl()), RSRC_IMAGE_BESTFIT);
            flush();
        }
    }.start();
}
```

Java 5 Executor

Java 5 introduced the java.util.concurrent package, which allows much greater flexibility on managing how threads are run.

The old-style Java 4 threads above preceding code will still work in Java 5, but the new executor functionality can also be used to manage how many threads are running and how threads are reused. Thread re-use can be a very useful tool if there are many threads being created in an application.

Converting the preceding example to a Java 5 example is straightforward. First, the WeatherScreen class needs an executor. All of this code can be found in Example 10-2 in the accompanying source code on the web site.

```
private ExecutorService exec;
```

The exec member should be defined in the WeatherScreen class and initialized in the constructor:

```
exec = Executors.newCachedThreadPool();
```

Then the doZip() method becomes:

```
public void doZip(final String zip) {
    this.zip = zip;
    FeedGrabTask task = new FeedGrabTask();
    exec.execute(task);
}
```

And a separate class FeedGrabTask is written to encapsulate the task:

```
public class FeedGrabTask extends Thread {
    public void run() {
        try {
            feed = new WeatherFeedReader(zip);
        } catch (IllegalArgumentException e) {
            e.printStackTrace();
        } catch (FeedException e) {
            e.printStackTrace();
        } catch (IOException e) {
            e.printStackTrace();
        }
        feed.parse();

        String titleStr = feed.getTitle();
        String forcastStr = WeatherScreen.this.join (feed.getForcast(), "\n");
        String currentlyStr = WeatherScreen.this.join (feed.getCurrentConditions(),
"\n");

        title.setValue(titleStr);
        forcast.setValue(forcastStr);
        currently.setValue(currentlyStr);

        icon.setResource(getResource(feed.getImageUrl()), RSRC_IMAGE_BESTFIT);
        flush();
    }
}
```

Of course, there is much more to take into consideration when writing concurrent applications, but that is a topic best covered in a book on Java.

Stopping Threads Correctly on Application Exit

One other area of threading that is useful to know is how to exit threads correctly when closing an application.

Suppose for some reason you wanted to display the time on the Zip code screen. Adding a text field and changing `handleEnter()` to start a thread to display the current time could accomplish this:

```
public boolean handleEnter(Object arg, boolean isReturn) {
    if (arg != null && arg instanceof WeatherScreen) {
        myWS = (WeatherScreen) arg;
        button.setResource(createText("default-20.font", "0xFFFFFF", "Continue"));
        button.setBarAndArrows( BAR_HANG, BAR_DEFAULT, "pop", null, H_UP, null,
false);
    }

    new Thread() {
        public void run() {
            while(true) {
                Date d = new Date();
                timer.setValue( d.getHours() + ":" + d.getMinutes() + ":" +
d.getSeconds() );
                flush();
                try {
                    sleep(500);
                } catch (InterruptedException e) {}
            }
        }
    }.start();

    return super.handleEnter(arg, isReturn);
}
```

This thread, however, runs forever. In this case, you probably only want to run this thread when this screen is active, so you can check to see if the current screen is active, and if not, exit the thread:

```
public boolean handleEnter(Object arg, boolean isReturn) {
    if (arg != null && arg instanceof WeatherScreen) {
        myWS = (WeatherScreen) arg;
        button.setResource(createText("default-20.font", "0xFFFFFF", "Continue"));
        button.setBarAndArrows( BAR_HANG, BAR_DEFAULT, "pop", null, H_UP, null,
false);
    }

    new Thread() {
        public void run() {
            while(getBApp().getCurrentScreen().equals(getMyScreen())) {
                Date d = new Date();
                timer.setValue( d.getHours() + ":" + d.getMinutes() + ":" +
d.getSeconds() );
                flush();
                try {
                    sleep(500);
```

```
                } catch (InterruptedException e) {}
            }
        }
    }.start();

    return super.handleEnter(arg, isReturn);
}
```

What if the thread was running in the application class, providing data to multiple screens, or to a background task of the application itself? The `Application.isApplicationClosing()` method would provide a good `while` condition for a thread running in the application:

```
new Thread() {
    public void run() {
        while(!getApp().isApplicationClosing()) {
            System.out.println("Still running");
            try {
                sleep(500);
            } catch (InterruptedException e) {}
        }
    }
}.start();
```

If this code is placed in the application's `init()` method, the thread will run as long as the application is running. When the user exits the application on the TiVo box, the thread will be stopped.

Keeping Shared Threads Running between Applications

Like shared data, threads that process data to be shared among application instances can be placed in the factory.

The factory object has a boolean, `isActive`, which is an appropriate flag to use when terminating a thread that is running in the factory.

Calling Other Applications

One of the new features added in the HME 1.4 SDK was the ability to transition to other applications from within a TiVo HME application. Basically, one application can tell the TiVo box to load another application.

Yahoo has another service that displays traffic alerts, given a Zip code, so it might be useful to have the weather application be able to transition to the traffic alert application sending along the same Zip code used in the weather application.

Transitioning to Another Application

In order to transition to another application, the `transitionForward()` method from the Application class is used. The parameters are shown in the following table:

Parameter	Type	Description
Location	String	This is the URL of the application to transition to.
Params	TeDict	TeDict is essentially a hash, allowing for key/value pairs. Params is passed to the application being started as its parameters.
memento	byte[]	The `memento` is used when transitioning back to the current application — it can be used to restore the state of the application being transitioned back to. The `byte[]` is limited to 10KB in size.

To add transitioning capabilities to the BWeatherApp, add a button to the WeatherScreen that will get the traffic information for the current Zip code as well by calling the BTrafficApp application and sending the Zip code information along. In the `handleEnter()` method of WeatherScreen, the following code will add a button for retrieving traffic information:

```
BButton traffic = new BButton(getNormal(), 300, 350, 250, 48);
traffic.setVisible(true);
traffic.setResource(createText("default-20.font", "0xFFFFFF", "get traffic
alerts"));
traffic.setBarAndArrows(BAR_DEFAULT, BAR_HANG, null,"traffic",  H_UP, H_DOWN,
true);
setFocusDefault(traffic);
```

This new button will fire off a "traffic" action (the `setBarAndArrows()` makes the button send the "traffic" action when the right key on the remote is pressed while on the traffic button), so in the WeatherScreen's `handleAction()` method, the following code will transition to the traffic application:

```
public boolean handleAction(BView view, Object action) {
    if ("quit".equals(action)) {
        getBApp().setActive(false);
        return true;
    }
    if ("zip".equals(action)) {
        getBApp().push(new ZipScreen(getBApp()), TRANSITION_LEFT, this);
        return true;
    }
    if ("traffic".equals(action)) {
        TeDict parms = new TeDict();
        parms.add("zipcode", ZipCode.getZipCode().getValue());
        getBApp().transitionForward("http://192.168.1.103:7288/traffic/", parms,
null);
        getBApp().play("thumbsup.snd");
        return true;
    }
    return super.handleAction(view, action);
}
```

The traffic application's IP address is hard coded here, but this would likely be derived dynamically in a real application. See Example 10-4 in the accompanying source code for the full implementation.

In the traffic application, the application must look for information that comes in the parameters from a transition application. This means you need to do the following:

❏ Listen for the InitInfo event.

❏ Push initial screens in the `handleActive()` method instead of `init()` so you can retrieve data from the InitInfo event before pushing screens.

`handleEvent()` in the BTrafficApp handles the InitInfo event to grab the data passed in the parms object:

```
public boolean handleEvent(HmeEvent event) {
    if (event instanceof HmeEvent.InitInfo){
        HmeEvent.InitInfo iiEvent = (InitInfo) event;
        TeDict parms = iiEvent.getParams();
        ZipCode.getZipCode().setValue(parms.getString("zipcode", 0));
    }
    return super.handleEvent(event);
}
```

`handleActive()` in BTrafficApp pushes the screens based on the ZipCode, which was set in InitInfo if it received parameters from a transition:

```
public boolean handleActive(boolean active) {
    if (active) {
        String zipString = ZipCode.getZipCode().getValue();

        if ("".equals(zipString))
            push(new ZipScreen(this), TRANSITION_FADE);
        else
            this.push(new TrafficScreen(this, zipString), TRANSITION_FADE,
"first");
    }
    return super.handleActive(active);
}
```

This method will work both if the application is started directly on a TiVo box, or via a transition from another application.

Running the Example

This is probably the most complex example to date, in that two HME applications must be running in order for the example to work. Because you are transitioning to the traffic application, that should be run first.

Try It Out

Setting up Eclipse to run this application is similar to other examples. To set up a new application to be run by Eclipse, select Debug... from the Run menu. In the main class field, enter `com.tivo.hme.host` `.sample.Main`, and in the Arguments tab, enter `com.wiley.hme.ch10.traffic.BTrafficApp` (see Figures 10-2 and 10-3).

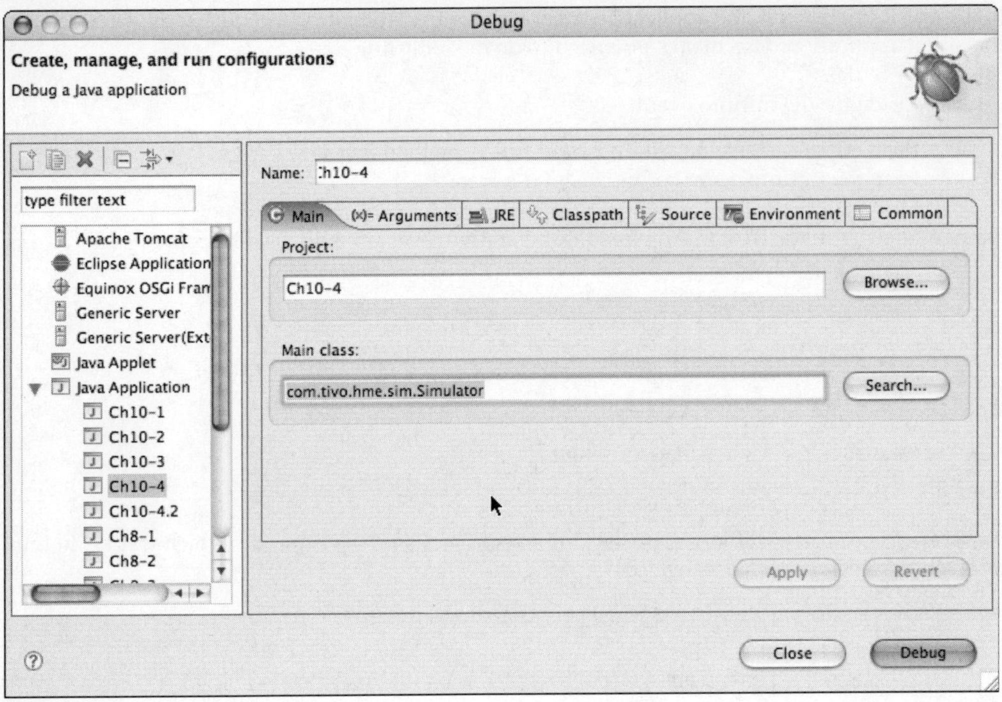

Figure 10-2

Click the Debug button to start the Traffic application. The Console tab in Eclipse will show:

```
Title will be: Traffic
LOG: added factory
MDNS: http://192.168.1.12:7288/traffic/
RUNNING: http://192.168.1.12:7288/traffic/

LOG: HME receiver connected
```

The URL after the MDNS and RUNNING lines is the URL of the traffic application. HME applications start on port 7288 if it is available. This is why you want to start the Traffic application first: so that it will start on port 7288, which is coded into the transition in the Weather App.

Now the weather application must be started. Again, follow the preceding steps, but in the arguments field, enter com.wiley.ch10.BWeatherApp. Click Debug to start the Weather application. The Console tab in Eclipse will show:

```
HME SDK 1.4 (TiVo, Inc.)
Title will be: Weather
LOG: added factory
MDNS: http://192.168.1.12:62515/ch10/
```

This time, a random port (not 7288) was chosen to run the application.

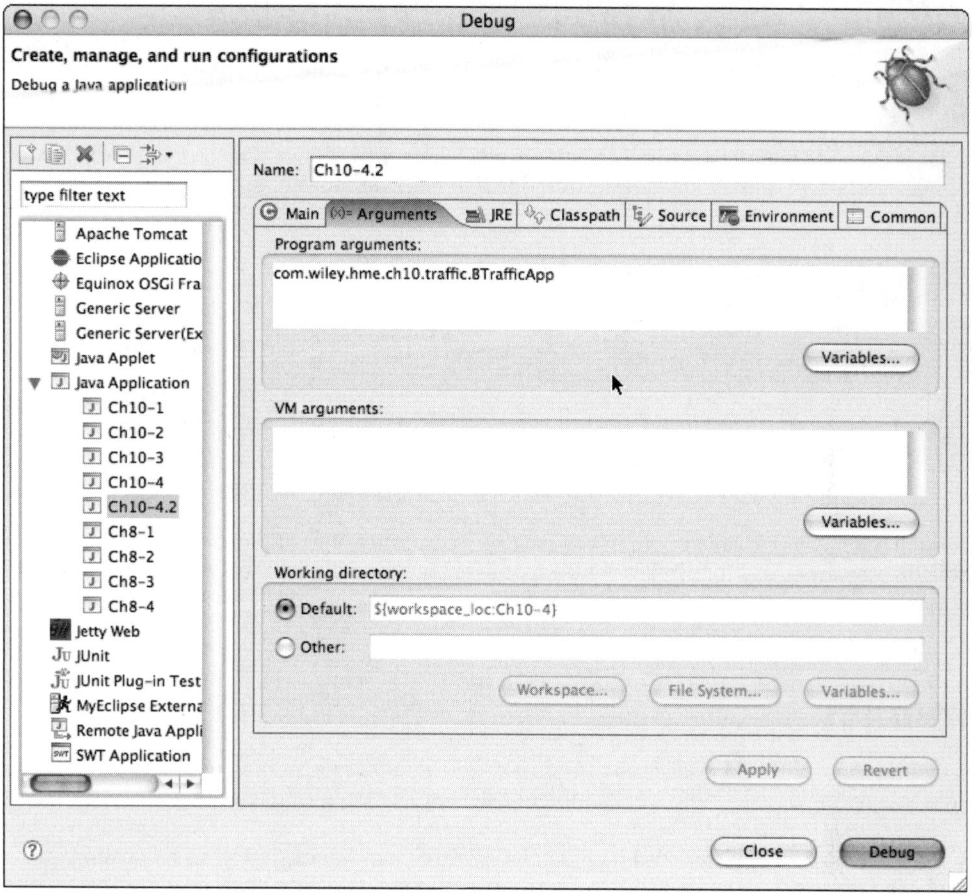

Figure 10-3

How It Works

Navigate to the Weather application on your TiVo box. Transitions between applications do not work in the Simulator application, and must be tested and run on a real TiVo box. After entering a Zip code, and retrieving the weather, you will see the "get traffic alerts" button that was added to the Weather information screen. Pressing the "right arrow" key on that button will transition to the Traffic application. Once in the Traffic application, pressing "left arrow" will exit the traffic application, which will cause a transition back to the weather application.

The TiVo box will actually run the two applications separately, stopping the first application when the transition to the second application takes place, and will re-run the first application when the transition back occurs.

Transitioning between applications is a useful tool for providing a suite of applications, such as weather and traffic, or transitioning from a local application to an application running on a server on the Internet.

Transitioning Back to the Original Application

Transitioning back to the original application will take place by calling `transitionBack()` in the transitioned-to application or by simply exiting the transitioned-to application.

Similar to how the parameters can be retrieved when an application is transitioned to, the memento (originally set when transitioning away from the first application) can be retrieved from the InitInfo event:

```
public boolean handleEvent(HmeEvent event) {
    if (event instanceof HmeEvent.InitInfo) {
        HmeEvent.InitInfo iievent = (InitInfo) event;
        byte[] memento = iievent.getMemento();
        // process any data needed to
        // restore the application state...
    }
    return super.handleEvent(event);
}
```

Although the method is called `transitionBack()`, the "previous" application is no longer running — it is actually re-started and the HmeEvent.InitInfo event is sent with the memento to assist in restoring the previous state.

Summary

Overriding some of the lifecycle classes adds more flexibility in terms of where data is stored and capabilities to alter previously static information like the application's Title (name).

Adding threads to an application can greatly increase responsiveness to the user. Locating certain threads and data in the Factory can also centralize processing of common data across instances of the application.

Transition from application to application can be a little clumsy, and requires some creative handling of events and of lifecycle methods, but provides a good way for a single application to aggregate access to applications.

Questions

1. What are the main reasons for overriding the Factory?

2. Will the following code work? If so, how does it work? If not, why not?

```
/**
 * Assume that myBText is defined and set up correctly as a BText
 */
public class BApp extends BApplication {

    public void init(IContext ctx) {
```

```
        String data = ((MyBAppFactory)getFactory()).getMyData();
        myBText.setValue(data);
    }

    public static class MyBAppFactory extends Factory {

        public String getMyData() {
            return "Test";
        }

    }

}
```

3. What is the difference between a thread started in the Application and one started in the Factory?

4. What event does an application need to wait for to determine if it is being started as a transition?

Application Preferences

In the previous chapter, the weather application asks for the user's Zip code each time it starts. The application definitely needs this information to operate correctly, but it seems like a waste of the user's time to force it to be entered each time. Saving the Zip code information so that it only needs to be entered once would make for a much better user experience. This chapter provides a few different options for saving preferences for an HME application, and reasons why to choose each.

Per-TiVo Preferences

Storing per-TiVo preference information is appropriate for many applications, and for all that intend to run on a server, providing an application to many different users over the Internet. Per-TiVo preferences allow information about the preferences the user has selected while running the application on the TiVo to be saved.

Per-TiVo preferences saves data that can be retrieved between runs of an application. The data, however, is only available to the same application running on the same TiVo box. If you run the BWeatherApp on a TiVo box in your living room, the TiVo box in your bedroom will still prompt for Zip code information because the application is being run on a different TiVo.

Using Per-TiVo Preferences

Preferences are only able to be set in a running application, and are saved by the hosting environment. The data is not saved on the TiVo box itself; although the preference data is keyed to a specific TiVo box and application, it is saved on the machine that is hosting the HME application.

The object used to communicate information from the hosting environment to the application is the Context object. If you recall, every application's `init()` method looks like this:

```
public void init(IContext arg0) throws Exception {
    super.init(arg0);
}
```

The IContext interface describes an object that provides information about the application from the hosting environment. Information the application would not otherwise be able to know, such as the application host URL and access to the persistent data that is used to store preferences, are items provided by the context.

Persistent data (this is what the IContext API calls preferences) consists of the following:

Call	Parameters	Notes
getPersistentData	String key	Retrieves persistent data from the context
setPersistentData	String key, String value	Saves the value to be retrieved by the key

As you can see, the only data that is saved is in the form of a String object, and all keys are in the form of a String object. Even with this limitation, the persistent data store will vastly improve the BWeatherApp HME application.

Try It Out   Setting and Retrieving Persistent Data

Following is a simple application that sets and retrieves persistent data:

```
package com.wiley.hme.ch11;

import java.awt.Color;
import com.tivo.hme.bananas.BApplication;
import com.tivo.hme.bananas.BScreen;
import com.tivo.hme.bananas.BText;
import com.tivo.hme.interfaces.IContext;

public class PrefApp extends BApplication {

    public class PrefScreen extends BScreen {
        PrefApp app;

        public PrefScreen(BApplication arg0) {
            super(arg0);
            this.app = (PrefApp) arg0;
            init();
        }

        private void init() {
            BText bt = new BText(getNormal(),0,0,640,480);
            bt.setColor(Color.white);
            bt.setFont("default-20.font");
            bt.setValue(app.getContext().getPersistentData("data"));
        }
    }

    public boolean handleActive(boolean isActive) {

        if (isActive) {
```

```
                    push(new PrefScreen(this), TRANSITION_FADE);
            }
            return super.handleActive(isActive);
        }

    public void init(IContext arg0) throws Exception {
        super.init(arg0);
        getContext().setPersistentData("data", "test saved data");
    }

}
```

How It Works

When the application's `init()` method is called, the context argument is passed along to the call to `super.init()`. The next call to `getContext()` relies on `super.init()` being called first. It retrieves the context object and saves the string "test saved data" to the key "data" in the persistent data store.

When the application is started, the `handleActive()` handler is called, and the PrefScreen is pushed and retrieves the saved data from the context data store.

How the Data Is Stored

For the data to be persistent, as the API name would suggest, the data has to be stored somewhere on the host system in a file to be retrieved later.

On Mac OSX, Linux, and other Unix-based operating systems, the data is stored in the user's home directory in the `.tivo` directory:

```
john@macbuk~/.tivo$ ls -la
total 112
drwxr-xr-x    9 john  everyone    306 Sep 17 10:58 .
drwxr-xr-x   72 john  501    .   2448 Sep 15 16:25 ..
-rw-r--r--    1 john  everyone     82 Sep 17 10:59 00000000000000000000-and-
com.wiley.hme.ch11.PrefApp.txt
-rw-r--r--    1 john  everyone  31973 Sep 17 10:59 sim-cookies.txt
john@macbuk~/.tivo$
```

In Windows, the data is stored in the user's home directory in `\Application Data\TiVo`.

As you can see, the files are named as follows:

```
[TSN]-and-[classname].txt
```

In the preceding listing, you can see the data from the PrefApp that was saved. Because it was run in the Simulator, the TSN (TiVo Service Number) is set to all zeros. Inside this file is the data that was saved by the application while it was running:

```
#http://192.168.1.4:7288/ch11/
#Sun Sep 17 10:59:46 EDT 2006
data=test saved data
```

The data is simple key/value pairs, which is why the persistent data methods take String objects for both the key and the value. The TSN from the file name is used to match the TiVo box that is running the application, and the class name from the file name is used to make sure data is being provided to the correct application.

To update the BWeatherApp converted to use the persistent data store provided by the context, the `init()` method of the application should be updated to retrieve the data from the persistent data store:

```
public void init(IContext context) throws Exception {
    super.init(context);
    getRoot().setResource(Color.white);
    String zipString = getContext().getPersistentData("zip");

    if (zipString != null && !"".equals(zipString)){
        ZipCode.getZipCode().setValue(zipString);
    } else {
        zipString = "";
    }

    if ("".equals(zipString))
        push(new ZipScreen(this), TRANSITION_FADE);
    else
        this.push(new WeatherScreen(this, zipString), TRANSITION_FADE, "first");
}
```

The `zipString` value is retrieved from the context first, and then used in the same manner it has been previously used in the application.

The ZipScreen also must be updated to save the data to the persistent store when the Zip code is changed. This will require updates to `handleAction()` in the ZipScreen:

```
public boolean handleAction(BView view, Object action) {
    if ("getweather".equals(action)) {
        ZipCode.getZipCode().setValue(keyb.getValue());
        getBApp().getContext().setPersistentData("zip", keyb.getValue());
        getBApp().push(new WeatherScreen(getBApp(), keyb.getValue()),
TRANSITION_LEFT);
        return true;
    }
    if ("pop".equals(action)) {
        myWS.doZip(keyb.getValue());
        getBApp().pop();
        return true;
    }
    return super.handleAction(view, action);
}
```

Now the BWeatherApp can make use of persistent data and reuse the Zip code information obtained the first time the application was run. Example 11-2 on the accompanying web site contains the full source code for this example.

Per-Application Preferences

Although the per-TiVo persistent data is useful, there are probably situations in which per-application preferences would be more useful. Preferences saved per application would apply to all instances of the application, run on all TiVos.

For instance, if you are running BWeatherApp on your desktop at home, and have three TiVo boxes in your house, using the per-TiVo preferences, you would have to enter the Zip code on all your TiVos. Unless you are very wealthy, and your home spans multiple Zip codes, this probably doesn't make a whole lot of sense. Rather, saving the data for the BWeatherApp so that all instances of the application are able to access the same Zip code would make much more sense.

Using Persistent Data

If by chance you were looking over the Javadoc API information during the discussion of per-TiVo application preferences, you probably noticed that there is actually a second `setPersistentData()` method that takes an application identifier and boolean argument.

The boolean indicates whether the key/value pair is global. If it is global, then the data is available to all instances of the application that use the same application identifier. This means that all the BWeatherApp instances run on all the TiVos in your home could share the same persistent data about the Zip code. Updating the BWeatherApp to use per-application preferences instead of per-TiVo preferences would be as easy as adding a boolean indicating the value is global and a global application identifier.

The ZipScreen would need to be updated to save the information globally:

```
public boolean handleAction(BView view, Object action) {
    if ("getweather".equals(action)) {
        ZipCode.getZipCode().setValue(keyb.getValue());
        getBApp().getContext().setPersistentData("zip", keyb.getValue(),
getBApp().getFactory().getFactoryData().get(IFactory.HME_APPLICATION_CLASSNAME).toS
tring(), true);
        getBApp().push(new WeatherScreen(getBApp(), keyb.getValue()),
TRANSITION_LEFT);
        return true;
    }
    if ("pop".equals(action)) {
        myWS.doZip(keyb.getValue());
        getBApp().pop();
        return true;
    }
    return super.handleAction(view, action);
}
```

And the BWeatherApp would be changed to

```
public void init(IContext context) throws Exception {
    super.init(context);
    getRoot().setResource(Color.white);
```

```
    String zipString  = getContext().getPersistentData("zip",
getFactory().getFactoryData().get(IFactory.HME_APPLICATION_CLASSNAME).toString(),
true);
```

```
    if (zipString != null && !"".equals(zipString)){
        ZipCode.getZipCode().setValue(zipString);
    } else {
        zipString = "";
    }

    if ("".equals(zipString))
        push(new ZipScreen(this), TRANSITION_FADE);
    else
        this.push(new WeatherScreen(this, zipString), TRANSITION_FADE, "first");
}
```

You can find this example in full in Example 11-3 in the code samples on www.wrox.com. The application ID String that is passed to the preferences must begin with the application class name; in BWeatherApp's case, this would be com.wiley.hme.ch11.BWeatherApp. Any application ID that does not at least start with that string will fail to save any preferences, and give no indication that the data was not saved.

In this case, you obtain the application ID using the Factory's data map, which stores the application ID in the map under the key HME_APPLICATION_CLASSNAME. Although the call to obtain the class-name is very convoluted, it is by far the safest way to retrieve it for the purpose of setting persistent data. Otherwise, changing package names or class names would cause preference data to simply disappear and make it very hard to track down problems, because the API fails silently.

Using the Java Preference System

If persistent data that can be shared across applications is already present in the HME API, then why would any other means of saving preferences be necessary?

There are other limitations of using the HME persistent data methods. For instance, these preferences can only be accessed or updated with an IContext object, which is created only when the application is running on a TiVo box. If a custom factory requires access to preference data, there is no way to obtain it until the application is running.

Details of Java Preference API

The Java Preference API is a built-in API in Java for storing preference information. It is not tied to the HME SDK at all, and is available anywhere in your application, including a custom factory class, and any supporting code for your application.

AudioFaucet, the authors' application, uses the preferences API to store preference information set up in GUI Swing screens shown on the host computer. Because no application is running on the TiVo at the time this preference information must be saved, the Java Preference API is a natural solution.

```
            e.printStackTrace();
        }
        throw new IllegalArgumentException( "Unable to load image: " + imageName );
    }

    public JPanel createPanel()
    {
        if (jpanel1 == null) {
            jpanel1 = new JPanel();
            m_imagecomponent1 = loadImage("welcome.jpg");
            JLabel l = new JLabel(m_imagecomponent1);
            jpanel1.add(l,BorderLayout.CENTER);
        }
        return jpanel1;
    }
}
```

Because the splash screen should be displayed when the application is started on the host system, not on the TiVo box, the splash screen should be kicked off from a custom factory:

```
public static class UsableAppFactory extends Factory implements IFactory {
    public UsableAppFactory() {
        super();
        new SplashScreen().display();
    }
}
```

This causes the application to start up and stop bouncing once the Factory has been created. It solves the problem of the never-ending dock bouncing, and displaying a splash screen is a fairly common occurrence when starting an application, and so remains in line with a user's expectations of an application starting up.

Packaging

Apple recommends that developers make use of disk images to distribute their software bundles to Mac OS X users. Creating a disk image is fairly easy. However, there are a few things you can do to make your packaging have a more professional look and feel. These include creating disk images that are compressed to save distribution bandwidth, utilizing custom background images, disk image icons, and finder views, automatically mounting the disk image when downloaded via a web browser, and also the ability to show license agreements before the image is mounted, if needed.

Creating the Disk Image

The first step in creating a professional Mac OS X distribution package is the creation of the disk image (.dmg file) itself. To create a disk image, you need to make use of Disk Utility, which is provided with every version of Mac OS X and can be found in your Applications/Utilities folder.

Choose the New Blank Image option from the File New menu in Disk Utility. Disk Utility opens a dialog box that asks you for the specifics needed to create your initial disk image, as seen in Figure 14-5.

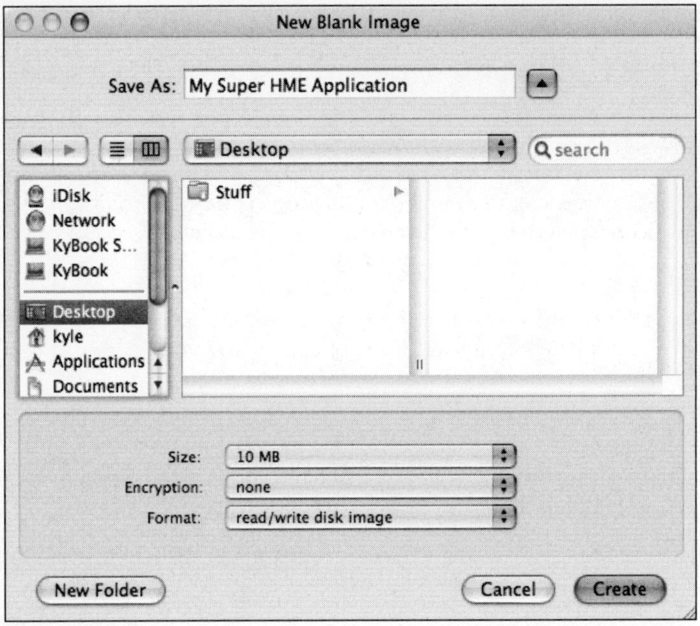

Figure 14-5

In this dialog box, set Save As to the name of your new disk image. This is the name that people will see when they mount the image on their computer, as well as the file name that the .dmg file will be saved as.

In the Size drop-down list, select a file size that is large enough to hold the target application, as well as any support documents (ReadMe Files, Links to your Website, Software Licenses, Graphic background files, and so on).

Setting encryption on your disk image will require that the end user enter a password in order to mount the image. It is highly recommended by the authors that this setting not be set to avoid distribution complexity.

Finally, make sure that the initial disk image that you create is read/writable. Select "read/write disk image" from the Format drop-down menu and click the Create button.

You will now have a new .dmg file and mounted disk image on your desktop to place all of your application and support files into.

Stylizing the Disk Image

Mac OS X allows Disk Images to define how they are shown when mounted in the Finder. You can customize your Disk Image with a custom .dmg and mounted drive image, add custom graphical backdrops to the finder window, and also set the size and display properties of your folder.

Custom Disk Icons

The easiest modification is adding a customized icon to the .dmg disk image file and the resulting mounted drive. Doing this is fairly straightforward.

Find the application Icon (ico file) that you created earlier. Rick-click the ico file and select Get Info from the resulting menu. The Get Info dialog box will open. From this screen you will see some specifics about your file including the icon itself at the top of the dialog box. Click it to give it a blue halo. This means that this file icon is selected. Then from the Edit menu choose Copy to place the image into the Mac OS X clipboard.

Get Info on the .dmg file on the desktop and repeat the steps to select the disk image icon. Then from the Edit menu choose Paste to paste the icon image you have in your clipboard into place, as seen in Figure 14-6.

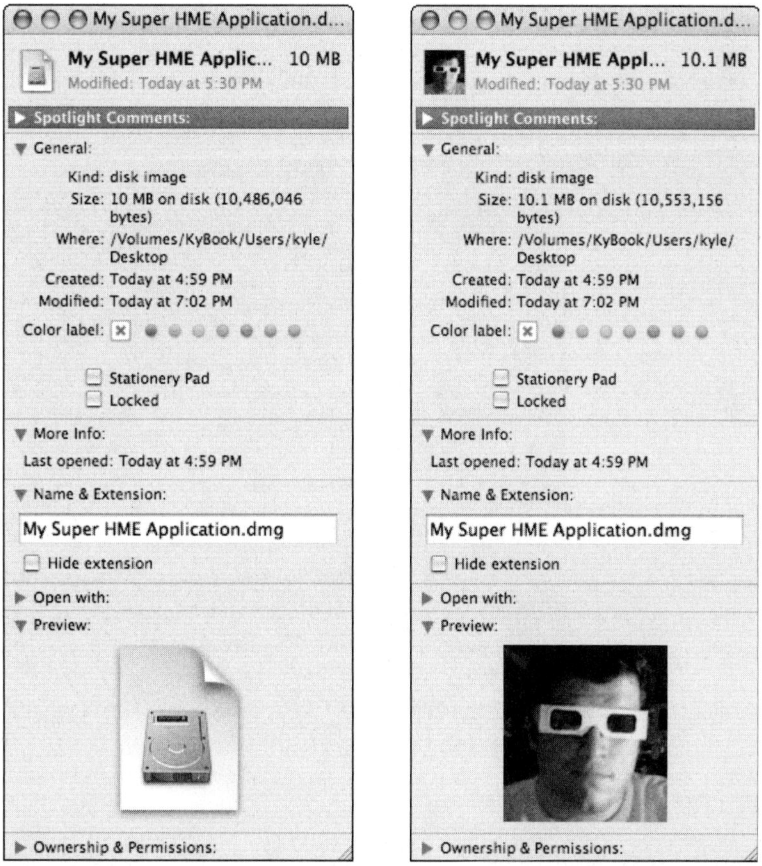

Figure 14-6

To revert the change, simply click the new icon and press Delete on your keyboard. This removes your new icon resource from the file and reverts back to the default icon. Close the dialog box to save the change. Repeat the same steps for any other icons you would like to customize within your bundle.

Custom Finder View

You may also want to change the look and feel of the window that opens when your disk image is mounted. You can change the view options such as the background image of the window, font size, and the layout for the icons and toolbars in the finder window.

You can place an image as the background of your finder window. Before you make modifications to your finder window view, if you plan on using a background image, create one using your favorite image-editing program and create the backdrop for your folder and save it as a jpeg file. Place the file in a folder inside of your disk image; don't worry about the visual placement of that folder for now because that folder will be ultimately hidden from the user once you are done.

To change the standard view options of the window, simply open the disk image in the finder and use the View menu to hide the toolbar and finder extras around the window. Then go back into the View menu to Show View Options. This will open the View Options dialog box, as seen in Figure 14-7.

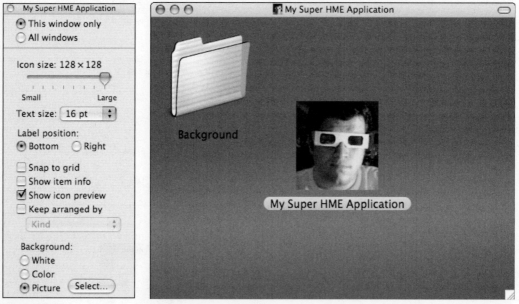

Figure 14-7

Select "This window only" to make sure you are not changing the window views for your entire system, and then customize the icon size, text size, label position, and layout of your window. Once you have your layout settled, choose the background you would like for your window. The example shown in Figure 14-7 utilizes a `background.jpg` file that is inside of the Background folder in my disk image. It also has a custom colored text background label around the application name; selecting the application icon and then using the Color Label option in the Finder's File menu configures this. Closing the dialog box saves the custom settings for the disk image folders.

Finally, if the configuration utilized a background image and folder, you will want to hide this from the end user. To do so, simply rename the Background folder to add a period in front of the file name. From the command prompt in Mac OS X, change the directory to the mounted volume that you just created and rename the folder. Run the command as follows:

$ cd /Volumes/My\ Super\ HME\ Application/

$ mv Background .Background

Finder does not show files whose names begin with a period. The view settings will follow the file when the name of its containing directory is changed. To change the file in the future, simply go back to that directory and change the name back to `Background`, replace the file, and rename it again to `.Background`.

Compressing and Locking Down the Disk Image

Once you have your disk image loaded with all the appropriate files for your application and behaving the way you intended, it is highly suggested to compress the image and lock it down to a read-only state.

Return to Disk Utility and choose Convert... from the Images menu. From the following dialog box, navigate to your dmg file and click the Convert button. This opens a dialog box very similar to the one used to create the Disk Image in the first place. By default it will be set to a "Save As" name of disk1 and an "Image Format" of compressed. The file name is not important in this step; you will be converting the disk image again to read-only shortly. Click Convert to compress your disk image to a file called `disk1.dmg` and place it in the same folder as the source dmg file used to create the compressed image.

Now that the image is compressed, you will want to make it read-only so that users cannot easily change the contents and behavior of the disk image. To do this, go back into Disk Utility and again choose Convert... from the Images menu, locate the `disk1.dmg` file you just created, and this time set the "Save As" file name to a recognizable and distinguishable name. Select an "Image Format" of "read only" and then click Convert to lock down the final compressed disk image for distribution.

Once the image is locked down, you can always rename the file to anything you like. Often for ease of download from web sites it is better to rename the document without spaces and to include a version identifier in the file name as well. The authors adopted the naming convention of ApplicationName_Version_Platform_YearMonthDay.dmg for distributing between downloaded versions of their program AudioFaucet. The mounted disk image will always contain the original name that was chosen when creating the initial image when mounted and opened in the Mac OS X finder.

Launching a Disk Image Automatically Upon Download

Once you have your disk image locked down, you may choose to Internet-enable your disk image, meaning that the image will automatically mount itself when a user downloads it from your web page. To Internet-enable a disk image, you will have to make use of a tool provided by Apple called hdiutil.

From the command prompt, type "hdiutil internet-enable –yes <path to dmg>" as follows:

$ hdiutil internet-enable -yes ~/Desktop/MySupperHMEApp_1_OSX_20060923.dmg

hdiutil: internet-enable: enable succeeded

You can disable the Internet-enable flag by using the same command with a "-no" argument instead.

If you make any modifications to your disk image in Disk Utility after setting the Internet-enable flag, the file will revert back to being a normal DMG image and will not auto-open when downloaded from a browser.

Displaying a Software License Agreement

Because most applications show a license agreement as part of the installer activities, it might be necessary for a developer to display a software license agreement to users before allowing them access to the mounted DMG image. Apple provides an SDK and instructions on how to do this as part of its free developer program. The SDK, called "Software License Agreements for UIDFs," can be downloaded from the Apple Developer Connection web site located at http://developer.apple.com/sdk/index.html.

Windows Native App

Packaging a Java application for Windows is a complicated task. Unlike Web Start, jars, or packaging for OS X, there is no single way to approach building a Windows application.

There is a vast amount of software available to create Windows native exe applications from jar files. The options covered here are the choices made by the authors when bundling their HME applications for Windows.

Creating an Application Icon

You may want to create an icon for the Application and also the Installer used to distribute your application. Each application platform has its own distinct icon format requirements. Windows uses ico format to store application icons.

First find the image files that you would like to use as icons. As with Mac OS X, the authors suggest that this image file be similar to that of your application's "Music, Photos, and More" icon. The best choice is a PNG file with a transparent background, but any graphic file will do.

Then simply convert the image to the ico format. Many applications are available to convert png graphic images to ico format. The authors prefer to use a freeware program called Imagicon, which can be found at http://www.deviouscodeworks.co.uk.

Once the ico file is created, save it in your resources folder for your application so that you can easily find it in the future when necessary.

Bundler

As for Web Start applications, first a jar file must be created with all the classes and resources needed for the application. As with Web Start, all the supporting jars must also be gathered: `hme.jar`, `bananas.jar`, `hme-host-sample.jar`, and any other libraries the application uses. If you are using any external binaries or code in your application, make sure you have the right to redistribute them before they are included with your application's distribution. Many times you will also be required to include any licenses or other acknowledgments within your application's documentation package as well.

There are a few open source projects that accomplish this sort of bundling, and several commercial products.

Xenoage JEStart is an open source project hosted at sourceforge (`http://sourceforge.net/projects/jestart`). Xenoage is GPL licensed, so there may be restrictions against commercial use. JPackIt (`http://sourceforge.net/projects/jpackit`) is another open source solution, which accomplishes the same task; it is Apache licensed, so it may be more friendly for commercial use. JavaService allows Java programs to be used as a Windows service. It is LGPL licensed, and is available from `http://javaservice.objectweb.org/`. All of these packagers are good, but some of the commercial packagers allow for additional flexibility.

The authors use Exe4j (`http://www.ej-technologies.com`) for packaging AudioFaucet. Though it's a commercial product, the exe builder has some very useful features. The exe can be created to contain all the jar files, so that no extra jar files or libraries are needed — everything is contained within the exe file. Exe4j also has options to allow "pass-through" command-line options to the Java JVM. This can be particularly useful if the application may need additional memory for large data sets, or to tweak the behavior of the application using command-line arguments. Exe4j also allows your application to be installed and run as a background Windows service if you choose.

Each application has a different workflow for creating executable files for Windows, and the one you choose will likely depend on what level of flexibility is needed for your application, and the level of polish your users will expect.

Installer

Most Windows applications come with an installer. Many tools are available to create installation packages. The authors' choice for generating an installer is Advanced Installer (`http://www.advancedinstaller.com/`). Depending on the level of complexity required for the installer, there are free versions up through enterprise versions that can create installers and bundles for both Mac OS X and Windows.

The features of the installer will largely be dependent on how much setup is required to be done before the application is started, but in most cases, the free version of Advanced Installer will likely be able to create an installer that can copy an application to the correct place, set up shortcuts in the Start menu, and add any registry keys that are needed. The Nullsoft Scriptable Install System (NSIS) is an open source solution to create installers, and is a powerful and free alternative. NSIS is available from `http://nsis.sourceforge.net`.

Additional steps following the installation of an HME application on Windows will likely require opening up firewall ports so that the HME application can broadcast to the TiVo box, and to allow for the application to run on the TiVo box. David Staas has a great tutorial on setting up firewall exceptions for HME applications, which is available at `http://bitrazor.com/content/tivo/hme/howtos/windowsfirewall/wf.php`.

Chapter 14

Packaging

Normal conventions suggest that developers make use of ZIP archive files to distribute their applications to Windows users. By using a ZIP archive, your application installers will require less disk space and make for easy and quick downloads from your distribution web sites.

Creating a ZIP file of the installer application is fairly easy. Windows XP has a built-in ZIP archive file creation tool called Compressed Folders. To create a ZIP archive in Windows XP, right-click the installer application of the folder that contains the application and other supporting documents and select Send To and then Compressed (zipped) Folder from the resulting menu. This will make a compressed ZIP file with a zipper icon with the same name as the file or folder you compressed with the .zip extension in the same directory as the selected contents. In other versions of Windows, you can use many tools that are available for creating ZIP archive files; WinZip is suggested by the authors.

Selling Your Application

There are, of course, many options for selling an application as well. A simple PayPal donation link from your site may be all you want to use. For a more complicated sales and registration number system, the eSellerate system is excellent.

eSellerate will host the application as well, which saves on bandwidth costs. Integration with Java applications is mildly difficult, but can be accomplished easily enough by using Java Native Interface (JNI) to place calls to the native DLLs or libraries, and eSellerate is available for several platforms.

Summary

Making a Java program into a native-feeling application is really the last mile to getting your application into the hands of your user. Any good application will take into account the user's experience from downloading to running the application, and should make every effort to make the process work as the user expects.

In some cases, the convenience of a Web Start application, which requires nothing to be installed on the user's system except Java, is the best option. In other cases, an installer and full bundled application is the best route to take.

Whatever your application, presenting it with polish both when it is run on the TiVo box and during the installation and startup process will make the application more usable for a wider audience, and will make for happier users.

Questions

1. Why does `hme-host-sample.jar` need to be modified for use in Web Start?
2. Why would you create a jar for your application?

Tips and Troubleshooting

No matter how carefully you write an application, or how many unit tests you write to make sure classes are working correctly, there will likely come a time when looking at the application variable while the application is running will be the quickest, and perhaps only, way to fix some troublesome code.

Developing in Eclipse makes visual debugging of code pretty simple. Because the source code for the HME SDK and the Bananas library are available from the Sourceforge site, Eclipse can step into the SDK's code to see how events are being processed in the HME code itself.

Eclipse allows for setting break points (places to stop code execution) and for stepping through the code as it is running. To set a breakpoint, select Toggle Line Breakpoint from the Run menu, then run your application from the Run, Debug... menu; the application will stop when the point in code is reached, and allow you to examine variables and visually see the status of the code while the application is running (Figure 15-1).

Debugging code is extremely useful while code is under development, and to check on behavior even after development has been completed, but other tools are useful for determining what your users are doing with your application to help sort out any problems or bugs.

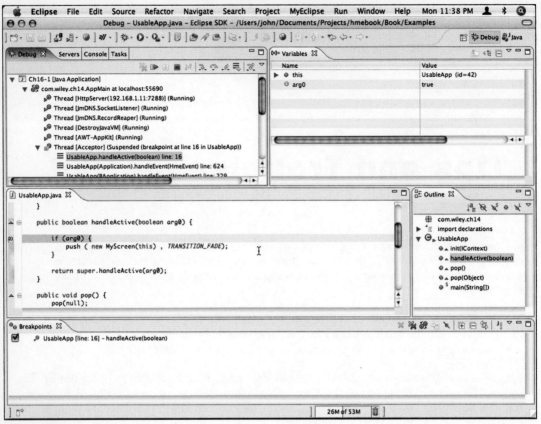

Figure 15-1

Logging

Any application that is made available to users will likely run into problems that never happened when the application was being tested. In addition to being a Murphy's Law scenario, the HME SDK is also sensitive to the configuration of the system it is running on. From the version of Java to network problems, there are a fair amount of unforeseen problems that HME applications come up against when running on machines other than your home system.

The HME SDK's `hme-host-sample.jar` includes logging classes. The Logging classes are available via the context, but unfortunately do not allow for much flexibility like most modern logging systems do.

Try It Out   Using the Built-in ILogger

The HME SDK has a built-in logging mechanism that any application can access. The messages logged are printed to standard output.

The logger also supports "levels" that indicate the severity of the messages.

```
ILogger log = getBApp().getContext().getLogger();
log.log(ILogger.LOG_DEBUG, "entering myscreen");
```

How It Works

The ILogger is created by the hosting environment, and a reference to the logger is saved in the context. Any screen can retrieve the context through the application, and get a reference to the logger object. The preceding code will output the following on the standard output:

```
HME SDK 1.4 (TiVo, Inc.)
LOG: added factory
MDNS: http://192.168.1.11:7288/ch15/
LOG: 192.168.1.11 icon.png HTTP GET - to factory /ch15/
LOG: HME receiver connected
LOG: entering myscreen
```

The built-in logging can be overridden by extending the com.tivo.hme.host.sample.Main class:

```
package com.wiley.hme.ch15;

import java.io.IOException;

import com.tivo.hme.host.sample.Main;
import com.tivo.hme.host.util.ArgumentList;
import com.tivo.hme.interfaces.ILogger;

public class AppMain extends Main implements ILogger {

    public AppMain(ArgumentList arg0) throws IOException {
        super(arg0);
    }

    public void log(int arg0, String arg1) {
        System.out.println("AppLog: ["+arg0+"] :" + arg1);
    }

    public static void main(String argv[]) throws IOException
    {
        new AppMain(new ArgumentList(argv));
    }
}
```

The constructor is required to be present because Java requires it. The `log()` method is the method that must be overridden, and the `main()` method will be the new entry point into the application (`com.wiley.hme.ch15.AppMain` instead of the `com.tivo.hme.sim.Simulator` or `com.tivo.hme.host.sample.Main` that was previously being used).

This update to the logging system will output:

```
AppLog: [2] :added factory
MDNS: http://192.168.1.11:7288/ch15/
```

```
AppLog: [2] :192.168.1.11 icon.png HTTP GET - to factory /ch15/
AppLog: [2] :HME receiver connected
AppLog: [1] :entering myscreen
AppLog: [2] :connection to receiver closed
AppLog: [2] :HME receiver disconnected
```

Overriding the log() method in this manner, however, can allow for the integration of much more sophisticated logging frameworks, such as Log4J, Apache Jakarta Commons Logging, or Java Logging API, which all have greater flexibility in terms of turning on or off different levels of logging, writing to files, obtaining their configuration from files, and other capabilities that are useful when attempting to get logging information from users of your application.

Common Problems

Description	Suggestions
My HME Application doesn't show up on the TiVo.	Check to see if a firewall on the system is blocking the application. Also make sure that if the system is using multiple interfaces (multiple network cards or addresses), the HME application is using the correct interface. Passing the -intf flag to the Factory with the specific interface will force the HME app to bind to a specific network interface.
The Application starts on the local machine, but says it cannot find the application.	Make sure your application class files or jar file are in the classpath when it is run. If you are running from a Web Start application, check to make sure you updated hme-host-sample.jar.
Images disappear from the TiVo box screen.	This is normally a resource problem — check to make sure you aren't using too many images or images that are too large.
I'm using MP3 audio, and the application is slow.	MP3 audio decoding uses approximately 30% of the CPU power on the box. Optimizing the resources you are using in the application can help mitigate slowness, but it may not be entirely avoidable.
The application keeps exiting on the TiVo box.	Check the log files on the host system. If Java errors are reported, these are likely the cause. Any Java error the application reports will cause the hosting environment to kill the application. A slow network link between the TiVo box and the application may also cause failures because a constant connection is required between the TiVo box and the HME application.
	My list shows up onscreen, but nothing is selected, and the keys don't do anything.
	Call setFocusDefault() to set the default focused item in the screen. If no default is set, the focus cannot be changed.

Additional Resources

The TiVo HME SDK comes with a developer guide PDF file. The guide is a quick run-through of the HME environment, and is a good place to look first.

The HME SDK and Bananas libraries come with a complete Java Doc documentation package. Though not 100 percent of the methods are explained in the same detail, there is good information available in the Java Doc as well as a complete listing of the classes that make up the HME SDK.

The HME SDK home page is `http://tivohme.sourceforge.net/`, and additional TiVo developer information is posted at `http://www.tivo.com/developer`. The HME developer mailing list is also a good resource to bounce ideas off other HME developers, and get clarification on any questions you may have. Finally, the "HME Developers Corner" forum at `http://www.tivocommunity.com` is a great place to ask questions.

Summary

Having a good understanding of how the HME SDK works will assist you in tracking down problems in your application. Logging is an important consideration when developing your application—tracking down errors that a user of your application is running into is much easier when your application is able to provide a log of what is going wrong.

Exercise Answers

Chapter 1

1. TiVo HMO was designed as a simple and standardized user interface for accessing music and photos stored on a personal computer within the household network or a server hosted on the Internet. Because the user interface on the TiVo itself was templates, all music and photo applications that pushed their content to the TiVo box shared the same look and feel. TiVo HME gives developers the freedom to design user interfaces, feature sets, and application display behavior to meet their specific needs.

2. TiVo HME does not allow the overlay of information over any video content nor does it allow access specifically as part of the SDK to use or manipulate program data or recording preferences on the TiVo box.

Chapter 2

1. The TiVo HMO and HME feature set is enabled in software for use on the Series2 and Series3 hardware references platforms. However, DirectTV has chosen to software-disable USB ports on its Series2 boxes in an attempt to protect their content; therefore, DirectTV receivers with TiVo built in cannot make use of any network-enabled applications.

2. TiVo enables network applications with any paid TiVo service. This includes Lifetime and Monthly subscription options. TiVo does not enable network applications with the free minimized TiVo Basic service that is included by some third-party manufacturers.

3. Music, Photos, Products, & More.

Chapter 3

1. The `hme.jar` and `hme-host-sample.jar` are needed to run HME applications. They must be part of your Eclipse project or your CLASSPATH to be able to compile and run Java code for your HME application.

2. All HME applications are essentially a server program using an IP communications link to the TiVo box. Running the HME application using the correct network interface ensures that the TiVo box can see and communicate with the application.

3. MDNS (Multicast Domain Name Resolution) is the technology that an HME application, running on a computer, utilizes to announce the availability of the application to the TiVo box. Without MDNS, the TiVo box would not display the application in the "Music, Photos, Products & More" menu.

Chapter 4

1. An HME application responds to a key press by overriding the `handleKeyPress()` method to receive the message from the receiver that a remote control button was pressed.

2. The `handleActive()` method and the `destroy()` method are called when an application is closing. The `destroy()` method is always called, even when a warp key is used to exit the application, whereas the `handleActive()` method is called only when the application is exited by calling `setActive(false)`.

3. A custom icon can be set by placing a PNG graphic named `icon.png` in the root directory of the application CLASSPATH with the dimensions 34px X 26px. A custom name for the application may be set by defining the public String TITLE in the Application class.

Chapter 5

1. The text color is set when the text resource is created.

2. A view determines the alignment of the text. This is because the view defines where the text will be on the screen, and so is responsible for setting the alignment of its contents.

3. Built-in sounds are retrieved using `getResource()` and played using the `play()` method in HMEObject. Custom resources are created using `createSound()`.

Chapter 6

1. The `sendEvent()` method communicates with the TiVo box, while the Ticker callbacks run a thread on the host system.

2. `handleIdle()` informs the application that the TiVo box is about to time out to live TV. The application can take action to perform screensaver-type animation at this point.

3. The application will not see any KEY_FORWARD or KEY_REVERSE events that are sent to `handleKeyPress()` because those events are handled, and true is returned. The application will see all other key events. Although there is code for KEY_SELECT, the `handleKeyPress()` method still returns false, so it too is sent to the application's `handleEvent()` method.

4. The SDK will send an event to whichever view has focus. Both views could receive the event if, for example, viewA was the parent of viewB and viewB did not handle the KEY_SELECT event, or chose to pass it to the parent view as well.

Chapter 7

1. BList cannot be instantiated directly. It is an abstract class, so BList must be subclassed in order to be used.

2. The BApplication subclass's `init()` method should call the superclass's `init()` method as the first action in the `init()` method. This is because the BApplication's implementation of `init()` creates the layers used when setting up an application. If `init()` is not called, NullPointer Exceptions will likely be thrown when the application is run.

3. The `setBarAndArrows()` method takes as parameters the actions the button will take for the up, down, left, and right keys. In order to be managed by the focus manager, the H_UP, H_DOWN, H_LEFT, and H_RIGHT constants indicate that focus manager should process the key to move the focus in the screen.

Chapter 8

1. An Action is a type of BEvent used in Bananas to pass control between widgets, BViews, and BScreens.

2. Like HME, events first enter the Bananas toolkit via the `dispatchEvent()` method. BApplication overrides the HME Application's `dispatchEvent()` to gain access to the event stream.

3. `sendEvent()` sends an event on a round trip to the TiVo box whereas `postEvent()` drops the event immediately into the event processing system on the local machine without sending the event on a round trip to the TiVo box.

Chapter 9

1. The HME runtime environment will create a new connection to retrieve streamed resources, separate from the application's connection.

2. The HME Simulator includes an interactive hierarchical view system to aid developers with the process of optimizing their user interfaces. There is also an HME runtime debug mode that allows a developer to see exactly which resources within their application are not being directly rendered in hardware and could possibly be causing a degradation of performance.

Chapter 10

1. The main reasons for overriding the factory are:

   ❑ Changing the name of the application dynamically

   ❑ Using the factory for storing shared data

   ❑ Handling arguments to the application

   ❑ Allowing access to files outside the classpath

2. The code will not function properly. Because the factory does not follow the naming convention <ApplicationName>Factory, and the application has no getAppFactory() method, the default factory will end up being used. The application's init() method will receive a class cast exception when it attempts to cast the default factory to the custom factory because the custom factory could not be found and the default factory was created.

3. A thread started in the application will run only while the application is running on the TiVo box (assuming it is terminated correctly), and a thread started in the Factory will run even after all TiVo boxes have exited the application.

4. The HmeEvent.InitInfo event will contain the data that determines if the application was started as part of a transition or directly by the TiVo box.

Chapter 11

1. Global preferences are a good idea if the same data is going to be shared among all instances of the application. It is not a good idea to use global preferences when deploying a server-based HME application, as any user who accesses the application could change the preference information.

2. In general, the Factory would not be able to save or retrieve data from the SDK's persistent data calls. The setPersistentData() and getPersistentData() methods are part of the Context object, which is not created until an application is started on the TiVo box.

Chapter 12

1. Calling getResource("*500,0") will return a Resource object that represents an animation. This resource can be passed to any method that accepts an animation. The "*" part of the string indicates to getResource() that an animation resource must be generated, the 500 portion of the string indicates the animation should last for 500 milliseconds, and the 0 portion of the string tells HME that the animation will take place linearly (not accelerate or decelerate).

2. The following properties of HME objects may be animated:

   ❑ Changing the bounds of a view

   ❑ Changing the scaling factor of a view

   ❑ Changing the translation of a view

   ❑ Changing the transparency of a view

   ❑ Changing the visibility of a view

   ❑ Removing a view

   ❑ Sending an event

3. Animated Events allows events to be sent back to your HME application after a specified period of time. These are most commonly used for chaining animations.